Invisible Forms

KEVIN JACKSON spent the months before writing *Invisible Forms* on a fishing trawler in the North Atlantic, on board HMS *Illustrious* in the Eastern Mediterranean, on an oil rig in the Caspian, on a cattle station in Western Australia, on a university campus in Ankara, on the Great Wall of China and on the town in Benidorm.

During the months of writing *Invisible Forms*, he also studied social anthropology and made documentaries for BBC Radio 3 on Camões, Potocki, Rousseau, Hölderlin and Leopardi.

In the months since completing *Invisible Forms*, he has been working on a two-part film about Anthony Burgess and a biography of Humphrey Jennings, as well as studying Latin and photography.

He divides his time inefficiently.

All of the above is perfectly true, but has been massaged a bit to make him seem more interesting.

By the same author*

Schrader on Schrader, an interview

The Humphrey Jennings Film Reader, an edition

The Oxford Book of Money, an anthology

The Risk of Being Alive, a memorial

The Language of Cinema, an orismological† essay

---

* The 'By the same author' page is an Invisible Form which would merit lengthier study elsewhere. Think of the possible permutations: arrangement by genre or by order of publication? If the latter, should the list run forwards or, as in a c.v., in reverse? With dates? Publishers? How about suppressing the one that had all those embarrassing reviews? . . . The model I've chosen here is adapted from Barry Humphries' *More Please* (Penguin edition, 1993).

† Orismology: 'the explanation of technical terms' (OED).

Invisible Forms

A Guide to Literary Curiosities

KEVIN JACKSON

THOMAS DUNNE BOOKS
ST. MARTIN'S PRESS ❧ NEW YORK

THOMAS DUNNE BOOKS.
An imprint of St. Martin's Press.

INVISIBLE FORMS. Copyright © 1999 by Kevin Jackson.
All rights reserved. Printed in the United States of
America. No part of this book may be used or
reproduced in any manner whatsoever without
written permission except in the case of brief
quotations embodied in critical articles or reviews.
For information, address St. Martin's Press,
175 Fifth Avenue, New York, N.Y. 10010.

www.stmartins.com

ISBN 0-312-26606-5

First published in Great Britain by Macmillan,
an imprint of Macmillan Publishers Ltd

First U.S. Edition: November 2000

10 9 8 7 6 5 4 3 2 1

To Her Majesty

Queen Elizabeth II

This work is respectfully dedicated

by a loyal subject. ⋆

⋆ Since Her Majesty only authorizes dedications in exceptional circumstances, this must unfortunately be considered a somewhat illegitimate
example of the form. It appears, however, that Her Majesty does not
positively forbid such dedications, so I am in small risk of the Tower. My
thanks to Mrs Mary Francis for clarifying this point of protocol.

Acknowledgements

Earlier, considerably shorter versions of the chapters on Footnotes, Marginalia, Pseudonyms, Heteronyms, Follies and Stage Directions first appeared in the *Independent*; my thanks to Tom Sutcliffe and Tristan Davies for commissioning them, and to Newspaper Publishing plc for giving them their freedom. The chapter on Footnotes published here also incorporates extracts from my interviews with Nicholson Baker, Patricia Duncker and Prof. Anthony Grafton, recorded for broadcast on the 1997 series of the Radio 3 books programme *Reading Around*. 'Enoch's Castle', in the chapter on Appendixes, is reproduced from *Enoch Soames: The Critical Heritage*, which was published in an extremely limited edition (one copy) and deposited in the British Library in June 1997.

My thanks are also due to Michael Schmidt, who commissioned the earliest version of this book for Carcanet Press, was then gracious enough to pass it on to Macmillan, and even came up with its title; to my editor Richard Milner, whose shrewd and tolerant supervision has, I suspect, saved me both blushes and the attentions of libel lawyers; to my agent, Georgina Capel, without whose powers of negotiation that wolf would by now be right through the door and into the living room; and to Gilbert Adair, for encouraging me to hope that some of my *disjecta membra* might be worth gathering. Among the specialists I consulted en route, I'm particularly indebted to Mr Michael Billington and Prof. Anne Barton for their knowledge of the history of stage directions, and to Dr Greg Dart for information about Rousseau's prefaces and afterwords.

Among the friends and colleagues who have helped me out on the project, I'm particularly grateful to Abigail Appleton (who produced *Reading Around*), Ian Irvine, Tom Lubbock, Robert Mayer, Simon Pettifar, Adrian Poole, Claire Preston, Peter Swaab, Clive Wilmer and Martin Wallen. All the lapses of taste, intelligence and scholarship which have survived into the final draft are, of course, the fault of Society.

There are books in which the footnotes, or the comments scrawled by some reader's hand in the margin, are more interesting than the text. The world is one of those books.

George Santayana, *Realms of Being*

Some of the means I use are trivial – and some are quadrivial.

James Joyce, responding to accusations of triviality

Contents

Introduction, or Preface

> Don't put a preface at the head of your work, or the
> critics won't talk about anything else.
>
> George Moore

There's a fairly well-known detective story by Edgar Allan
Poe entitled 'The Purloined Letter'. It goes something like
this: D_____, a wicked minister of the French government,
has stolen a compromising letter from a certain female
member of the royal family and is blackmailing her into
doing his evil political bidding. The Paris police have tried
everything they can think of to find and recapture this
scandalous document, but their clandestine searches of the
minister's apartment, though painstaking to the *n*th degree,
have yielded nothing. In desperation, the Prefect of Police
consults an oddball genius who has proved handy before,
one C. Auguste Dupin, an unemployed nocturnal visionary
and occasional poet, who can see far more deeply into the
nature of things than other mortals. For Dupin, a case like
this is a piece of *gâteau*. When the Prefect returns a month
later, he calmly produces the letter, trousers the reward, and
sits back basking in the sycophantic admiration of the story's
narrator. How did Dupin perform the trick? Simple: a recce
of the minister's apartments confirmed his theory about
how the dastardly fellow had fooled everyone. Rather than

concealing the letter in some obscure cranny, D_____ had just turned it inside out, crumpled it up a bit, and stuffed it in his letter rack. The police had overlooked it, not because it was hidden but because it was right in front of them. Astounding, Dupin.

Frankly, this has never struck me as a particularly convincing plot, but 'The Purloined Letter' is an interesting story for a number of reasons, not least the rather sad light it throws on Poe's narcissistic fantasy-life. With its companion stories about Dupin, 'The Murders in the Rue Morgue' and 'The Mystery of Marie Roget', it presented the fiction-reading world with the first of the Great Detectives, and served as a direct inspiration for Conan Doyle in creating Sherlock Holmes (so direct that there's a passage in *A Study in Scarlet* which, in my view rather nervously, dismisses Dupin as a precursor). American universities have often assigned 'The Purloined Letter' as set reading, since it's useful for teaching Freshman English students about point of view and narrative structure; and it excites literary theorists, or at any rate used to excite them, because the psychoanalyst Jacques Lacan once wrote an essay showing that the story was really about the phallus or something. My particular reason for referring to it here is the hope of justifying and explaining my title, *Invisible Forms* – 'forms' meaning pretty much the same as the posher critical word *genres* and 'invisible' meaning ... well, strictly speaking, things that aren't really invisible at all, but which have none the less tended to escape the attention of readers (even professional readers) in much the same way that the filched letter escaped the attention of the Parisian *gendarmerie* – or, to use a British example, in much the same way that the postman in one of G. K. Chesterton's Father Brown stories got away with murder, because people are so used to the sight of a postie doing his rounds that he is, in effect, an invisible man.

For the most part, these Invisible Forms are the parts of books that we see every time we take a hardback or paperback from the shelf and flick through it: *titles, dedications, epigraphs, prefaces, footnotes, indexes* and so on – in short, all the minor elements and dressings which help serve up the principal content of a book to its readership, and which are known to scholarly specialists as 'paratexts'. But I've cast my net a little wider than a strict adherence to that term would permit, and have classified as Invisible Forms (hereafter: IFs) some species of literary creation which are only mildly or occasionally paratextual, such as *pseudonyms*; a subject which leads inevitably, at least in my mind, to another kind of IF, *heteronyms*; a topic which in its own turn demands a supplementary note on the IF of *imaginary books and imaginary authors*. Similarly, a discussion of footnotes is followed by a discussion of the theatrical counterpart of the footnote, the *stage direction*, and this piece on notes that are never (or almost never) meant to be read out loud is complemented by an essay about notes that are always (or almost always) meant to be read out loud, *lectures*. There are essays on the unspoken conventions to be found in *first lines* and *last lines*, in *marginalia* and in *blurbs*. In each case, I've tried not only to give some indication of what those conventions have been, but to offer a fair sampling of some of the more entertaining, moving, eloquent, elegant, horrifying or simply odd examples of each IF, and to mention some of the writers who have excelled at such kinds of literary artifice:

Coleridge at marginalia, T. S. Eliot at epigraphs, Samuel Johnson at prefaces, Freud at lectures.

Why am I interested in such unconsidered trifles? Let me try to justify myself with a brief excursion into what a Hollywood screenwriter might call my Back Story. Or, more precisely, with two excursions. The first goes back twenty years or more, to the day when I first read Paul Fussell's splendid book *Samuel Johnson and the Life of Writing* and experienced a minor epiphany, somewhere in the middle of its third chapter. I think it came with this sentence: '. . . we recognise a piece of writing as literature only through our prior acceptance of the convention that its genre is literary; otherwise we do not notice it, or we do not notice it artistically.' Now, it was no newsflash that all literature is written in genres. But his implication that a great deal of the writing we don't often acknowledge as literary is also largely shaped by the force of genre, from a letter home from summer camp (Fussell quotes his young daughter's epistolary request for liquorice) to an end-of-term school report to a job reference to a mash note to a 'Dear Diary' entry – *this* was a novelty.

Fussell was obviously on to something, and he proceeded to explain some of the things that he was on to. For example, just about everyone with enough education to read a book with no pictures knows that certain bits of writing – such as this Introduction – have particular jobs to do, and will feel duly gratified when the job is well done or vaguely irritated when it isn't. But why? No one's ever shown us the rules. You can buy a How To book for writing a novel or a play or, in the last couple of years (this is not a joke), a diary, but you'll have to search long and hard to find a book which shows you how to choose an epigraph or phrase a dedication. Despite this glaring gap in the self-help market, though, writers happily go on dedicating and epigraphing and writing blurbs about themselves, and their readers appreciate perfectly well what is going on. In short, we understand a good deal more about the rules of (extremely) minor literary genres than polite society generally admits.

Fussell's remark also had certain implications which he didn't trouble to spell out: . . . *otherwise we do not notice it, or do not notice it artistically.* If you took this phrase as an invitation rather than a dismissal, it meant that the world must be full of buried literary treasure – countless thousands of small but perfectly formed works of literary art out there, just waiting to be noticed and enjoyed as such. Very well, then, I would try to start noticing. *Invisible Forms* is, in part, a record of some of the things I've since noticed in and around the relatively neglected parts of books. It's easy once you start, anyone can do it, and, far from diluting one's enjoyment of main texts, it's a way of multiplying the already vast pleasures of reading.

My alternative or supplementary Back Story is closer to the present. In the late 1980s and early 1990s, I worked on the arts pages of the *Independent*. Its Arts Editor of the day, Thomas Sutcliffe, had taken as one of the guiding principles of those pages a motto coined by the fashion designer Paul Smith: 'classic with a twist'. What this meant in practice was that we would try wherever appropriate to vary the standard arts pages diet of reviews and interviews with features that had more or less mainstream subject matter but which were approached in a less orthodox manner: parodies and pastiches, essays in unusual formats, verse, fiction, cartoons.

The subject matter was classic, the twist came in the approach. As far as I was concerned, it was a highly congenial approach, which gave a great deal of scope for the kind of Noticing I'd been doing in off-duty hours. At various times, I was assigned to review a concert by Status Quo in the style of the 'Ancient Mariner', to write a retrospective of the year's principal events in the arts world as they might have been viewed by Alexander Pope in his *Dunciad* period, and to come up with acrostic sonnets on the name WOLFGANG MOZART with both Petrarchan and Shakespearean rhyme schemes. I was also commissioned to write articles about the moon, gifts (at Christmas), food (ditto), parties (ditto), hangovers (New Year's Day), madness, genius and many other phenomena, all as represented by writers, dramatists, film-makers and other artists. I wrote an interview with Bugs Bunny and an angry riposte by Daffy Duck, a soliloquy by Frankenstein's monster, a spoof get-rich-quick guide to churning out violent, sexy screenplays *à la* Joe Esterhaz, short essays on palindromes and sequels and screams and Arcadias and lost books and . . .

After a while, my friend Gilbert Adair, who had just published a collection of his own journalism under the enviably smart title *The Postmodernist Always Rings Twice*, suggested that I might think about collecting these assorted pieces into a book. I was flattered, and even more flattered when a distinguished publisher, Michael Schmidt, spontaneously made the same proposal. Tempted as I was by the almost effortless challenge of putting together a book out of my tatty old cuttings, however, I saw that it really wouldn't do. Questions of merit aside, the *Independent* pieces were far too miscellaneous to add up to a book with a properly coherent set of concerns; and on the whole, the articles one writes in haste are better left alone to be repented in leisure, not exhumed, stuffed and put on display. Still, even after throwing out the majority of candidates as unfit for any kind of perfect-bound afterlife, there were about half a dozen articles which did suggest the germ of a proper book. Most of them were written as exercises in the form they discussed: a heavily footnoted piece about footnotes, a copiously defaced article on marginalia, and an introduction to the work of the Oulipo – that admirable Parisian body dedicated to the composition of literary works obeying strict formal constraints – in accordance with a simple alphabetical constraint. All of them were written with the aim of showing some of the pleasures that may be hidden in plain sight right beneath our reading eyes, and of relishing the artistry that might be achieved within genres which seldom receive their due.

. Obviously, these half-dozen or so journalistic scraps – few of them much more than 1,300–1,500 words long – would have to be rewritten and expanded, and I'd have to write more than a dozen new ones. As I settled to my agreeable task, it dawned on me that this Force of Genre or Classic with a Twist way of looking at the edges of books was so beguiling, and in one or two cases so enlightening, that I couldn't believe someone hadn't written about my IFs before. Someone, I soon discovered, had. His name was Isaac D'Israeli, he flourished in the nineteenth century, and his deliciously vagrant book of rambles around the folklore of writers and writing, *Curiosities of Literature*, includes essays on prefaces, titles, dedications and one or two other paratexts. At a pinch, you could also claim that his article 'follies', about lipograms and the like, unwittingly predicts (or, as Oulipians would put it, 'plagiarizes by anticipation') the twentieth-century activities of the Oulipo. I felt that D'Israeli's example conferred an unexpected air of ancestral dignity on my enterprise, and so resolved to cheat slightly on my own self-imposed rule that each of the chapters of *Invisible Forms* should be about an IF by devoting a chapter to this amiable bibliophile and *bibliognoste*.

I was slightly less thrilled, a few months later (by which time my book-in-progress had acquired a new publisher), to be alerted to the existence of a book by the theorist Gerard Genette with the knowing title *Seuils* ('Thresholds'). 'Knowing', because Genette's work is published by Éditions du Seuil. *Seuils*, it appeared, was all about paratexts; worse, it was so ferociously erudite as to pre-empt all further comment on the subject; worst of all, it had not been translated, so I was going to have to slog through the better part of 400 pages of densely argued French. Daunted, but remembering the example of that other Parisian sage C. Auguste Dupin, I investigated, and was relieved. On the one hand, yes, *Seuils* was all about paratexts and it was ferociously erudite. On the other, no, it *had* just been translated, with the slightly less snappy title *Paratexts: Thresholds of Interpretation*; and, despite aforementioned ferocious erudition, it did not pre-empt my project, since Genette had wholly different ambitions, and was (mostly) writing about very different authors. So I simply fiddled here and there with my own interim conclusions, acknowledged Genette where appropriate and otherwise steamed ahead regardless.

As with Genette's work, so with that of other authorities: I've drawn on the appropriate works of scholarship where it seemed valuable and ignored them where it didn't, since *Invisible Forms* is also intended as an entertainment of sorts. Since I'm not an academic and don't have to fret about tenure, I've felt at liberty to write throughout in much the same vein as I've been writing here – that is, to digress, reminisce, speculate, make cranky assertions and crack daft jokes as much as I wanted. That isn't to say that I've played fast and loose with the usual decencies: I've tried to quote accurately, cite sources where required and generally give as reliable a representation of each topic as was within my powers. (Unless it meant sacrificing some of the daft jokes.) Obviously, none of the essays is meant to be anything like exhaustive: many of its topics might be, probably should be, and with any luck will one day be the subject of book-length studies in their own right.

Actually, one of my minor hopes for *Invisible Forms* is that it might provoke one or two real scholars into writing such studies. My major hopes include vast royalty cheques, the sale of film rights, a record-breaking advance for the sequel (working title: *IF2: The Sequel*), the possibility that a fair number of people might find the process of reading this book as informative as I have found researching it, and the remote possibility that they might even enjoy a small frisson of recognition here and there. Oh, and by the way: I trust that no one will assume that my paying attention here to some of the most minuscule forms of literature indicates that I'm not interested in more substantial genres. But in case they do: I am.

Finally, since a main purpose of *Invisible Forms* is to grant some of the lesser amenities of books a dignity usually reserved for those fully grown genres, I had better conclude my introductory remarks by suggesting a suitable generic name for the parts of which it is composed. Here and elsewhere in the book I've lazily called them 'pieces' or 'essays' or, closest to the mark, 'digressions', but in the course of writing them I began to suspect that there must be a more accurate term somewhere in the lexicons. 'Lucubrations', though it has its charms, is a bit of a mouthful and has other drawbacks. (It comes from the Latin *lucubrare* and *lux*, 'light': to lucubrate is, literally, to work by artificial light, and a lucubration is the study or writing so produced; 'Now somewhat derisive or playful', cautions the *OED*.) In the end, I decided that it was best to wallow in the mild eccentricity of the project and admit that it smacks here and there of, to put it mildly, idiosyncrasy. So I filched an old term from the worlds of music and abnormal psychology, and began to think of each component part of *Invisible Forms* as a maggot. (*OED*: 'A whimsical or perverse fancy: a crotchet.') Here it is, then, or rather here they are: *Invisible Forms*: a bunch of maggots.

K.J.
St Cecilia's Day,
1998

Titles

I'm not interested in titles;
making titles is snobbish.

Shuntarō Tanikawa, 'At Midnight in the
Kitchen I Just Wanted to Talk To You'

It took me ages to come up with a suitable title for this book, and in the end someone* had to come to my rescue. But in the months before I finally threw in the towel, I beguiled many a half-hour by seeking inspiration in the titles of other gatherings of essays, particularly those by some of my favourite modern writers, from grand and solemn Americans such as Lionel Trilling (*The Liberal Imagination, Beyond Culture, The Opposing Self*), Edmund Wilson (*The Shores of Light, The Triple Thinkers*) and Susan Sontag (*Against Interpretation, Styles of Radical Will* and – most beautiful – *Under the Sign of Saturn*) to the jokier or more oblique Britons: Anthony Burgess (*Homage to QWERTYUIOP*), Gilbert Adair (*The Postmodernist Always Rings Twice*), Bruce Chatwin (*What Am I Doing Here*; and what happened to the question mark?).

Eventually, and inevitably, I turned to Cyril Connolly, who seemed able to summon up or track down titles for his

* Michael Schmidt. *Gratias ago.*

collections of journalism (*The Condemned Playground*, *Previous Convictions*) that were almost as memorable as those of his through-written works: *Enemies of Promise*, *The Unquiet Grave*. The best of all his titles for the former group was surely *The Evening Colonnade*, with its subdued play on the journalistic and architectural senses of the word 'column' and its pleasing assonance of 'Colonnade' and 'Connolly'. He found the phrase in Pope:

> What are the gay parterre, the chequr'd shade
> The morning bower, the ev'ning colonnade
> But soft recesses of uneasy minds
> To sigh unheard in, to the passing winds?

Pope was not, however, Connolly's first choice. His introductory essay to this late collection reveals that he had also toyed with, and rejected, *Penultimatum*, Iago's *Nothing If Not Critical*,* *The Meeting Rivers* (too flat), *The Voiceless Worm* (from Wordsworth: too self-loathing), *The Surface of Past Times* (also Wordsworth: too Proustian), *Time and the Bell* (from T. S. Eliot: too suggestive of the boxing ring), *The Downright Epicure* (Henry Vaughan; too downright) and others. In the course of his vain searches, he grew envious of the dead: 'Some writers have no problem: their title descends in tongues of flame, it's just a matter of choosing a book. *Paradise Lost – Vanity Fair – War and Peace – Farewell to Arms – The Waste Land . . .*'

Fine titles, all of them, yet Connolly's suggestion that this select band of writers had 'no problem' in finding a name is as disconcerting as his slovenly omission of the indefinite

---

* Which has since been bagged by Robert Hughes.

article from that Hemingway title. Just about everyone who reads Eliot nowadays, and quite a few who don't, will recall that *The Waste Land*, far from descending in tongues of flame* was originally entitled 'He Do The Police in Different Voices'.† As a devotee of high modernism, Connolly was almost certainly aware of this himself, since Faber had published the facsimile of Eliot's drafts, with annotations by Ezra Pound, in 1971, two years before *The Evening Colonnade*. And in any case, *The Waste Land* wasn't exactly a coinage, but – as one would expect of such an allusion-ridden work – a sort of double quotation, from Malory's *Morte D'Arthur* (Book 17, Chapter 3) and from Book II of St Augustine's *Confessions*.‡

This odd lapse of attention on Connolly's part set me to

---

* Anyway, doesn't 'tongues of flame' suggest the *Four Quartets* rather than *The Waste Land*?

† I oversimplify. As far as I can make out, 'He Do . . .' seems to be a kind of subtitle to *The Waste Land*, for which 'The Burial of the Dead' is therefore sub-subtitle (1) and 'A Game of Chess' (or, originally, 'In The Cage' – an allusion to Henry James) is sub-subtitle (2). What is beyond dispute is that the phrase is an allusion to *Our Mutual Friend*, chapter xvi. An old widow, Betty Higden, says of her adopted son Sloppy that he is '. . . a beautiful reader of a newspaper. He do the Police in different voices.'

‡ Or, possibly, a triple quotation: the June 1915 issue of *Poetry Chicago*, which published 'The Love Song of J. Alfred Prufrock', also boasted a poem called 'The Waste Land' by the now forgotten Madison Cawein. *The Waste Land* must be one of the most commonly misspelled titles of the century; I've lost track of the number of times I've seen it cited as *The Wasteland*, but it must rival or exceed the number of times that *Finnegans Wake* is rendered as *Finnegan's Wake*.

wondering quite how firey or tonguey the titles of the rest of his short list might have been. *Paradise Lost*? One of the early outline drafts of the poem suggests that Milton was considering the alternative title *Adam Unparadized*.* *Vanity Fair*? Thackeray appears to have begun writing his novel in February 1845, and it wasn't until October–November 1846 – after it had been rejected by Colburn and other publishers – that the Bunyanesque title finally struck him. He was staying in Brighton, and it 'came upon him unawares in the middle of the night'. He 'jumped out of bed and ran three times round his room, uttering as he went, "Vanity Fair, Vanity Fair, Vanity Fair" '.† Before this revelation, he had referred to his work-in-progress as 'Novel Without a Hero' and 'Pen and Pencil Sketches of English Society'; both of these, as John Sutherland observes, 'survive as sub-titles' in the final version.

War and Peace? When Tolstoy began work on the novel, it was set in the 1820s, and he planned to call it *1825*. Then, after it dawned on him that he would have a far more impressive tale to tell if he transported his characters back two decades to the height of the Napoleonic Wars, he changed the title to *1805*, and it was duly published under this heading in the *Russian Herald*. Still uncomfortable, and suspecting that it might be a good idea for all his heroes and heroines to enjoy happy endings, he resolved to lift one of

---

* See *Paradise Lost*, edited by Alastair Fowler (London: Longman, 1968), p. 4.

† See John Sutherland's introduction to the World's Classics edition of *Vanity Fair* (Oxford: Oxford University Press, 1983), p. xxxvii.

Shakespeare's finest titles and call it *All's Well That Ends Well*. It was only when the epic implications of his theme became fully apparent that he settled on the stately, all-encompassing *War and Peace*.

A Farewell to Arms? On the face of it, another odd modern choice for Connolly, since Hemingway was well known to fiddle and fidget with his titles to a neurotic degree. He once claimed that 'I make a list of titles *after* I've finished the story or book – sometimes as many as a hundred. Then I start eliminating them, sometimes all of them'.* His memoir of Paris, *A Moveable Feast*, was given its name by his widow Mary, who discovered that he had referred to the City of Light by that phrase in a letter; the alternative titles Hemingway had contemplated included *The Eye and the Ear*, *To Write it Truly*, *Love is Hunger*, *It is Different in the Ring* and *The Parts Nobody Knows*. Curiously, *A Farewell to Arms* just happens to be one example of a title which Hemingway settled on and stuck to unswervingly, but it certainly didn't come to him in a blinding flash – he set himself to trawling through Sir Arthur Quiller-Couch's *Oxford Book of English Verse* in search of inspiration when he had already completed a 600-page manuscript of the novel. The phrase comes from the Elizabethan poet George Peele, and is itself a title or sub-title, for the well-known verses which begin 'His golden locks time hath to silver turn'd . . .'

Adam Unparadized, *Novel Without a Hero*, *1805*, *He Do The Police in Different Voices* . . . While it would be a trifle

---

* See André Bernard, *Now All We Need is a Title* (New York and London: Norton, 1994), p. 62.

harsh to suggest that, with a strike-out rate of 80 per cent or higher, Connolly could hardly have picked a more wobbly set of titles had he tried,* his feeble score can serve to remind us that memorable titles are much more likely to be the product of long deliberation, search missions and the application of talent than some painless Pentecostal descent.

Anyone interested making a swift trawl through the lore of classic titles and some of their earlier avatars is warmly recommended to consult André Bernard's *Now All We Need is a Title: Famous Book Titles and How They Got That Way* (1994), an entertaining little volume from which I learned that *East of Eden* was once called *The Salinas Valley*, *Gone With the Wind* was once called *Pansy* (also *Tote the Weary Load*, *Tomorrow is Another Day*, *Jettison*, *Milestones* and *Ba! Ba! Black Sheep*), *Tess of the d'Urbervilles* was once called *The Body and Soul of Sue* (also *Too Late, Beloved!* and *A Daughter of the d'Urbervilles*) and *Bleak House* was called, among several other scarcely less odd possibilities, *Tom-All-Alone's Factory that Got Into Chancery and Never Got Out*. Mr Bernard's book also includes some useful authorial hints on the nature of a memorable title, such as Walker Percy's maxim that it 'should be like a good metaphor; it should intrigue without being too baffling or too obvious', or John O'Hara's proposal that one way to arrive at a haunting title is to juxtapose two

---

* He might, for example, have picked *The Great Gatsby*, which began life as *Trimalchio in West Egg*. Fitzgerald, who had also suggested the possibilities of *Gold-hatted Gatsby* and *The High-Bouncing Lover*, continued to lament the loss of his Petronian allusion long after the novel's successful publication.

simple words in an unexpected way, as he did for his own novel, *A Rage to Live*.*

Whether or not they indulge in public discussion of the subject as O'Hara did, however, most authors will be aware that a title is, or should be, a small work of art in its own right. (Similarly, most publishers will recognize that, though an apparently uncommercial title need not sink a book that people want to read,† a good title can be the commercial making of a book.)‡ One of Connolly's favoured quintet, T. S. Eliot, acknowledged as much when he wrote that Nathaniel Hawthorne had possessed even that minor token of literary genius, the genius for titles,§ and Eliot's general

---

* A juxtaposition he found ready-made in Pope's 'Moral Essays'. Eric Korn, who collects such trifles, has pointed out that John O'Hara's earlier novel *Appointment in Samara* is one of that happy breed of books in which author and title rhyme: other examples include *Omphalos* by Philip Gosse, *The Golden Gate* by Vikram Seth . . . See his collection, *Remainders*, (Carcanet, 1989).

† As becomes clear from Mr Bernard's book, publishers have objected to many a subsequently successful title, such as *The Rise and Fall of the Third Reich*, *The Catcher in the Rye*, or *Smilla's Sense of Snow* (the American title for what the British know as *Miss Smilla's Feeling for Snow*).

‡ True story: an English publisher went to an American book fair to try to sell a book entitled *An Anthology of Surrealist Humour*. 'No, that's no good,' he was told. 'Why don't you call it something like, oh, I don't know, *This Fish is Loaded*?' He did. It sold very nicely.

§ I owe this point to Christopher Ricks, *T. S. Eliot and Prejudice* (London: Faber and Faber, 1988), p. 1. Ricks is, as ever, wonderfully acute and illuminating on Eliot's own weird genius for titles, notably *Prufrock and Other Observations*. Eliot's verses have spawned many other memorable titles: *A*

proposition sounds right whether or not you agree with him that Hawthorne was a titular whizz. One working definition of a great title might be that it manages to pass into common literate currency, and only one of Hawthorne's titles, *The Scarlet Letter*, has achieved that distinction – you need to be fairly well read to be able to reel off two or three others without hesitation (*The House of the Seven Gables*, *The Blithedale Romance*, *The Marble Faun* – Hawthorne had a penchant for the adjective/noun template), and a fairly advanced student of American literature to dredge up the title of his first novel.* By contrast, Edgar Allan Poe, whose prose can be garish and creaky and downright silly compared to the best of Hawthorne's, had the gift of coining title after title that has lodged firmly in the popular imagination: 'The Fall of the House of Usher', 'The Gold Bug', 'The Murders in the Rue Morgue', 'The Masque of the Red Death', 'The Premature Burial', 'The Purloined Letter', 'The Conquerer Worm', 'The Raven' . . . but then, these were titles for short stories and poems: Poe's novel has a more lumbering, not to mention oddly punctuated title: *The Narrative of Arthur Gordon Pym. Of Nantucket*. (I have no idea. Why he put the full stop in the middle.)

And there is one sense in which both American writers must be regarded as primitive geniuses. However self-conscious they may have been about other aspects of their artistry, Hawthorne and Poe both wrote in the plain-

---

Handful of Dust, *The Grass is Singing*, and – as Nicholas Lezard pointed out to me – Julian Sensitive's autobiographical novel *My Trousers Rolled*.

* *Fanshawe* (1828).

dealing days before the rise of the modern title – the title, that is, which conspicuously puns or alludes or dazzles or provokes curious thoughts; the title that *knows* quite well that it should aspire to the condition of a free-standing work of art, rather than state its case frankly and let the reader decide about the attractiveness or otherwise of becoming acquainted with a chap called David Copperfield, a lady called Jane Eyre, a place called Wuthering Heights or the embodied interplay of pride and prejudice.* Personal names, place names, statements of theme: the vast majority of classic titles before the twentieth century fall into these ranks and files.† By the time Eliot was reviewing Hawthorne in the early twentieth century, such titular innocence had been lost. One quick way of watching the old order yielding to the new is to run through a chronological list of the works of Hawthorne's admirer Henry James: places and people – *Roderick Hudson* (1876), *The American* (1877), *Daisy Miller* (1879), *Washington Square* (1881) and *The Princess Casamassima* (1886) – give way to abstractions and evocations: *What Maisie Knew* (1897), *The Turn of the Screw* (1898) *The Awkward Age*

---

* The practice of calling a novel after its hero or heroine has become so unfashionable among serious writers that when we come across such a title we suspect deliberate anachronism or pastiche, as in Peter Carey's recent reworking of themes from *Great Expectations*, *Jack Maggs*.

† I overstate the case, though not very much. This seems as good a place as any to observe that some classic English titles aren't in English: *Areopagitica*, for example. Off-hand I can only think of two or three twentieth-century books with Latin titles: Wittgenstein's *Tractatus Logico-Philosophicus*, Russell & Whitehead's *Principia Mathematica*, and Barthes's *Camera Lucida*.

(1899), *The Wings of the Dove* (1902) and *The Golden Bowl* (1904).* This isn't just a matter of James's personal development. Broadly speaking, as the Victorian age wanes, book titles wax more lyrical, more loquacious, more conspicuously literary. A small emblem for the changing times: Samuel Butler's autobiographical novel *Ernest Pontifex* had grown up, by the time of its posthumous publication in 1903, into *The Way of All Flesh*.

Hasty as they are, such observations none the less hint that a sufficiently industrious scholar could write a critical history of this IF, one that might be broken down into quite clearly distinct periods, showing just which fashions and patterns prevailed where and when;† and, therefore, that a sufficiently well-informed reader could work out the likely date of a book on the evidence of its title alone. Actually, some eras are already sufficiently distinct for ready identification by averagely well-tuned ears. Only the sixties or early seventies, surely, could have spawned the likes of Peter Weiss's *The Persecution and Assassination of Marat as Performed by the Inmates of the Asylum of Charenton under the Direction of*

---

* This was first pointed out to me by Dr Adrian Poole, who also provided many other valuable observations, including his suggestion that one of the finest titles ever given to a work of history was *To the Finland Station*, by Edmund Wilson. Among the other scholarly titles for which I nurse a fondness are *Traces on the Rhodian Shore*, by Clarence J. Glacken, and *All That Is Solid Melts into Air*, by Marshall Berman.

† It would have to include a discussion of the practice of double-titling, once commonplace – *Frankenstein, or The Modern Prometheus*; *Twelfth Night, or What You Will* – now perilously close to extinction.

the Marquis de Sade,* or Tom Wolfe's *The Electric Kool-Aid Acid Test* or Timothy Leary's *The Politics of Ecstacy* or Jerry Rubin's *Do It!*. And it must have been some time in the late 1970s or early 1980s that the Modern Languages Association of America sent out its hit-squads to kneecap any academic in the humanities who refused to follow the iron rule that all monograph titles *must* use a present participle, preferably with some suitably lame pun on the word 'gender': *Engendering Possessions, Declining Genders, Gendering Genres, Generating Genders, Regenerating Gendered Genres from Genet to Genette* . . . that sort of thing.

One thing you're unlikely to find in any of these participled studies is the reason why at least one or two titles of films, books and songs should seem to exercise an appeal, even a magic, greatly in excess of their face-value merits or appeal. Some triumphs are easy enough to understand: *Catch-22*† entered the language of the lettered and unlettered alike thanks to its having, for the first time, memorably tagged a maddening double-bind from which almost everyone has suffered; *The Right Stuff* gave a laconic, macho label name to a complex of laconic, macho virtues that were easier to grasp instinctively than to define succinctly; *The Man Who Mistook His Wife for a Hat* was a little fable in its own right; *The Female Eunuch* managed to be at once oxymoronic and punchy.

---

* No room here, alas, for a discussion of preposterously long titles.

† Simon Pettifar pointed out to me that the titles of all Heller's subsequent novels and memoirs are calculatedly unremarkable – clichés, stock phrases, scraps of phatic communion: *Something Happened, Good as Gold, No Laughing Matter, God Knows, Picture This, Closing Time, Now and Then*.

And, of course, an otherwise unpromising or uncompromising title sometimes becomes widely known simply because it is blazoned across the spine and cover of a bestseller or a cult book. It hardly occurs to us now that *Ulysses* is hopelessly unsexy, or that *Of Human Bondage* is unsaleably pompous,* or – to take a brief canter through some culty American best-sellers – that *The Catcher in the Rye* isn't very eye or rye-catching, or that *On The Road* sounds like a manual for itinerant tarmac salesmen, or that *Gravity's Rainbow* ought to be the title of a slim volume of verse by a high school physics teacher. *My Struggle* (oh, all right, it's more chilling in the original: *Mein Kampf*) isn't particularly distinctive, either. Though some people dissent, I can see far greater commercial potential in Herr Hitler's more obviously loony *ur*-title *Four and a Half Years of Struggle against Lies, Stupidity and Cowardice.*

Other titles attain a fame that is only partly due or reducible to their robust sales figures. What makes *The Unbearable Lightness of Being*, chunky mouthful that it is, such an unforgettable title? Why did the Savonarolan severity of *The Bonfire of the Vanities* set the world alight? (Talking of bonfires, why was *Fahrenheit 451* so catchy?)† Or, to turn from

---

* Maugham took the phrase from Spinoza's *Ethics*. He probably wouldn't have risked it nowadays; the public has a filthier collective mind.

† Ray Bradbury has other splendid titles: *The Silver Locusts*, *The October Country*, *The Illustrated Man* and – a nod to Whitman – *I Sing the Body Electric*. But then, many science fiction writers have had a pronounced knack for titling: Ursula Le Guin's *The Left Hand of Darkness*, Robert Heinlein's *Stranger in a Strange Land*, Fritz Leiber's *Conjure Wife*, Aldous Huxley's *Brave New World* (the Bard) and *After Many a Summer* (Tennyson)

the metropolis to the country, the down-home lilt of *A River Runs Through It*? Or Eco's Shakespearean/Gertrude Steinian *The Name of the Rose*? Why do *Tropic of Cancer* and *Tropic of Capricorn* lodge in the mind so firmly, whether read or unread? Or *Lord of the Flies*? Or *Waiting for Godot*?* Or *A Long Day's Journey Into Night*? Or *The Caucasian Chalk Circle*? Or almost any of William Faulkner's titles: *The Sound and the Fury*,[†] *As I Lay Dying*, *Absalom, Absalom!*, *Intruder in the Dust*, *Requiem for a Nun*, and, probably the most lyrical of the bunch, *Light in August*?

Without resorting to questionnaires and teams of impoverished graduate students, it would hard to establish reliable statistics for the tenacity and diffusion of these and similarly

---

... and, however posterity eventually comes to judge the novels of Philip K. Dick, his titles were fabulous: *The Man in the High Castle*, *Do Androids Dream of Electric Sheep?* (filmed as *Blade Runner*, a different kind of good title), *A Scanner Darkly*, *The Three Stigmata of Palmer Eldritch* ... My personal favourite: *Flow My Tears, the Policeman Said*, quite probably the only SF title to allude to John Dowland (1563–1626). For a complete list of Dick's titles, see his biography, *Divine Invasions* (by Lawrence Sutin, London: Paladin, 1991).

* There's probably already a book on Beckett's titles, but let's just have a swift revision session: he begins in bawdy with 'Whoroscope' and *More Pricks Than Kicks*, occasionally relapses (*Krapp's Last Tape*), passes through proper names (*Murphy*, *Watt*, *Molloy*, *Malone Dies*) to *The Unnamable*, and ends up with eerie phrases, non-words and bad puns: *The Lost Ones*, *Lessness*, *Worstward Ho*, *Stirrings Still*, *Ends and Odds*. His most chilling title: *How It Is* (in the French, a pun: *Comment C'Est*: 'Commencer': 'To begin'). His most wholly unexpected title: *Ohio Impromptu*.

† Yes, I know it's from Shakespeare. So was *Music, Ho!*, by Constant Lambert.

charmed titles, but a rough rule of thumb might be the number of times they have been cited or twisted in head-lines, stand-up routines or political speeches – such as Mrs Thatcher's declaration that 'The Lady's Not for Turning!'. Hard to believe that she or her speechwriters are actually fans of Christopher Fry's *The Lady's Not for Burning*; easier to suspect that there is something in the turn of his title which has made it stick like a burr to the synapses of generations.

*

That bright elusive 'something', Gilbert Adair has suggested in his essay 'On Titles',* is a quality of ambiguity, which gives *The Lady's Not for Burning* a 'weird compacted force' that makes it the peer of six other exceptionally haunting play titles: *The Importance of Being Earnest*, *The Playboy of the Western World*, *Six Characters in Search of an Author*, *A Streetcar Named Desire*, *The Trojan War Will Not Take Place* and – in Adair's view, the most beautiful title in the English language – *Mourning Becomes Electra*.† Adair's is a persuasive enough account of the play-titles in question, but it isn't much help with those titles which seem to have become memorable almost despite themselves: *Out of Africa* is about as bland as a set of words can be, but I saw it used and punned on for dozens of newspaper headlines in the 1980s, when its closest rival was the not especially witty or remark-

---

* *Surfing the Zeitgeist* (London: Faber and Faber, 1997), pp. 88–91; this collection was originally to be called *Variations Without a Theme*.

† A phrase of which I hear a distant echo in the title of Michael Ondaatje's *Coming Through Slaughter*, which I find so spellbinding that I don't want to risk reading the novel in case the contents don't live up to it.

able paradox *Back to the Future*. (Earlier cinematic and literary-cinematic contenders: *A Bridge Too Far*; *Mean Streets*; *Rebel Without a Cause*; *From Russia With Love* . . .)*

Old-style methods of close reading might do a lot to unpack the reasons why a given title might tickle the ear, but I suspect that the only people who could hope to reduce this mysterious matter to more or less reliable and recyclable formulae are off making their millions in the advertising trade, and are too shrewd to share their secrets. You can sympathize with the authors cited in Mr Bernard's book who despaired of ever finding their own titles, and so farmed out the job to others;† and you might suspect that a lot of authors have privately wished they could adopt the radical policy hatched by Enoch Soames‡ who planned to issue a book of poems with no title at all: 'Rothenstein', Max Beerbohm reports, 'objected that the absence of title might

---

* This is neither the time nor the place to go into the vast subject of film titles, but there are a couple of oddities I can't bear to miss. Isn't it weird that the titles of a highly successful, intensely violent film of the seventies and a highly successful, intensely violent film of the nineties both contain the word 'dogs' and are both incomprehensible to the uninitiated? (Neither film 'explains' its cryptic title anywhere in its running time.) I refer, of course, to Sam Peckinpah's *Straw Dogs* and Quentin Tarantino's *Reservoir Dogs*. The first is a recondite allusion to the Chinese Taoist philosopher Lao Tse; the second is a private joke about a mishearing of the title of Louis Malle's film *Au Revoir les enfants*.

† He mentions, for example, the case of Ann Beattie, who sends her untitled stories to the *New Yorker*, where her editor, Roger Angell, may sometimes reject it, but will always give the rejections a 'perfect' name in his accompanying letter.

‡ See below, p. 230 and pp. 265–72.

be bad for the sale of a book. 'If,' he urged, 'I went into a bookseller's and said simply "Have you got?" or "Have you a copy of?" how would they know what I wanted?'*

Rothenstein's point is well taken. To the best of my knowledge, the only established author ever to have issued a book with no title was e. e. cummings, who in 1930 published a sixty-three-page volume which bibliographies list as '[Untitled]'† with the house of Covici-Friede. It did not set the market on fire, and one major copyright library I visited did not possess a single volume, as though to slap cummings down for his temerity. Instead of dreaming of such perverse escape routes, the suffering author should simply knuckle down to the task with a will, reflecting that every ounce of sweat expended on a title may one day prove to be worth it: sometimes all that survives in general memory of an author's entire *œuvre* is a title or two.‡ And those readers who lead busy and careworn lives can take a certain kind of

---

* *Seven Men*, p. 9.

† See Richard S. Kennedy, *Dreams in the Mirror: A Biography of E. E. Cummings*, pp. 316–17. Many of cummings's titles pose headaches for the librarian or bibliographer – *&* and *½*, among others – and even the ones that can be spelled are pretty rum: *Is 5*, *CIOPW*, *ViVa*, *Eimi*, *1 x 1*, and χαῖρε.

‡ I'm sure, for example, that thousands of people are still enjoying the works of Thomas Heywood (?1574–1641), but I'm not aware of ever having seen or read so much as a single scene from his plays, and at present feel only the feeblest inclination to put that right before I die. And yet Heywood does occupy a small chink of my grey matter, and many others', because he achieved the durable titles *A Woman Killed With Kindness* and *The Fair Maid of the West*.

heart, as well: even if you, Overworked Reader, have never found the leisure to read *The Decline and Fall of the Roman Empire* or *Don Quixote* or *Faust* or the *Commedia*, you can console yourself with the reflection that you have at least read – and, in the last second or so, just re-read – a minute but essential part of those books.

Pseudonyms (a.k.a. Noms de Plume)

She's picking out names
I hope none of them are mine

Elvis Costello,* 'Green Shirt'

Before John Wilson could make a name for himself as a novelist, he had to make a name for himself as a novelist. His full legal name was John Anthony Burgess Wilson, but there were already too many Wilsons in the literary world (Angus, Colin, Edmund . . .); besides, the terms of his contract as a teacher for the Colonial Office did not allow him to publish fiction under his own name. And so, as he later put it with characteristic verbal *sprezzatura*, Wilson peeled off the carapace of his nominal shrimp, or pulled his own nominal cracker, and his first published novel *Time for a Tiger* was credited to one Anthony Burgess. It would be tempting to call this act of creative slicing one of the most inspired moments of a prodigiously fertile literary career, were it not that credit for the name should really be handed to Wilson's editor at Heinemann, Roland Gant.† Thanks to Mr Gant, the

---

* A.k.a. Declan McManus, Napoleon Dynamite, Spike the Beloved Entertainer, etc. etc.

† See *You've Had Your Time*, p. III.

big novelist called 'Anthony Burgess' could enjoy all sorts of possibilities denied to little John Wilson.

'Burgess' translates smoothly into other European languages, so that his future mother-in-law, the Contessa Maria Lucrezia Pasi della Pergola, could content herself by thinking that her daughter was marrying a man with the perfectly decent Italian name Antonio Borghese,* and so that Jorge Luis Borges – with whom Burgess once swapped verses from Cædmon at a cocktail party in Washington DC, to the consternation of security men – could playfully suggest that they must be distant relations. Wilson/Burgess was a composer as well as a novelist, and the initials A and B can, like the component letters of Bach, be rendered into a musical signature, as they are on the cover of his memoir *This Man and Music*. He was a poet as well as a composer, and wrote an ingenious book about Keats and the Roman dialect poet Belli incorporating English versions of Belli's obscene verses and entitled *ABBA ABBA*, the rhyme scheme for the octave of a Petrarchan sonnet. True, there were also some disadvantages to this rechristening, especially after Guy Burgess tainted the assumed surname with connotations of treason. Burgess, A. once made a sly punch back at the widespread journalistic assumption that he was closely related to, or indeed one and the same man as, the Soviet stooge by asserting a, presumably fanciful, family connection to a far more obscure Burgess, G. – the American humorist Gelett Burgess, now remembered, if at all, for his verse about the

---

* More decent, perhaps, than the name she had so far worn, Liana Macellari, since 'Macellari' has associations of hacking through flesh: better a bourgeois than a butcher, the contessa may have reflected.

purple cow and for having coined the word 'blurb'.* Yet
even in death, Anthony Burgess's created name continues to
work hard and play hard for him: the same letters ABBA
ABBA are inscribed on his gravestone in Monaco, where
they now evoke the agonized dying cry to Big God of
another well-known subject of Burgess's fiction, the Man of
Nazareth; in Aramaic, the words mean 'Father, father'. And
these are by no means all the conceits† that Mr Wilson
managed to spin from the fourteen letters of his assumed
identity.

To be sure, 'Anthony Burgess' is an unusually fertile
name: it was a rich creative resource for its bearer as well as
a working convenience, and not every literary pseudonym
deserves to be considered so respectfully as an IF. Many are
quite dull. Even so, to discuss the art of pseudonyms at
adequate length would require a study so large that few
could be bothered to read it, let alone write it. One of the
best reference books on the subject, Adrian Room's *Naming
Names*,‡ for example, is a compendious and often fascinating
Who's Who of the pseudonym, running to some 350 closely
printed pages and containing countless thousands of examples from the worlds of showbiz, politics, art, religion and

---

* See the blurb for the hardback edition of Burgess's *End of the World
News* (London: Hutchinson, 1982); for more on Gellett Burgess, see the
chapter on blurbs, pp. 52–62.

† To borrow Mansfield Forbes' epigram on the obscure metaphysical poet
Thomas Phillipot: Burgess scattered his *concetti* like *confetti*.

‡ *Naming Names: Stories of Pseudonyms and Name Changes with a Who's
Who* (London and Henley: Routledge and Kegan Paul, 1981).

war as well as literature, yet even this painstaking work is a long way from being exhaustive.* For the purposes of this brief digression, then, here are just six things that the example of 'Anthony Burgess' might suggest about pseudonyms, beginning with a kind of inverted Gresham's Law.

1. Good Names Drive Out Bad

When a pseudonym catches on, it tends to obliterate the true name from popular memory. An onomastic arriviste, as it were, the successful pseudonym hushes up its obscure origins, snubbing and denying its precursor as cruelly as Pip betrays poor honest Joe in *Great Expectations*. Plainly, there are several well-known exceptions to this first rule, notably those in which the writer has become a classic of some kind, so widely known, discussed and dissected that – to hop metaphors – the long-neglected ghost of the true name is troubled in oblivion and returns to haunt the pages of an oeuvre. Thus, every reasonably literate Anglophone is aware that George Orwell was really Eric Blair, that Christopher Caudwell was Christopher St John Sprigg, that George Eliot

---

* Among a few omissions I noted: Ezra Pound's persona as an art critic, B. H. Dias; A. E. Ellis, author of *The Rack*, whose real name escapes me; Pauline Réage, see the following discussion; another of Burgess's personae, Joseph Kell; 'Professor Pitman' of the *Daily Worker*, a.k.a. Allen Hutt; Gordon Brown, the Anglicized form of Giordano Bruno, which was James Joyce's proposed stage name for his career as a tenor ... But this is to quibble: Room's research is assiduous and indispensable.

was Mary Ann Evans,* that Currer, Ellis and Acton Bell were Charlotte, Emily and Anne Brontë, that Lewis Carroll was Charles Lutwidge Dodgson, that Hugh MacDiarmid was Christopher Murray Grieve, that Flann O'Brien, Myles na gCopaleen and Myles na Gopaleen were Brian O'Nolan, that Palinurus was Cyril Connolly and Elia was Charles Lamb and 'Q' was Sir Arthur Quiller-Couch and Beachcomber was J. B. Morton, that Mark Twain was really Samuel Langhorne Clemens,† that O. Henry was William Sydney Porter, that Tennessee Williams' real first names were Thomas Lanier and, though the pronunciation may be a touch tricky, that Joseph Conrad was Józef Teodor Konrad Nalecz Korzeniowski. Conversely, in the rather less numerous instances where the true name has continued to outshine the pseudonym – usually one briefly adopted for a specific purpose – these hypothetical bookish persons will probably be aware, too, that Oscar Wilde went under the name of Sebastian Melmoth during his exile after discharge from Reading Gaol, that Samuel Taylor Coleridge enlisted in the army as Silas Tomkyn Comberback (he also called himself Nehemiah Higginbottom), that Swift wrote as Isaac Bickerstaff (see below) and Pope as Martinus Scriblerus (ditto). Stepping outside the strictly Anglophone world, the

---

* Though probably not that her lover, George Henry Lewes, sometimes published as Slingsby Lawrence.

† Though, as Adrian Room points out, not everyone knows that the yarn about Mississippi river pilots and their depth soundings isn't the full story; Clemens had begun by satirizing an older writer who also called himself Mark Twain; the man's real name was Isaiah Sellers. *Naming Names*, p. 151.

same readers are also likely to know that Stendhal was Marie-Henri Beyle, that Molière was Jean-Baptiste Poquelin, and perhaps that Voltaire was François Marie Arouet (again, see below).

But there are far more cases in which true names have vanished from literary memory almost as completely as the enemies of Stalin.* You can count yourself as thoroughly genned-up in the art of authorial onomastics if you can effortlessly reel off the real names of all or most of the following writers: François Villon? (François de Montcorbier or, possibly, François des Loges; he also called himself Michel Mouton – Michael Sheep.) George Sand? (Amandine-Aurore-Lucille Dudevant.) Maxim Gorky? (Aleksei Peshkov; Gorky, which means 'bitter', had previously been adopted by other radical writers.) Alberto Moravia? (Alberto Pincherle.) Italo Svevo? (Ettore Schmitz.) Aleksandr Herzen? (Aleksandr Yokovlev; Herzen also wrote under the mono-pseudonym of Isksander, the Turkish form of his given name.) André Maurois? (Emile Herzog.) W. N. P. Barbellion? (B. F. Cummings, the slowly dying author of *The Journal of a Disappointed Man*, one of the greatest diaries ever published; he explained that the initials stood for Wilhelm Nero Pilate; Barbellion comes from the barbel, a freshwater fish.) Pablo Neruda? (Ricardo Reyes Neftali.) George Santayana? (Jorge Ruis de Santayana y Borrais.) Novalis? (Friedrich

---

* Joseph Stalin, *a.k.a.* Iosif Vissarionovich Dzhugashvili; he adopted the pseudonym, generally taken to mean 'steel' (from the Russian *stal*) in 1913, but also published and passed as K. S. or K. Salin (*sic*, with no 't'); as Koba, Kato, David Bars, Gayoz Nizheradze, I. Besoshvili, Zakhar Gregoryan Melikyants, Ogoness Vartonovich Totomyants . . .

Leopold von Hardenberg.) Feel equally free to indulge in smugness if you are aware that Louis MacNeice once published under the name Louis Malone, that Schiller posed as Dr Schmidt (he was on the run from his employer, the Duke of Württemberg), H. G. Wells wrote as S.B., Shelley as John Fitzvictor, Alfred, Lord Tennyson as Alcibiades and as Merlin, Gore Vidal as Edgar Box, Alexander Pope as Dick Distich and Matthew Arnold as Baron Arminius von Thunder-Ten-Tronckh . . .

Wherever and whenever a pseudonym can be seen to grow tall and walk alone, it is no more than fair to include that name among the list of its author's hard-won creations, even when others assisted at the birth. For partial demonstration of which, consider some of the examples for proposition (2):

2. A Good Name is Hard to Find

'Anthony Burgess' was not the earliest suggestion for John Wilson's pseudonym. His first wife Lynne was keen on two other possibilities: devoted to the memory of her uncle and aunt, William and Gwenllian Powell, she proposed Anthony Powell and was disappointed to hear that another prolific novelist had already bagged that one. The late Mr and Mrs Powell had kept a pub in Gilwern, near Abergavenny, so her second suggestion was Anthony Gilwern. Posterity evidently has good reason to be grateful to Mr Roland Gant; not all editors and agents have made quite such felicitous choices. Eric Blair's agent Leonard Moore proposed the pseudonym 'X' for *Down and Out in Paris and London*, but Blair had understandable objections,* saying that if the book didn't 'flop, as I anticipate', it would be better to have a marketable pseudonym he could use again when he came to publish his novel-in-progress, *Burmese Days*.

It's not altogether clear why Blair was so keen to publish pseudonymously, though the wish to spare the feelings of his family or to escape them seem to have been among his motives. He felt that Eric was too Norse and Blair too Scottish, Scotland being at the time the Holy Land of a peculiar snobbish cult in the Home Counties.† In place of his legal name, he proposed instead one of four possibilities: P. S. Burton, or Kenneth Miles, or George Orwell, or H. Lewis Allways.‡ Quite interesting, this trio of also-rans: what could have been on Blair's mind? To my mind, at any rate, P. S. Burton – 'a name I always use when tramping' – carries associations of ruin (as in the slang expression 'gone for a Burton'), afterthoughts ('P. S.') and maybe, given the writer's rather lugubrious disposition at times, Robert Burton, the author of *The Anatomy of Melancholy*. 'Kenneth Miles'? Reference books – Blair loved to browse for useless information in such tomes – tell us that the Christian name Kenneth derives from St Kenneth, a.k.a. Cainnech and Canicus, an Irish hermit noted for his love of wild animals and his eloquent preaching; both of these attributes fit snugly onto Blair, who was passionately fond of country pursuits and

---

* *The Collected Essays, Journalism and Letters of George Orwell*: Volume 1, *An Age Like This, 1920–1940*, p. 129.

† A cynic might add that 'Blair' is an unlikely name for a socialist.

‡ Op. cit., p. 131.

became one of the century's great secular preachers.
Schooled in the classics at Eton, he presumably took Miles
from the Latin *miles*, 'soldier' – again, a fine name for a
militant writer, albeit one who had not yet fought in a real-
life war. H. Lewis Allways is the mystery, and the dud; it's
faintly bathetic, in the vein of J. Alfred Prufrock,* and the
word Allways is redolent less of heroic endurance than of
chronic irritation.

Whether the final choice was made by Mr Moore or by
the publisher Victor Gollancz, Blair pretty much decided the
outcome of the nominal lottery by concluding 'I rather
favour George Orwell'. As well he might: George Orwell is
a splendid creation. George, the name of England's patron
saint for this most cantankerously English of writers, Orwell
after the river† in Suffolk, where he had lived for a while,
but also containing a muffled echo of the rejected Allways
(and 'all's well?') and a good, solid internal rhyme with the
'or' of George. 'George Orwell' is plain, unpretentious,
robust and inevitable, and Orwellian is also a very plausible
adjective. Imagine having to read about 'Allwaysian dysto-
pias' or whatever.

---

* For a funny and searching discussion of how and why and whether
J. Alfred Prufrock is a funny name, see Christopher Ricks' *T. S. Eliot and
Prejudice*. Professor Ricks points out that the author of 'The Love Song
of J. Alfred Prufrock' used sometimes to sign articles with the name
'T. Stearns Eliot'.

† Curiously enough, I have only been able to come up with one other
well-known pseudonym derived from a river: Rock Hudson, *né* Roy
Fitzgerald. The name was given to him by a talent scout for Selznick
Studios; see Room, op. cit., p. 108.

I was pleased to discover* the small coincidence that
Lewis Carroll was also one of four names that Charles
Lutwidge Dodgson offered as a pseudonym to Edmund
Yates, the editor of a comic paper entitled the *Train*. On
11 February 1856 Dodgson confided to his diary: 'Wrote to
Mr Yates sending him a choice of names: 1. *Edgar Cuthwellis*
(made by transposition out of 'Charles Lutwidge'). 2. *Edgar
U. S. Westhill* (ditto). 3. *Louis Carroll* (derived from Lutwidge
. . . Ludovic . . . Louis, and Charles). 4. *Lewis Carroll* (ditto).'
These are the coinages of an inveterate word-gamesman,
based on the truffling out of nominal roots and the juggling
of letters into anagrams – the latter a doubtful practice for
pseudonymists, adopted by few major authors save Balzac,[†]
and not very successfully even by him, unless you care for,
say, 'Lord R'Hoone' (from 'Honoré'). For the most part,
anagrammatic or semi-anagrammatic pseudonyms tend to be
gawky or ridiculous, yielding the galumphing likes of Olphar
Hamst (Ralph Thomas) or Rudolf Otreb (Robert Fludd). Like
Gollancz or Moore, Yates made the right choice in opting
for the translations instead of the transpositions. Had he
plumped for the latter, the bookshelves of the western
world's genteel nurseries might have been infested with the
name Edgar U. S. Westhill.

Before offering Yates this tricksy quartet, Dodgson had
been hunting around for other possibilities. He had so far
been contributing to the *Train* under the pseudonym B.B. –
one of the several all-initial pseudonyms he had used for his

---

* In *Room*, pp. 83–4.

† See *Room*, pp. 188–9.

schoolboy squibs in the *Rectory Magazine*, produced by and for the members of his family; others included FLW, FX, JV, QG and VX.* The significance of B.B. has never been settled, though the likeliest decodings are either Bobby Burns – the Scottish bard was an evident influence on young Dodgson's ballad style – or Beau Brummell, which may have been one of his childhood nicknames. The novelist Francis King has pointed out that Dodgson seemed to have rather a penchant for the letter B, citing the crew of the *Snark* – Barrister, Beaver, Bellman, Billiardmarker, Broker – and the pseudonymous creature itself, which proves, of course, to be a Boojum. Dodgson/Carroll had also proffered Yates the name Dares, derived from his birthplace, Daresbury, but his editor felt that it sounded 'too much like a newspaper signature' – not to say a verb with inappropriate connotations. Whether or not Dodgson required pseudonyms for emotional as well as professional reasons is a matter for biographical speculation, but the mellifluous, romantic Lewis Carroll seems far more likely to have written classic books for children than a character with the plodding moniker of Dodgson, who taught maths at Christ Church. On which point:

3. New Name, New Hat

John Wilson is not the only writer to have been contractually obliged to seek a new name for his part-time employ-

---

* For a list of the authors who have published under initials only, from AE (George William Russell) to Z.Z. (Louis Zangwill), see Room, p. 218.

ment.* As Burgess himself pointed out, a near-contemporary called David John Moore Cornwell, working by day in the Foreign Office and moonlighting as an author of novels about espionage, was similarly advised to disguise his identity and came up with John Le Carré, reputedly finding it on a shop front in the West End of London. Direct orders from one's bosses to adopt a new name comes relatively infrequently, however, and most writers with a respectable day job take on a pseudonym quite voluntarily, so as to make it clear to their readers that they are wearing a different professional hat. Thus the anthropologist Ruth Benedict wrote poetry as Anne Singleton; the historian Eric Hobsbawm discussed jazz as F. Newton; J. I. M. Stewart, a university lecturer in English, published detective novels as Michael Innes; and Joseph Needham, the great polymath who conceived and executed much of the titanic, multivolume study of *Science and Civilization in China*, wrote about the Levellers and the English Civil War as Henry Holorenshaw.†

Even when a writer has no day job, he or she may be driven to a pseudonym to distinguish one aspect of his or her writing from another, usually the popular from the

---

* Burgess was, however, permitted to publish his short history of English literature under the name John Burgess Wilson. This makes his nominal career the opposite of D. H. Lawrence's; the one textbook written by the author of *Sons and Lovers*, *Movements in European History* (London: Oxford University Press, 1921), was credited to Lawrence H. Davison.

† See Maurice Goldsmith, *Joseph Needham: 20th Century Renaissance Man* (Unesco Publishing, 1995), pp. 45–6.

serious, the entertainment from the art work.* Hence Julian
Barnes's cover as Dan Kavanagh for his raffish thrillers about
the bisexual Duffy, Paul Auster's as Paul Benjamin for his
Chandleresque early novel *Squeeze Play*, C. Day Lewis's
detective stories, attributed to Nicholas Blake and – a remarkable instance of a cover identity that was apparently conceived as an experiment in literary reputation – Doris
Lessing's creation of a Mills & Boony romantic novelist
called Jane Somers.† Disreputable writings of all kinds have
tended to be handed to the world pseudonymously or
anonymously – even William Burroughs, whose *Naked Lunch*
helped change the climate in such matters, published his
debut work *Junkie* as William Lee – and pornography is
generally pseudonymous when credited at all. Hence Georges Bataille as Lord Auch, Christopher Logue as Count
Palmiro Vicarion, and – for several decades, one of the great
pseudonym mysteries of the century – Dominique Aury‡ as
Pauline Réage, the creator of *L'Histoire d'O* (1954), a work
variously attributed across the years to a variety of authors,
always male, including Alain Robbe-Grillet, Raymond Queneau, André Malraux,§ Pieyre de Mandiargues and Mme
Aury's lover Jean Paulhan, editor of the *Nouvelle Revue*

---

* Stephen King takes them because he is too terrifyingly prolific always
to publish under his own name.

† Who was actually very readable, even distinguished.

‡ Whose death was announced on the morning I began writing this essay,
30 April 1998.

§ Who, as a soldier of the Resistance, took his *nom de guerre* from a
character in one of his own novels: Colonel Berger.

Français. Mme Aury, *née* Anne Desclos, only stepped forward with the true story in 1994, when she told the *New Yorker* that she had composed *O* serially, as a sharpener of Paulhan's flagging carnal appetites. She confected the name Pauline Réage in homage to Pauline Roland and Pauline Borghese (presumably no relation of Antonio Borghese?) and picked Réage from an estate agent's brochure.

At the very base of the literary totem pole lies a form of writing even more despised and disreputable than pornography or confessions of drug addiction: criticism. Small wonder that Ezra Pound should have wanted to disguise himself as B. H. Dias (for art criticism) and William Atheling (for musical criticism), that George Bernard Shaw* sheltered behind the by-line Corno di Bassetto (also for music criticism: it means 'basset horn'), that the young Paul Auster signed his book reviews Paul Quinn and the young Tom Stoppard wrote dramatic notices as William Boot (in homage to the hapless hero of Waugh's *Scoop*;† both Stoppard and Auster later recycled these pseudonyms into their creative work). Understandable reticence, but the practice also has its hazards. What would happen if the creative and the critical personae were brought face to face? – something which actually did happen in the case of our master-pseudonymist, since:

---

* Seemingly the inspiration for one of Lawrence of Arabia's various alter egos, T. E. Shaw; it became his legal name in 1927.

† A young friend of mine, who prefers to remain nameless, sometimes publishes journalism under the by-line Keith Boot.

4. Pseudonymists Tend to be Repeat Offenders

In his capacity as book reviewer for the *Yorkshire Post*,
Anthony Burgess was once sent a novel called *Inside Mr
Enderby*, by one Joseph Kell. This was, as is now well known,
his own novel; he had adopted the name to disguise quite
how many books he was turning out each year.* Sensing a
practical joke by his editor, he played along with the gag by
giving *Enderby* a stinking review. Alas, it was not a joke, and
within a week Burgess became briefly notorious as the man
who reviewed his own novels.† Some people even began to
wonder, shrewdly, whether 'Anthony Burgess' existed at all,
or was merely the creation of 'a paralytic Irish soak named
Joseph Kell'.‡ One suspects that something of this kind was
bound to have happened to Burgess sooner or later, since
the writer who learns to relish the freedoms of one new
identity will soon start to hanker for another, and all those
multiplying alter egos will end up causing mischief. Kell and

---

* When I interviewed him, he told me that Kell referred to the Book of
Kells, but was unenlightening on the Joseph.

† There were distinguished precedents. As Burgess points out, Walter
Scott had reviewed the first of the *Waverly* novels at great length; as Gore
Vidal points out, Walt Whitman had done the same for *Leaves of Grass*; as
both point out, a man who reviews his own book will at least have read
it, which is more than some critics manage. Walter Scott, incidentally,
used many pseudonyms, including Jedediah Cleishbotham, meaning
'bottom-whipper', Malachi Malagrowther, Captain Cuthbert Clutterbuck,
and the Rev. Dr Dryasdust.

‡ *You've Had Your Time*, p. 72.

Burgess were not the only names under which Wilson wrote; he also composed a series of crank letters to the editor of the *Daily Mirror* in the guise of an outraged Pakistani moralist whose name, thirty units long, began with Mohamed Ali. These letters were about the newspaper's hyper-democratic habit of calling Lord Snowden Mr Jones ('no man have two names if he is not criminal',* thundered the writer), which Mohamed Ali took to be proof of bigamy on the part of Princess Margaret. Though Mohamed Ali was a spoof identity, Burgess/Wilson had, a decade or so before, seriously contemplated converting to Islam so as to be permitted to stay on in Malaya after Independence, and had a name ready for his new faith: Yahya bin Haji Latiff, Yahya signifying John and Haji Latiff being the name of a friend who urged the conversion.

Awesomely prolific as he was in every other respect, however, Burgess/Wilson was almost costive in the matter of pseudonyms. A significantly less gifted writer, the self-styled Baron Corvo, whose real name was extraordinary enough in its own right – Frederick William Serafino Austin Lewis Mary (yes, Mary) Rolfe – easily out-distances Burgess in the *nom de plume* stakes, having published as, *inter alia*, George Arthur Rose, Frederick Austin, Nicholas Crabbe and, still more vaunting than Baron, King Clement; by shortening his given name of Frederick Rolfe to Fr. Rolfe, he also tried to pass himself off as an ordained priest.

Swift used some seventeen pseudonyms, including T. N. Philomath, Dr Andrew Tripe, Gregory Miso-Sarum and

---

* *You've Had Your Time*, p. 150.

the weirdly Monty-Pythonish S.P.A.M., as well as the better-known Isaac Bickerstaff and M. B. Drapier. Thackeray used twenty-five, including George Savage Fitz-Boodle, esq., Master Molloy Molony and – a rare example of male to female cross-dressing in a major author – The Honorable Wilhemina Amelia Skeggs. But these are relatively piffling efforts compared to the big boys of the pseudonym form, who easily ran into three figures. Voltaire employed at least 173 pseudonyms, or 174 if you include Voltaire, including Genest Ramponeau, Dominico Zapata, George Aronger Dardelle, Catherine Vade and Guillaume Vade, Abbé Tamponet, Robert Covelle, George Avenger, Dom Calmet, Don Apueleius Risorius, Abbé Maudit, Major Kaiserling, Dr Good Natur'd Wellwisher and – a curious one for fans of the Great Detective – Mr Sherloc.* And still the reigning world champ, with at least 198 known pseudonyms, is Daniel Defoe (*né* Daniel Foe?). Here goes: Solomon Waryman, Miranda Meanwell, Hen. Antifogger, Jr., Count Kidney Face, Jeffrey Sing-Song, Theophilus Lovewit, Anthony Impartiality and Jack Indifferent, Fello De Se, Boatswain Trinkolo, Anglipolski of Lithuania, Tom A. Bedlam, Christopher Careful, Sir Malcontent Chagrin, Frank Faithfull, Tea-Table, Nelly, Sir Fopling Tittle-Tattle, Protestant Neutrality, Anthony Quiet, Tom Turbulent, Wallnutshire, Jeremiah Dry-Boots, Obadiah Blue Hat and – appropriate surname in the circumstances – Nicholas Boggle . . .

---

* For the complete list, see Room, pp. 332–334. For Defoe, see ibid., pp. 335–337.

5. Mother's Name's Best

Burgess was the maiden name of John Wilson's mother, Elizabeth Burgess, a dancer and singer 'pleonastically', as her son was later to note, billed as the Beautiful Belle Burgess. By taking her real maiden name as his authorial name, Burgess was following in a well-established tradition: Room has hunted down no fewer than fifty-eight pseudonyms formed on the same principle, so many that he resorts to the abbreviation 'mmn', though most of these are stage names – Mel Brooks, Anthony Hopkins, Elsa Lanchester, Shirley Maclaine, Anna Neagle, Simone Signoret – rather than *noms de plume* (Christopher Fry, Elizabeth Jane Howard). Freudians and post-Freudians may care to muse about the symbolic patricide involved in casting off the Name of the Father in this way, though the only instance I've come across of a pseudonym coined in wilful defiance of a male parent is that of Anna Akhmatova, *née* Gorenko. She looked back a couple of generations when her father angrily told her that her decadent verses were bringing shame on the family name, and took her authorial surname from her great-grandmother. Finally:

6. One's a Crowd*

For the purposes of the Inland Revenue, the name Anthony Burgess designated not one person but two – John Wilson

---

* Or, as Mr Room puts it, *e pluribus unum*.

and his wife Lynne. Mrs Wilson, whose logic was not always of the most orthodox order, took this to mean that she was in some metaphysical sense the actual author, or at least co-author, of the novels published under that name.* Her point was debatable, but the principle is at least as well established as that of the mmn model. Smectymnuus, a name once familiar to everyone who took a degree in English History or Literature, was the collective pseudonym of five Presbyterian ministers who, in 1641, issued a pamphlet attacking Bishop Hall's claims of divine right for the episcopacy; 'Smectymnuus' was built from their initials, or a slight fudging thereof: Stephen Marshall, Edmund Calamy, Thomas Young, Matthew Newcomen and William (or UUilliam) Spurstow. Adrian Room lists some forty other examples, of which the most famous are Peter Anthony, the name taken by the playwright brothers Peter and Anthony Shaffer for their collaborations, Martinus Scriblerus (Pope, Swift & co.), the detective-fiction writer Ellery Queen (Frederic Dannay and Manfred B. Lee) and Caroline Lewis, a named coined by way of a nod to Lewis Carroll by the political wits Harold Begbie, M. H. Temple and Stafford Ransome for their political skits *Clara in Blunderland* and *Lost in Blunderland*.

At the risk, or dead certainty, of courting bathos I might add that I have swelled these particular ranks myself on more than one occasion: a decade or so ago, I collaborated with my friend Roger Parsons on some squibs which were published under the unimaginative pseudonym of Jackson

---

* *You've Had Your Time*, p. 57.

Parsons. Moreover, I am also – in accordance with principle (3) – a multiple offender, and have used at least half a dozen *noms de plume* for a variety of reasons. Most of them are dull and better forgotten, but one has been troubling me a little of late. Having called his name into existence, I've found myself wondering what he's really like: how old is he? Where does he come from? And would he perhaps like to start writing things of his own? This last thought suggests either that I am going off my trolley or that this pseudonym has started to mutate, and is struggling towards the condition of a full-blown heteronym. And that term deserves a chapter of its own.

Heteronyms

My name is Legion, for we are many.

Mark v: 9

Largely unnoticed by Britain and the rest of the anglophone world, Portugal has quietly gone about the task of producing at least three of the century's greatest poets: Alberto Caeiro, Ricardo Reis, and Alvaro de Campos. The members of this accomplished trio have, on the face of it, little in common beyond the accident of nationality. Caeiro (b. 1889), who writes on pastoral and philosophical themes, has been praised – by no less an authority on matters spiritual than the writer and Cistercian monk Thomas Merton – for the 'Zen-like immediacy' of his work. Others have found in his writings an anticipation of the early pages of Sartre's decidedly un-Zen-like *L'être et le néant*; Caeiro has also and more plausibly been compared to Wordsworth, and to the classical nature poets of Japan. Ricardo Reis (b. 1887) could be considered as a modern reincarnation of Horace, reprising many of the Latin poet's themes – the vanity of human wishes, the brevity of existence, the *aurea mediocritas* – within exquisitely formal verses that mingle Stoicism and Epicureanism. Alvaro de Campos (b. 1890) is the wild man of the group, a ranting experimentalist strongly influenced by Marinetti and his contemporaries of the Italian Futurist movement, and still more strongly by Walt Whitman; Roy Campbell amusingly said that de Campos's 'Maritime Ode' was 'the loudest poem ever written'. Despite their widely differing philosophies, styles, educations and temperaments, however, these three Portuguese giants shared one supremely important characteristic. They did not exist.

More exactly, they existed in much the same way that Hamlet, Don Quixote or Mr Pickwick* existed and exist. Messrs Caeiro, Reis and de Campos were imaginative constructions, forged in the melancholic and sometimes alcoholic brain of a flesh-and-blood poet, Fernando Pessoa (1888–1935), who also wrote a considerable body of work under his own name, thus bringing Portugal's total score of major twentieth-century poets to a very respectable four. Pessoa referred to himself and his three imaginary friends as an 'inexistent coterie', and he coined a useful technical term for a full-blown literary alter ego: not a pseudonym, but a heteronym. He also gave cerebral birth to a similarly 'inexistent' prose writer, Bernardo Soares, to whom he grudgingly granted the status of 'semi-heteronym', and to as many as sixty-eight additional other characters with rather less secure ontological status: a regiment of, so to speak, semi-, demi-semi-, and hemi-demi-semi-heteronyms. There could well be more of these insubstantial beings lying in wait. Pessoa's principal legacy to the world was a domed wooden trunk in

---

* 'Mr Pickwick belongs to the sacred figures of the world's history. Do not, please, claim that he has never existed . . .': Fernando Pessoa, undated fragment: cited in *A Centenary Pessoa* (Manchester: Carcanet Press, 1995), pp. 122–3.

which he kept all the scraps and jottings he wrote; when its contents were inventoried after his death, they were found to number 25,574 items. Unsurprisingly, his complete works have yet to be published.

It has sometimes been said of Pessoa that if he had not existed, Jorge Luis Borges* would have been obliged to invent him, since his career is without precedent or peer anywhere in literary history,† though not, perhaps in works of morbid psychology, anthropology or demonology. It is not simply that Pessoa wrote sublimely in many different voices, for the same might be said of Browning and Tennyson in their dramatic monologues. Come to that, it might be said of Shakespeare, the writer admiringly described by Pessoa, for reasons too bizarre to outline here, as 'the greatest failure in literature'.‡

What Pessoa did was something far more radical than the occasional adoption of a fictional mask for purposes of satire, stylistic experimentation or fun. To appreciate the full

---

* John Hollander said it plain, and Harold Bloom said it approximately. Borges admired Pessoa, by the way; he wrote a respectful 'letter' to him on the occasion of the fiftieth anniversary of Pessoa's death. See the *Centenary Pessoa*, p. 297.

† I can think of quite a few other examples of writers imagining some other writer whose works they then purport to translate or publish: John Peck's contemporary Chinese poet Hi-Lo, Christopher Reid's Katherina Brac, possibly – in a different vein – Anthony Burgess's F. X. Enderby . . . but not, so far, of any other writer who has created full-blown, independent alternative selves in the manner of Pessoa.

‡ See Pessoa, *Always Astonished* (trans. Edwin Honig), pp. 55–63: an extraordinary essay.

magnificent eccentricity of his career, one would have to compare him not so much to his beloved Shakespeare as to some hypothetical, alternative-universe Shakespeare who not merely conceived a Hamlet and brought him to the stage, but who went on to compose a sizeable oeuvre of prose and verse by that same Hamlet – verse of a far higher standard, one hopes, than the single piece of doggerel the lovesick prince inflicts on Ophelia.

This science-fictional Bard would then need to have published said writings under Hamlet's name, and sent the Prince out into the world to take part in cultural debates and write articles on a wide variety of philosophical, political and aesthetic matters, including the writings of this older chap William Shakespeare. Finally, our alternative Shakespeare would need to have imagined several more characters – a Falstaff, say, an Oberon and a Prospero – and then composed, published and distributed a collected works for each of these creatures, who would all have gone on to become friends, collaborators and rivals in the Jacobethan literary racket.

This little conjectural exercise is not meant to insinuate that Pessoa's lyric genius was of Shakespearean dimensions (though some have made the highest claims for him: in 1994, Harold Bloom was happy to include him alongside Shakespeare, Dante, Chaucer and Proust as one of the twenty-six authors essential to the Western canon) but to suggest that Pessoa might best be recommended to the newcomer as a kind of *sui generis* dramatist. He once distinguished his heteronyms from their far more vulgar cousins the pseudonyms in just such terms: 'A pseudonymic work is, except for the name with which it is signed, the work of an author writing as himself; a heteronymic work is by an author writing outside his own personality: it is the work of a complete individuality made up by him, just as the utterances of some character in a drama would be.'* And though Pessoa was a dramatist for the page rather than the stage, he had a decidedly Shakespearean capacity for submerging his own identity in that of his creations – a capacity Pessoa described as 'hysterical'.

There were other, more worldly senses in which Pessoa seems implicitly to have compared himself to Shakespeare. As a young man he nursed the ambition of becoming a national poet for Portugal – rather as Shakespeare, in the days when the British weren't embarrassed about talking in such terms, was Britain's national poet. This was an ambition all the more cheeky in that Portugal had already recognized its national poet in Luís de Camões, whose wonderful epic poem *The Lusiads* was a paean to the country's Great Discoveries of the fifteenth and sixteenth centuries, and particularly of Vasco da Gama's first voyage to India. In his first published article, 'New Portuguese Poetry Sociologically Considered', Pessoa prophesied the imminent arrival of a 'Supra-Camões in our land'. It's been suggested that one motive for Pessoa's self-multiplying was his suspicion that it would take a whole posse of poets to dethrone Camões.† He would have to become a poetic gang of one.

The attempt succeeded, or as near as makes no odds.

---

* From an article in *Presenca*, 1928; cited in the *Centenary Pessoa*, pp. 133–4.

† See Zbigniew Kotowicz, *Fernando Pessoa: Voices of a Nomadic Soul* (London: Menard Press, 1996), p. 21.

Portugal, sluggish and grudging in its appreciation of Pessoa for most of his lifetime, has long since acknowledged him as, if not a greater poet than Camões, at least its greatest writer since Camões. Pessoa studies are now a major Portuguese industry. You can see his image everywhere in Lisbon, even in your hands: he has been immortalized on the hundred-escudo banknote. And Portugal's upwardly revised opinion would be calmly received among the reading classes of France, Italy, Spain and much of Latin America.

Roman Jakobson, the Prague school linguistician and critic, confidently included him in the ranks of 'world-class artists born in the 1880s' – Stravinsky, Picasso, Joyce, Braque, Khlebnikov, Le Corbusier. Nor has he been altogether starved of English-speaking admirers. Apart from the afore-mentioned Roy Campbell (who called him 'the greatest literary figure of modern times') and Thomas Merton (who translated him – as, incongruous but true, did John Betjeman), that roll-call would include William Boyd, Anthony Burgess, Cyril Connolly, Gabriel Josipovici, P. J. Kavanagh and George Steiner. And yet, despite enjoying the applause of such a high-megaton claque, despite dozens of translations since the early 1970s, despite the fact that a good part of the work Pessoa published in his own lifetime was actually written in English, he remains stubbornly obscure in Britain and North America. When Harold Bloom included Pessoa's name in *The Western Canon*, the reviewer for *Time* magazine, who'd never heard of the dude, concluded that Bloom must simply be swanking as usual.

How to set about spreading the word of Pessoa's singularity? Perhaps with a few words of biography, both real and heteronymic, which might begin with the observation that names can be destiny: the Portuguese word *pessoa*, meaning 'person', is derived from the Latin *persona*, an actor's mask. Our capsule biography could begin, not with the literal birth date of Fernando Pessoa in 1888 but with the literary birth date of Alberto Caeiro on 8 March 1914, when the poet began, 'in a kind of trance whose nature I cannot define', to write some thirty-odd poems in an alien voice at a single stretch: this was, he later wrote in an extraordinary letter to a (three-dimensional) friend, 'the appearance of someone in me, to whom I at once gave the name "Alberto Caeiro". Forgive the absurdity of this sentence: my Master had appeared inside me.'* Reacting violently against the scary experience of obliteration, Pessoa rapidly composed half a dozen verses of his own, *Chuva Obliqua* (*Oblique Rain*); then he had a spectral vision of Caeiro's disciple, Ricardo Reis; and, with equal suddenness, became aware both of Alvaro de Campos and de Campos's poem 'Ode Triumphal', which poured unbidden out of his typewriter. 'It seems to me', Pessoa claimed, 'that it all happened independently of me. And it seems to me so still . . .'

It is a splendidly spooky yarn, and Pessoa may actually have believed it, though textual scholars have their doubts about its literal veracity.† One way in which he sometimes understood and described the experience of meeting or being possessed by his heteronyms was as a psychological anomaly, a form of identity crisis along the lines of the sort of 'dissociated personality' or 'multiple personality' disorders

----

* The *Centenary Pessoa*, p. 132.

† See Kotowicz, p. 87.

that Hollywood used to find so appealing, and hyped up in such melodramas as *The Three Faces of Eve*. This possibility frightened him, and it's not hard to guess why. Until recently, there was quite a vogue among literary theorists and latter-day psychoanalytical gurus for insisting that what the rest of us cheerfully call the 'self' is no more than a pernicious fiction, and that the human individual is not to be seen as an integral unit but as a site where many texts, many voices, many discourses intersect and overlap ... well, something along those lines. For poor Pessoa, this rather dismaying philosophical proposition was not a stick to poke into the ideology of the beastly bourgeois but a daily reality; and if it brought him occasional ecstasies, and furnished him with a life's work, it also caused him immeasurable anguish. At times, one of his critics writes, it actually drove him mad.

Pessoa's work amounts to considerably more than an exotic symptom of pathology, however, and a very different, (even) less intellectually reputable way of describing his heteronymic eruptions would probably be more appropriate. It's worth remembering that, in common with W. B. Yeats and other founders of modernism, he was a convinced, not to say passionate, believer in the occult. Pessoa was so fascinated by stellar influences that at one point, around 1916, he seriously considered setting himself up as a professional astrologer. He was similarly preoccupied with alchemy, with the Kabbalah, with Freemasonry and with Rosicrucianism – one of the few substantial poems he published under his own name was 'At the Tomb of Christian Rosenkreutz', a homage to the legendary, or perhaps one should say 'inexistent', founder of the Rosicrucian order. His sole collection of

self-attributed works, *Mensagem* (1934), gave an occultist reading of Portuguese history. He described it as 'abundantly
steeped in Templarian and Rosicrucean [sic] symbolism'.* He
translated Theosophical works by that movement's founding
mothers and father, Madame Blavatsky, Annie Besant and
C. W. Leadbeater.

In a half-comic, half-frightening episode which might
make a promising subject for a film, he became involved in
a bizarre adventure involving the English magus Aleister
Crowley and the Lisbon police, and subsequently translated
Crowley's 'Hymn to Pan' into Portuguese. Most significantly, he was, like the Surrealists, a dabbler in automatic
writing. Unlike the Surrealists, he was convinced that the
resulting texts were messages from the next world rather
than the unconscious, and he wrote excitedly to his Aunt
Anica – herself a keen spiritualist and fan of the Ouija and
the tarot – about his various experiences of telepathy, etheric
vision, aura-spotting and other paranormal bits and bobs.
'Such things', he told her with a rather excessive note of
emphasis, 'are abnormal but not *unnatural*'. When such a
thoroughgoing connoisseur of the Western hermetic tradition starts talking about the appearance of other poets
inside him, it would be rash to assume he must always be
speaking metaphorically, or just playing a fanciful bookish
game.

Whatever it cost him in fear and bewilderment, Pessoa
was also fortunate in being on such intimate terms with
preternatural forces, since in most other respects his life was

---

* Cited in the *Centenary Pessoa*, p. 264.

one of quite exemplary monotony, and may be readily summarized in a few sentences. Born in Lisbon on 13 June 1888, the son of a reasonably affluent civil servant, he is taken, in 1896, to live in Durban, where he learns English. (Note for the psychologists: his first 'heteronym', the Chevalier de Pas, manifests himself in 1894, after the deaths of young Fernando's father and his infant brother Jorge. Lots of lonely children dream up imaginary friends; how many six-year-olds have engaged in correspondence with a non-existent French aristocrat?) In 1905, at the age of seventeen, he returns to Lisbon and never leaves it again. After a couple of minor career setbacks, he settles to his lifelong employment as 'foreign correspondent', meaning that he scrapes a living of sorts as a freelance translator of commercial letters. He writes, but doesn't publish much – a total of about 430 pieces of occasional journalism and verse, almost all in fly-by-night periodicals, little magazines or flimsy pamphlets. He lives mostly in rented rooms, suffers from depression, drinks heavily but not riotously, is probably a discreet homosexual* – his one heterosexual liaison, with a young secretary, Ophelia Querioz, is brought to an end partly by an abusive letter from one Alvaro de Campos, telling her to leave Pessoa alone. (There's a tactic you seldom see recommended by agony columnists.) He dies of hepatic colic at the end of November 1935, thus contradicting his self-cast horoscope, which had given him another two years.

What tedium: compared to Pessoa, Philip Larkin was

---

* Though in 1922 he was happy to make a brave defence of his overtly homosexual fellow-poet, Antonio Botto, who had been charged with 'immorality'.

James Bond. But then, as his semi-heteronym Bernardo Soares writes in *The Book of Disquiet*: 'Wise is the man who monotonizes his existence, for then each minor incident seems like a marvel.' And the experience of heteronymic possession was marvellous by anybody's standards. Pessoa's occultist tastes included a belief in reincarnation, but in his own case the hankering after lives to come would have been sheer greed. In the space of his forty-seven years on earth, he had already experienced at least brief bursts of seventy-two lives, and existed for a time as, *inter alia*, Jean Seul, the satirical French journalist and occasional poet; Mr Cross, addict of newspaper puzzles; Antonio Mora, the metaphysician; Pacecho the poet, pale imitator of de Campos; Alexander Search, the Scottish engineer (Pessoa cast his horoscope, wrote works in his name, and had visiting cards printed up for him); the Baron of Tieve, who had fallen on hard times; Vicente Guedes; Robert Anon; M. H. F. Lecher . . .

And as his primary trio. In the blond-haired, blue-eyed shape of Alberto Caeiro (1889–1915), he skipped formal education and lived his brief life – brief as Keats's – reclusively in a hilltop villa in Ribatejo, brooding on the natural world like an Eastern sage. De Campos wrote of him, 'My master Caeiro was not pagan; he was paganism', and de Campos was not alone in his awed respect for Caeiro: Reis and Pessoa also regarded him as their mentor. His masterwork: *O Guarador de Rebandos* (*The Keeper of the Flocks*):

> If I die very young, let them hear this:
> I was never more than a child at play.

> I was as heathen as the sun and water,
> Of a universal religion only men do not have . . .*

As Ricardo Reis, the most obviously 'Mediterranean' of the three, he was born in Oporto in 1887, educated in Latin by the brothers at a Jesuit college and then attended medical school; he spent the years from 1919 onwards in exile in Brazil, and lived there for many years, until a telegram from de Campos informed him of Pessoa's death and he returned to Lisbon, where he met Pessoa's earthbound ghost – or so one gathers from a critically lauded novel, *The Year of the Death of Ricardo Reis* (London: Harvill, 1992), by a younger Portuguese writer, José Saramago.† Reis's principal work: the *Odes*:

> Ashen already over my vain brow
> The hair of that young man whom I have lost.
> My eyes are not so bright.
> My mouth no longer has a right to kisses.
> If you still love me, don't love for love's sake,
> Cuckolding me with me.

As de Campos he was tall, thin, possessed of a cosmopolitan air and given to sporting a monocle. Born in Tavira on 15 October 1890 of Jewish ancestry, de Campos studied naval engineering in Glasgow, travelled extensively in the Far East and appears to have dabbled with hallucinogenic drugs. By

---

* All of these poetic translations are by Keith Bosley, from the *Centenary Pessoa*.

† Who, I'm happy to say, won the 1998 Nobel Prize for Literature just a few weeks after I wrote this piece.

the end of his wandering life he had become a poverty-stricken vagrant, a self-disgusted rebel. His principal works: 'Tobacco Shop' and 'Triumphal Ode':

> In the painful glare of the factory's big electric lights
> I have a fever and I write.
> I write gnashing my teeth, a wild beast for its beauty,
> For its beauty quite unknown to the ancients . . .

Above or behind or beneath all of these other incarnations, Pessoa lived his own writing life, a far more eventful and impassioned affair than one might guess from a bare outline of his movements, busy with all the usual friendships, manifestos, jaunts into publishing, feuds and fads.* Take his fervent involvement with the political cult of Sebastianism, which flavoured much of his poetry and prompted him to write some unfortunate political diatribes in favour of military dictatorship. The death of King Sebastian at the Battle of Alcazar Kebir in 1578 led to the downfall of Portugal as the world's greatest colonial power; but since Sebastian's body was never found, he became reborn in myth as *O Encoberto*, the Hidden One, who will one day return in the morning mists to restore the nation's glory. In short, the melancholy, possibly demented zealot Sebastian is Portugal's *rex quondam, rex futurus*. Pessoa believed the myth, every word of it, and spent hours casting horoscopes of political leaders to see whether they might be the long-awaited reincarnation. Silly stuff, no doubt, though hardly any sillier

---

* In this respect, he is a spiritual brother of Kafka. Gabriel Josipovici has said that the essential spirit of modernism is embodied most clearly in 'five grey-suited gentlemen': Cavafy, Kafka, Eliot, Borges and Pessoa.

than a lot of other things major writers have believed, and critics have been inclined to handle Pessoa's Sebastianism kindly. It provides the substance for the forty-four poems of *Mensagem* (*Message*), probably Pessoa's masterwork and certainly the only poem which ever made him any money – it won second prize in a competition for verse on a patriotic theme. One of its poems, spoken in the voice of Sebastian himself, offers a proud rebuke to anyone inclined to dismiss Pessoa's writings as the aberrations of a lunatic, and makes a fine epitaph for his life's – or lives' – work:*

> Mad, yes, mad, for I wanted to be great,
> My assurance uncontained
> Within me, my design undreamed by Fate;
> Hence of me on the sand
> What used to be, but not what is, remained.
> My madness let the others take from me
> And with it all the rest:
> For without madness what can mankind be
> More than a healthy beast,
> A corpse that breeds before its juices waste?

---

* For a survey of other types of 'inexistent' writers, please turn to the chapter on 'Imaginary Authors and Imaginary Books', pp. 224–34.

Blurbs, Authorial and Otherwise

'Advanced, forthright, significant'

Nigel Molesworth's verdict on Colin Wilson, 'the new philosopher'*

You know the form, I know the form, everyone knows the form. It goes something like this:

> Kevin Jackson was raised by a herd of moose in the Arctic Circle. He holds degrees in Sanskrit, astrophysics and raffiawork. Large sections of his biography may not be made public for reasons of international security; try juggling with the letters A, C and I. He is the author of over seventy books, many of them in English, and his ceramics have been exhibited to universal acclaim. He divides his time between a Tibetan lamasery, a tree house in West Africa, a cold-water flat in Greenwich Village, a *dacha* in Karelia, a ruined *palazzo* in Venice, a yurt near Lake Baikal, a houseboat in Kathmandu, a geodesic dome in Antarctica, a geostationary satellite in orbit over the South Pacific, and Swindon.

---

* See Geoffrey Willans & Ronald Searle, *Back in the Jug Agane* (London: Pavilion Books, 1992), p. 17. As always, Willans's ear for literary cliché is impeccable: *Jug* was first published in 1959, but the triple-epithet blurb form continues to grace countless covers.

A few minor variations are possible, depending upon the author's egomania, diffidence ('I'd better not mention the Nobel, it only puts people's backs up') and Stalinist suppressions of awkward episodes (abandoned wives, sojourns in the loony bin, notoriously duff books), but anything which makes too marked a detour from the understood route is bound to look eccentric. In its classic mode, the author's blurb is simply a kind of miniaturized CV or *cursus honorum*, with the key facts laid down in plain chronological sequence rather than in the backwards mode favoured by most prospective employers. First, the date and place of birth;* then the education, especially if Oxbridge or Ivy League or Sorbonnish; then the more picturesque foothills and summits of achievement, such as war record, respectable jobs and earlier publications; and, finally, always finally, the domestic circumstances – spouse, offspring, number of Labradors and place of domicile. Or, better, places of domicile: it is the mark of a successful author that he 'divides his time'.

A reasonable logical format, though it strikes me as odd that an author's place(s) of residence is considered a detail of such keen interest to prospective readers (who, unlike prospective employers, presumably aren't too fussed about how early the author can reasonably be expected to show up for

---

* A former denizen of the London publishing scene in the early 1960s told me, in rather ungallant spirit, that lady authors of the day – *female* or *woman* authors were still a few years away – would always omit the 'date of birth' section on the questionnaires they were sent by the publicity department. I doubt many authors are particularly fussed about such revelations now, unless they're young enough for precocity to be a marketing point.

work) that its inclusion is all but compulsory. I'm not sure when this sense of uneasiness about the geographical finale first dawned, but it may have been some twenty-odd years ago, when Mark Booth made me laugh out loud with the author's blurb for his study of *Camp*, which read, *in toto*:

> Mark Booth lives in Solihull.

Mr Booth has since gone on to make a successful career in publishing, and no wonder; he plainly has an eye for the coming thing. Short, sharp, smart authorial blurbs were fairly thin on the ground two decades ago, except when they adorned slim and whimsical fictions by the likes of Richard Brautigan, but these days you can't browse through a bookshop without being quipped at from all sides by dust-jackets and back covers. In just the last week, I've encountered three characteristic japes:

> Tristan Egolf was born in 1967.
> And there isn't a thing he can do about it.

Then there was a novel entitled *Slaughtermatic* by a writer new to me called Steve Aylett, the succinct blurb of which concludes:

> . . . If he were any more English, he'd be dead.

And then there was the one for a debut novel by a young woman whose name escapes me just now, but which claims that she:

> . . . lives in London and is currently on holiday.

Not all blurb-jokes of this laconic order are particularly amusing, but one can sympathize with the desire to make them – at least when their flippancy doesn't reek of a callow *je m'enfoutisme* more offensive than plain old-fashioned arrogance.* For it has become harder and harder for writers to evade the realization that blurbs are a bit of an embarrassment. To put the matter bluntly, the task of writing a blurb amounts to an invitation to boast about oneself in the third person for a paragraph or two. No, really, I've checked the etymology. The word 'blurb' was coined in 1914[†] by the American humorist Gelett Burgess in his book *Burgess Unabridged: A New Dictionary of Words You Have Always Needed*, which offered his public a hundred neologisms, of which only 'blurb' has survived.[‡] Burgess defined a blurb as 'praise for oneself, inspired laudation', which is why I've begun this maggot by concentrating on authorial blurbs rather than the other kinds of promotional copy you find on dust jackets – 'The greatest book ever written by a biped' and so on; these borrowed the name 'blurb' from their cousins.

A blurb, then, is a temptation to vanity, and the unjust

---

* A speculation: the growth of the short, jokey author's blurb may have been encouraged by the explosion of glossy magazines in the last decade or so. These often feature a half-page of picture by-lines of contributors paired with snappy prose. I was amused to hear the then-editrix of *Arena* magazine refer to this section as the 'Flannel Panel'.

[†] Or maybe a few years earlier, in a book called *Are You a Bromide?*. My account here is lifted from Martin Gardner's annotations (1961) to C. C. Bombaugh's *Oddities and Curiosities of Words and Literature*, 1896 edition, p. 366. I can't be bothered to track Burgess's first editions. Sorry.

[‡] Though, in other books, Burgess also coined or mangled 'bromide', meaning a platitude, and 'goop', meaning a goop.

can be seen to succumb to this temptation greedily. A couple of weeks ago, a friend who works as a newspaper features editor phoned me up to read out the brief orgy of self-congratulation stuck on the rear cover of a paperback by some young chancer,[*] which slobbered over every detail of every minor distinction he'd won since he was potty trained. We fell silent for a moment, awed by this pyrotechnical display of naked conceit. '*Shiny* with smugness,' my friend eventually murmured. Small wonder that decent souls have come to feel doubtful about the received format, and try to overcome its awkwardness in one way or another. If a fetching little joke doesn't seem quite appropriate, such writers will generally opt for ditching the old schools-spouse-Labrador-and-house routine in favour of something brief, unostentatious and matter-of-fact.

> Anthony Grafton is Dodge Professor of History at Prince-ton University . . .

begins the author's blurb to *The Footnote: A Curious History*, which goes on to list a few of Prof. Grafton's many books, including *Cardano's Cosmos: The Three Lives of a Renaissance Magician*. Faultless. To borrow an analogy[†] from one of

---

[*] No, I'm not going to name him.

[†] Or, as I find on looking it up, to adapt one. What Prof. Grafton actually writes is something a little more alarming: 'Like the high whine of the dentist's drill, the low rumble of the footnote reassures: the tedium it inflicts, like the pain inflicted by the drill, is not random but directed, part of the cost that the benefits of modern science and technology exact'; op. cit., p. 5.

that book's chapters, this is a perfect example of the blurb as reassurance. Like the diplomas on a dentist's wall which tell you that there will be no needless suffering ahead, the mention of his distinguished academic post quietly affirms the potentially nervous reader that this guy is no cowboy, and really knows his stuff; the book-list is also soothing, and it would obviously be churlish to deny any author the right to put in a discreet plug for the back catalogue.

It doesn't solve all the problems, however. The main problem with keeping your blurb short and factual like Prof. Grafton's is that, while you won't offend anyone, you're also unlikely to lure any but the most discerning potential buyers for your wares. For those who admit the necessity to hawk yourself around the marketplace but hate to show off, the best option is to turn the whole business over to the publishers, who can spare your blushes by making all the nasty decisions about how much to brag, what to brag about and the appropriate vocabulary of bragging. Not that this decision will always be in your hands. A lot of publishers, recognizing rank amateurism in the art of publicity when they see it, will go ahead and write the blurb anyway, sometimes with results that surprise* the author as much as they entertain the reader. Handy hint for the habitual browser in bookshops: it can often be a diverting exercise to try and work out whether a particular blurb is the work of the author, the publisher, or both.†

_____

* Read: appal.

† My editor wisely told me to delete the examples which followed this observation. I still chuckle about them in private, though.

It is worth underlining the point that an authorial blurb
will not always be the unassisted work of the author, just as
it's worth pointing out to unregenerate devotees of the
politique des auteurs that it's not always useful to consider a
film as a virtuoso solo by its director. The authorial blurb,
that is to say, is quite a different creature from another IF it
otherwise closely resembles, the Lonely Hearts advert. This
is almost always the work of the person who filed it –
though I'd be interested in reading a critical history which
compared the rise of the hip and flippant tone in both forms,
and examined the ways in which the impulse to self-
advertisement in both forms is shaped by the need for
brevity and the demands of rhetoric:

> Bored? Lonely? Just Curious? Longing for quiet evenings or
> lazy Sunday afternoons alone with someone special who
> knows his index from his appendices? SWM writer, N/S,
> into Sanksrit and raffiawork, seeks open-minded readers of
> any age/sex/race/orientation with GSOH for paratextual
> healing, your place or mine. No timewasters or pedants,
> please.

Sophisticated reviewers, therefore, will duly recognize
the likelihood that an authorial blurb may either be the
outcome of collaboration or by some unknown hand, and,
when they come to review a blurb – an increasingly common practice,* by the by – will phrase their notices ambi-
guously, to allow for the fact that the writer credited on the
front cover may not have produced the miniature biography
on the back cover. Instead, they will concentrate, as I have

---

* Again, I have deleted examples to protect the guilty.

thus far been doing, on questions of literary convention and marketing. Though some blurbs continue to twinkle merrily with scholarships, fellowships, congratulatory Firsts and Chancellor's Medals as if we were all still living in the 1940s, that habit has been largely superseded by the practices of sheepishly glossing over all higher educational details (where the writer is guilty of having a degree or, God forbid, degrees) and of boasting that the author left school at fourteen, or eleven, or three, or eighteen months, to become a lumberjack, coal miner, mercenary, crack dealer or travelling bleach salesman.*

This *nostalgie de la boue* routine is most commonly found in the blurbs for newish authors; by the time an author is successful enough for smart blurbing to be an irrelevancy, he or she will usually be pressured by publishers to take on a new type of employment, this time unpaid: coughing up blurbs for less well-known writers. Stephen King, the world's best-selling novelist, is also one of its most prolific suppliers of jacket copy for writers in the same vein – with, or so I'm assured by horror fans, the predictable inflationary results. To sidle over to a more genteel district of American letters, the poet Marianne Moore was also generous with her blurbing – so much so that an entire section of her *Collected Prose* is given over to a gathering of copy for other writers'

---

* Some years ago, Tom Lubbock contributed, among other entries, the word 'Author' to an updated version of Flaubert's *Dictionary of Received Ideas* for the *Independent*. I'll précis, from imperfect memory: 'AUTHOR: The author has worked as a bartender, a raspberry picker, a night security guard and a labourer on a building site.' (Paraphrase: the author went to university and took some odd jobs in the vacations.)

dust jackets. It only takes the most cursory examination of these opuscules to realize that by today's standards she was a hopelessly naive practitioner of the art, too true to her own critical standards to write falsely pitched praise, no matter how worthy or dearly beloved the recipient. As a consequence, she may well be the supreme mistress of several blurbish sub-genres, including the blurb tepid:

> I find him prepossessing. [On John Ashbery.]

And the blurb left-handed:

> Hugh Kenner, upon technicalities of the trade, is commanding; and when intent upon what he respects, the facets gleam. Entertaining and fearless, he can be too fearless, but we need him.

And the blurb bizarre:

> To begin with, a poet. His absence of affectation is one of the rarest things on earth. *Towards a Better Life* is a book to annotate. Un-stodgy *he!* [On Kenneth Burke]

These quirky samples will not, I'm sure, be to everybody's taste, but I must say I find them rather refreshing after a sickeningly unrelieved diet of what we might as well call blurbs superlative – you know the sort of thing: 'groundbreaking', 'shatteringly original', 'awesome' – whether in the form of log-rolling plugs by chums,* or of extracted bits of reviews that have obviously been written with a view to easy extraction and placement on back or front covers,† or

---

* Guilty, your honour. But only once or twice.

† Yes, all right, but even less often.

of the type of artless screech-lines churned out by the second most junior person in the office. ('When I worked in New York in the 1980s,' another publishing mole told me, 'blurb-writing was considered just one step up from the worst job of all, which was writing reports on the manuscript slush pile. I think the first one I wrote was for a bodice-ripper, and it said something like "Torn between duty and desire . . .!" The general attitude was that it was a job which soon sorted out the men from the boys – if you had to *read* the book before you write the blurb, you obviously weren't going to get very far up the company totem pole.')

I'll admit, though, that I for one would have thought several times before asking Miss Moore to compose a plug for anything I'd written; and much as I may grump about the idiocy and monotony of blurbs superlative, I will clearly be narked if *Invisible Forms* goes as scantily adorned with glowing commendations as a collection of poems by Enoch Soames.* What's more, I have every intention of writing my own author's blurb for a change. The only question is, should I follow (a) the sober option:

> Kevin Jackson is the author of five previous books. He also works for newspapers, radio and television.

(b) the cute one-liner option:

> Kevin Jackson is a recovering werewolf.

or (c) the bragging, shiny-with-smugness option:

---

* See 'Appendix', pp. 264–72.

Kevin Jackson has a brain the size of Jupiter.

It's a poser. There's one thing I'm certain of, though. I'm damned if I'm going to tell anyone I live in White City.*

---

* 'A Note on the Author' can be found on p. i, above.

Dedications

This essay is for Dr Ernest Klein,
For reasons which will become evident

Should anyone call my dedication to Chatterton affected
I answer as followeth: 'Were I dead Sir I should like a
Book dedicated to me'

> John Keats, in the rejected preface to *Endymion*,
> 19 March 1818

Shakespeare's first published work was neither a play nor a poem but (as M. Genette would have it) a paratext: an IF. On opening the quarto of *Venus and Adonis*, handsomely printed in 1593 by the poet's fellow Stratfordian Richard Field, and flicking past the title page to find the poetic meat, the Elizabethan reader's eye would have been greeted by these honeyed words:

> To the Right Honourable
> Henrie Wriothesley, Earle of Southampton
> and Baron of Titchfield

Right Honourable,
    I know not how I shall offend in dedicating my unpolisht lines to your Lordship, nor how the worlde will censure mee for choosing so strong a proppe to support so weake a burthen, onelye if your Honour seeme but

pleased, I account my selfe highly praised, and vowe to
take advantage of all idle houres, till I have honoured you
with some graver labour. But if the first heire of my
invention prove deformed, I shall be sorie it had so noble
a god-father, and never after eare so barren a land, for
feare it yeeld me still so bad a harvest, I leave it to your
Honourable survey, and your Honour to your hearts
content, which I wish may alwaies answere your owne
wish, and the worlds hopefull expectation.

Your Honours in all dutie
William Shakespeare.

Hardly a promising fanfare for the most illustrious of all
literary careers. More like the best of all justifications for
Samuel Johnson's scornful *Dictionary* definition of a dedication as 'a servile address to a patron' and of a dedicator as
'one who inscribes his work to a patron with compliments
and servility'.

Most of us would side with Johnson. Our age has lost
the taste for elaborate formal compliments, especially compliments paid to a nineteen-year-old Hooray Henrie, and we
find it irritating that one of the very few scraps and shavings
of direct personal utterance from our greatest poet should
be either so horribly self-abasing or so flagrantly insincere.
Come on, we are tempted to carp at the Bard, *do you seriously
mean you'll stop writing verse if the kid doesn't give you a good
review?*

But in grumbling like this, we are betraying a streak of
stubborn literal-mindedness which makes us the spiritual
kinfolk of that legendary redneck who, when he saw what
was about to happen to the poor white lady on stage, drew

his pistol and, bellowing a vile racist oath, shot dead the actor playing Othello. In composing a dedication, Shakespeare is writing conventionally, writing within a clearly defined genre of his time. Whatever his true feelings towards Southampton – and let me immediately offer the reassurance that I have no plans to go into the umpteenth set of tiresome, half-loony speculations as to whether H. Wriothesley was really the 'W.H.' of the dedication to Shakespeare's *Sonnets*, and thus the adored Young Man – his apparently grovelling words here are, in their way, perfectly proper. They're a standard part of the courtship dance between plebeian author and aristocratic patron, written with an eye on social advancement and big cash prizes. Southampton seems to have understood the game every bit as well as Shakespeare, and there are signs that he condescended to being so wooed. Just a year later, in 1594, Shakespeare once again dedicated a narrative poem to young Henry/ie – that heavily trailed 'graver labour', *The Rape of Lucrece*; and between the lines of its routine hyperbole, one can detect some satisfactorily ripening business:

> To the Right Honourable
> Henrie Wriotheseley, Earl of Southampton
> and Baron of Tichfield

The love I dedicate to your Lordship is without end: whereof this Pamphlet without beginning is but a superfluous Moiety. The warrant I have of your Honourable disposition, not the worth of my untutord Lines makes it assured of acceptance. What I have done is yours, what I have to doe is yours, being part in all I have, devoted yours. Were my worth greater, my duety would shew greater, meane time, as it is, it is bound to your Lordship, to whom I wish long life still lengthned with all happinesse.

> Your Lordships in all duety
> William Shakespeare.

Still quite conventional, but the temperature is noticeably warmer. You can see why semi-scholarly tongues have wagged over the years about the possibility of there being something less than robustly hetero about these chaps. When we read comparably fulsome dedications nowadays, we see the memorials of true love and loss, and generally with good reason. An academic publisher recently told me the (authenticated) story of one monograph which passed through his press about ten years ago. In the manuscript, the author's dedication – I have tampered slightly, to spare further remorse – read something like this:

> To Ermintrude
> Let me not to the marriage of true minds
> Admit impediment . . .

By the time it reached the proof stage, this touching reference had been altered,* and now read

> To Ermintrude
> The old order changeth, yielding place to new.

The temptation to hunt for hidden love stories in dedications is all the stronger when the identity of the beloved dedicatee is veiled with the mask of initials or pet name, or

---

* Shakespeare's sonnet continues, you will recall, 'Love is not love/ Which alters when it alteration finds' . . .

obscure from some other cause. There has been endless puzzling, for example, about the person of 'S.A.', the addressee of T. E. Lawrence's homoerotic dedicatory poem for *The Seven Pillars of Wisdom* – a curiously haunting set of verses, for all their vainglory and (unwitting?) double entendre:

> I loved you, so I drew these tides of men into my hands
>   and wrote my will across the sky in stars
> To earn you Freedom, the seven pillared worthy house,
>   that your eyes might be shining for me
>   When we came . . .*

There has also been a fair bit of elbow-nudging about the precise nature of the intense friendship between T. S. Eliot and one Jean Verdenal, dedicatee of *Prufrock and other Observations*.† If the French medical student wasn't so much as a wee bit gay, it's sad that literary history should recall

---

* Another of Lawrence's dedications – or, more exactly, of 352087 A/c Ross's – is harder to take. It's the one in *The Mint*:

> To
> Edward Garnett
> You dreamed I came one night
> with this book crying, 'Here's
> a masterpiece. Burn it.'
> Well – *as you please*

† This dedication went through several metamorphoses. The 1917 edition read 'To Jean Verdenal, 1889–1915'. *Ara Vos Prec* (1920), Eliot's next collection, dropped the dedication and substituted an epigraph from Dante; by 1925, in *Poems 1909–1925*, the dedicatee was restored, with 'To' changed to 'For', and Verdenal's name had been tagged with the phrase 'mort aux Dardanelles'. See B. C. Southam, *A Student's Guide to the Selected Poems of T. S. Eliot*, pp. 43–4.

him only as a possible youthful flame of Eliot's, though probably a lot less sad than if he weren't remembered at all. Much the same could be said of Henry or Henrie Wriothesley, who would by now be the sole property of professional historians had his path not crossed Shakespeare's. According to some accounts, Southampton gave the poet £1,000 in return for his two dedications; even allowing for inflation, that seems like a bargain for a slice of immortality.

And yet, force of convention and so on taken into account, it is still fair enough to be disappointed by Shakespeare's brace of paratexts – not because they show him being servile, or insincere, but because he failed to make of them something which could delight and astonish posterity as well as tickle a lord. The *Lucrece* dedication is a step in the right direction, with its nice quibble on 'love without end' and 'pamphlet without beginning', but it's not much more than a step. Had he gone on to dedicate his later works, whether to noblemen or to other entities, Shakespeare would surely have found all manner of ways to make a few dedicatory lines as pregnant as any sonnet. 'Surely', because we know that his lesser contemporaries and near-contemporaries sometimes looked hard at the form, and played games with it. Ben Jonson, for one, whose rancorous, self-justifying dedication to *The New Inn* is aimed at 'the Reader'; or that intriguing weirdo John Marston, best known for his play *The Malcontent*.

A scholarly Buddhist friend once told me that Marston had dedicated his works 'To Oblivion'. I was suitably impressed by this premature punk-nihilism, though when I looked a little more closely into the matter I found his account slightly exaggerated. It's true that Marston did express such a sentiment, in his poem 'To Everlasting *Oblivion*':

> Thou mighty gulfe, insatiat cormorant
> Deride me not, though I seem petulant
> To fall into thy chops. Let others pray
> For ever their faire poems flourish may.
> But as for me, hungry *Oblivion*
> Devoure me quick, accept my orizon . . .

And he appears to have compounded the gesture with the self-composed epitaph on his tombstone in the Middle Temple:

> Oblivioni Sacrvm.

But neither the epitaph nor the poem was, strictly speaking, a dedication. Marston did, though, dedicate his play *Antonio and Mellida* (c. 1600) to nobody, or Nobody:

> To the only rewarder and most just poiser of virtuous merits, the most honourably renowned Nobody, bounteous Maecenas of poetry and Lord Protector of oppressed innocence, *do, dedicoque* . . .

Marston was an avant-gardist; not until the late nineteenth and early twentieth century did such dedicatory stunts become common.

A lightning history of the dedication. For the better part of two millennia, the story of dedications is the story of patronage. Elegant literary cadging begins at least as early as Augustan Rome – Horace and Virgil dedicated their works to Maecenas for much the same reasons Shakespeare sucked up to Southampton – and thrives throughout Europe until roughly the latter part of the eighteenth century, when writing starts to become a profession.* Throughout this time, personal dedications are certainly not unknown – Cicero dedicates *De officiis* to his son, *De oratore* to his brother, and so on – but they are relatively uncommon. Most dedications are contained somewhere within the body of the work, even after Gutenberg's handy invention comes along, and it's not until the sixteenth century that the form makes its declaration of independence and moves up to the front of the book, classically on the first recto page after the title page. Enter the eighteenth century, enter lots of bookish stunts and parodies, *Tale of a Tub* (Dedication: 'To His Royal Highness Prince Posterity'), *Tristram Shandy*, and we already know what Dr Johnson thought of dedications, but, because it's one of the finest poems in the English language, here's a pertinent couplet from 'The Vanity of Human Wishes':†

----

* See Genette, *Seuils* (Paris: Éditions de Seuil, 1987), pp. 110–33 (trans. in *Paratexts* (Cambridge: Cambridge University Press,1997), pp. 117–43); and Adrian Room, *Bloomsbury Dictionary of Dedications* (London: Bloomsbury, 1990), pp. ix–xiv. Somewhat miffed to find that the scholarly Mr Room has walked the path of dedications as well as pseudonyms before me, I have resolved not to cite any of the examples used in his entertaining anthology unless – like the Shakespeare dedications – they are so obvious or so famous that to avoid them would be perverse. On the occasions where he's put me onto something I didn't already have, I've tagged it with the letter R, thus: (R).

† As Paul Fussell has pointed out, Johnson's distaste for the form didn't stop him from writing dozens of brilliant dedications on behalf of others; see *Samuel Johnson and the Life of Writing* (New York: Harcourt Brace Jovanovich, 1971), p. 177. Johnson's rude letter to the Earl of Chesterfield (7 February 1755) may be taken as the symbolic, if not the literal end of

> For growing names the weekly scribbler lies,
> To growing wealth the dedicator flies . . .

Rise of the middle classes, decline of the aristocracy, unpleasant acts in France, et cetera et cetera. Jane Austen dedicates *Emma* to the Prince Regent in 1816, but by the mid-nineteenth century the idea of the Dedicatory Epistle to an aristocrat is already so dated that such effusions tend from now on to be offered self-consciously, in a spirit of deliberate anachronism or pastiche.* Hence Thackeray, opening *The History of Henry Esmond* (1852):

> To the Right Honourable William Bingham,
> Lord Asburton
>
> My Dear Lord,
>   The writer of a book which copies the manners and language of Queen Anne's time, must not omit the Dedication to the Patron; and I must ask leave to inscribe this volume to your Lordship, for the sake of the great kindness and friendship which I owe to you and yours . . .

A few years before this, in about 1844, Balzac began to dedicate his unfinished novel *Le Prêtre Catholique* to Mme Hanska with the seemingly self-cancelling words 'Madame, the time of dedications is past' – meaning, that is to say,

---

patronage in Britain: 'Is not a patron, my Lord, one who looks with unconcern on a man struggling for life in the water, and, when he has reached ground, encumbers him with help?'

* Adrian Room points out that only one or two literary works have been dedicated to Her Majesty Queen Elizabeth the Second, who, in principle, does not accept dedications at all. See above, p. v.

dedications to a ritzy patron. Love, friendship, respect and common or garden sycophancy now take over from ambition and covetousness as the principal incentives to dedication.

Writers, to be sure, had long been in the habit of dedicating books to other writers – Chaucer 'directed' *Troilus and Criseyde* to Gower, Spenser addressed the *Fairie Queene* to Raleigh – but from now on they felt free to dedicate their works to nations and nation-states ('*à la République de Genève*': the dedication of Rousseau's second *Discours*), to spouses, to dogs by the kennel-load and cats by the bucketful, to pubs, to abstractions (Levi-Strauss dedicates one of his works 'To Music'), to the dead, even to themselves. After completing the manuscript of a play entitled *A Brilliant Career*, the eighteen-year-old James Joyce scrawled across its title page:

> To
> My Own Soul I
> dedicate the first
> true work of my
> life

Such whole-hearted dedicatory egotism is rare, though F. R. and Q. D. Leavis famously, or notoriously, dedicated *Dickens the Novelist* to each other. Readers who have their doubts about the critical couple might care to know that a similar exchange of bouquets was made by the writer and illustrator of *Brute!*, a scabrous comic-book of the mid-eighties.

Given the chance, it seems, writers will aim their work at just about anything – Adrian Room's *Dictionary of Dedications* offers abundant and well-annotated evidence for this asseveration, spread across some 350 pages. To simplify matters, I'd like to propose breaking down this infinite variety of dedications into just six major categories.

(A) The Penny Plain

These need little or no explanation: they are the straight-forward nods 'To Bill', or 'To my old friend Bill', or 'To Bill, in memory of happy hours at the Stoat and Snapdragon', and they show such minimal distinctiveness as scarcely to count as fully grown IFs at all. Guessing which authors are likely to go in for this kind of degree-zero dedication is a pleasant way of whiling away one's lazier hours in a library. I won a small bet with myself by skimming through the dedications of about a dozen novels by Kingsley Amis, which, sure enough, are all straight category (a). It's also easy enough to make a stab at which sort of author is likely to go in for category

(B) The Tuppence Coloured

Half-remembering, half-guessing, I pulled out my copy of Cyril Connolly's *The Unquiet Grave* and found:

To

Peter Watson

A never writer to an ever reader. Newes!

The category (b) dedication – which might be re-christened the dedigraph, since it scrambles together the otherwise distinct forms of dedication and epigraph – is pretty much standard issue for what Gore Vidal calls Quality

Lit. productions; I'd lay money that one of the things which helped establish the vogue is the dedigraph to *The Waste Land*, probably the best-known such offering of the century, if not of all time:

> For Ezra Pound
> *il miglior fabbro**

(C) The Fancy

A category which encompasses all the gross and subtle games that have been played with the form, from Marston, via Swift and Sterne, to the age of the postmodernist pranksters. It includes all forms of dedicatory poems, a sub-genre so vast as to defy summary here. It can, or should, include Sir Walter Scott's quietly unconventional dedication to *Waverley* (1814), which was kept to an afterword or postface:

> . . . As I have inverted the usual arrangement, placing these remarks at the end of the work to which they refer, I will venture on a second violation of form, by closing the whole with a dedication: these volumes being respectfully inscribed to our Scottish Addison, Henry Mackenzie, by an unknown admirer of his genius.

It can also include Virginia Woolf's dedication to *Night and Day*, which – mock-seriously? – despairs of the assump-

---

* Slightly adapted from Dante, *Purgatorio*, xxvi, 117: 'the better craftsman' (or 'maker') – a tribute to the twelfth-century troubadour poet Arnaut Daniel. Eliot didn't publish the dedication until the 1925 edition, *Poems 1909–1925*; again, see Southam, op. cit., pp. 135–7.

tion that anyone literate enough to write an arty novel should have a choice erudite quotation ready to hand:

> To
> Vanessa Bell
> But, looking for a phrase,
> I found none to stand
> Beside your name

And it can include all those dedications which are phrased in such a way as to play against the title of the work, such as Allen Ginsberg's 'Howl', which is followed by the words *for Carl Solomon*, and thus suggests that the poet is howling for his chum, or perhaps that the reader should think about howling for him.*

Other poets have played the same trick: the title of Peter Robinson's 'Going Out To Vote' is tagged with 'for John Wilkinson' – a witty effect which borders on our next category:

(D) The Intentionally Funny

This encompasses everything from Robert Morley's dedication of his *Book of Worries* (R) to 'scrambled eggs on toast', to Stephen Potter's dedication of *Lifemanship* 'To Anon'. It

---

* 'Howl' the poem, that is. *Howl* the book bears a triple dedication to Jack Kerouac ('new Buddha of American prose, who spit forth intelligence into eleven books written in half the number of years . . .'), William Burroughs and Neal Cassady. For a list of the dedications to his other books, see the *Collected Poems 1947–1980*, p. 802.

is this book, by the way, which drew attention to an ingenious way of rendering your book critic-proof: simply open it with something along these lines:

> To PHYLLIS,
> in the hope that God's glorious gift of sight
> may be restored to her.

(Phyllis, the author's great-grandmother, was rather short-sighted, and ninety-six years old.)* The most surprising people have chosen to poke some fun at the slightly pompous convention of dedicating, including Dr Nikolaus Pevsner, whose *Buildings of England* guide to *Bedfordshire and the County of Huntingdonshire and Peterborough* is dedicated:

> To the
> Inventor
> of the
> ICED LOLLY

All that tramping around buildings in high summer must have been thirsty work.

(E) The Unintentionally Funny

or faintly eccentric dedication is the sort which has always attracted the connoisseur. John Julius Norwich conferred a fresh and richly deserved lease of life on two memorable instances in his *Christmas Cracker* for 1975. The first is from Colonel Angus Buchanan's *Sahara*, 1926:

---

* Potter, *Lifemanship* (London: Rupert Hart-Davis, 1950), pp. 77–8.

To Feri n'Gashi
Only a Camel
But steel-true and great of heart.

The second is from Mrs Frances Simpson, *Cats for Pleasure and Profit*, 1905:

To the many kind friends, known and
unknown, that I have made
in Pussydom.

Enough frivolity. The final category,

(F) The Memorial

shows the form at its noblest, and even the plainest examples of the kind have their own eloquence. Oscar Wilde's dedication for *The Ballad of Reading Gaol* is almost shocking in its spareness, and reads like a memorial not only for the hapless Guardsman but for all of Oscar's former linguistic charms, now overthrown:

In memoriam C.T.W.,
sometime Trooper of the Royal Horse Guards,
obiit H.M. Prison, Reading, Berkshire, July 7, 1896.

Where Oscar showed his sincerity with plain English, many memorial dedicators feel that the vulgar tongue is somehow inadequate for their needs, and reach for their Latin, safe in the knowledge that few are likely to sneer at the pretension, even if the dedicatee is a quadruped, as in Martin Greif's (*sic*) dedication for *The Gay Book of Days* (R):

For Molly.
Vale canis nobilis et fidelis. Sit tibi terra levis.

The Latin dedication is liberating: one can say things about the dead in a dead language that might seem a little too effusive in a living one. Take Valentine Cunningham's tribute to a former student, in *British Writers of the Thirties* (1988)

IN MEMORIAM DISCIPVLAE MEAE
MGBAFOR NWENA INYAMA
LITERIS ANGLICIS AMANTISSIME STUVDVIT
INGENIOSA HILARA HVMANA FVIT
OBIIT XXIV AETATIS ANNO

But – to bring these remarks full circle, to their dedicatee – the most moving and harrowing dedication I have turned up in the course of my rummagings was composed in plain English, by a scholar of our language. I encountered it quite unexpectedly, in an essay by Nicholson Baker, who himself encountered it unexpectedly when chasing after the word 'lumber' in a library. Baker recalls* consulting the first volume of Dr Ernest Klein's *Comprehensive Etymological Dictionary of the English Language*, and being prompted to furtive tears. No wonder. This is what he read:

DEDICATED TO THE SACRED MEMORY OF THE BEST PARENTS
MY DEAR *MOTHER*
WHO AFTER A LIFE OF SELF-SACRIFICE DIED IN SZATMAR IN 1940
AND MY DEAR *FATHER*,
THE WORLD-RENOWNED RABBI AND SCHOLAR

---

* *The Size of Thoughts* (London: Chatto & Windus, 1996), pp. 294–5.

RABBI IGNAZ (ISAAC) KLEIN OF SZATMAR,
WHO DIED A MARTYR OF HIS FAITH IN AUSCHWITZ IN 1944;
AND TO THE SACRED MEMORY OF MY *WIFE*
AND OF MY ONLY *CHILD JOSEPH (HAYYIM ISRAEL)*
WHO ALSO FELL VICTIMS TO NAZISM IN AUSCHWITZ IN 1944

Epigraphs

'Überhaupt hat der Fortschritt das an sich, daß er viel großer ausschaut, als er wirklich ist.'

Nestroy

He that condemns himself to compose on a stated Day, will often bring to his Task, an Attention dissipated, a Memory overwhelmed, an Imagination embarrassed, a Mind distracted with anxieties, and a Body languishing with Disease. . .

Johnson, *The Rambler*, No. 208

Considerate la vostra semenza:
fatti non foste a viver come bruti,
ma per seguir virtute e canoscenza.

. . . and education too, as Henry Adams always sez, keeps going on forever.

Thomas Pynchon, *Slow Learner*

Sad but true: whatever other functions it may supposedly serve, the epigraph (or page of epigraphs, or pages and pages of epigraphs)* will sometimes be little more than a display

---

* The longest example I know – though some may quibble as to whether these texts genuinely count as epigraphs – can be found in *Moby-Dick*, where the ominous opening words 'Call me Ishmael' are preceded by fifteen pages of extracts about whales from the likes of Montaigne,

of raw swank – the literary counterpart to name-dropping, as Madonna once said to me over Madeira and seed cake. Whatever apposite wisdoms a citation appears to offer about the recompenses of the examined life, the impossibility of recapturing past time, the lacerations of abandoned love or the advisability of giving a sucker an even break, it is also broadcasting a connotative signal far stronger than any of its overt, denotative content, with a far more basic burden: 'Me brainy. Me read clever books. Me someone to treat with heap big respect, O slack-jawed, demi-literate slob who by some freak of unearned good fortune happens to be perusing this quite remarkable, nay, epoch-making opus.' And the more recondite the citation – preferably in French, Latin, Tuscan, Attic Greek or Swahili – the louder the noise of territorial spraying.

Barry Humphries harpoons such affectation neatly in 'Alzheimer Remembers', the preface to his autobiography *More Please*:

> The Reader will be relieved, I hope, to see that this book is not prefaced by a page of pompous epigraphs; obscure apophthegms from Kierkegaard, Borges, F. Scott Fitzgerald, Kafka, Turgenev and the letters of Arnold Schoenberg. It is an indulgence of the provincial opsimath; a highfalutin' mannerism beloved of Australian and American authors keen to parade their multi-lingual skills and sophistication in the face of strong suspicions to the contrary.

Shakespeare, Bacon, Dryden, Milton, Goldsmith, Darwin and a bunch of jolly Jack Tars; and these pages are preceded by a couple of pages of etymology.

Who *can* he be thinking of . . . ? Well, to avoid the enmity and lawsuits of the living, let's pretend that his particular mention of American authors was an invitation to go back and look at, say, the compulsive epigraphizing of Edgar Allan Poe, who, whatever his other sterling qualities, seems to have been neurotically anxious to show Joseph Public just how astonishingly erudite he was. While Poe wasn't the first of the pretentious epigraphists, he does set a standard for the display of flashy polyglot scholarship – much of it bogus – that few have equalled in respect of its frequency and downright fraudulence.* A few samples: 'Eleanora' is tagged with the Latin phrase *Sub conservatione formae specificae salva animae*, which Poe attributes to one 'Raymond Lully', also known to the Western esoteric tradition and New Agers as the Mallorcan mystic Ramon Lull;† 'William Wilson' with two lines said, wrongly,‡ to be from Chamberlayne's *Pharron-ida* (*What say of it? what say of* CONSCIENCE *grim/ That spectre in my path?*); 'Ligea' with a passage from Joseph Glanvill that no one has ever been able to find in Glanvill's *Works*; 'A Descent into the Maelstrom' with another passage

---

* I suspect that Poe was one of the principal targets of Mark Twain's satire when he adorned each chapter of *The Gilded Age* with epigraphs in Phoenician, Ancient Egyptian, Old Norse . . .

† Poe swiped it from a Victor Hugo novel; Hugo swiped it from one Henri Sauval; Sauval claims he took it from Lull, but probably didn't. It means 'the soul is saved by the preservation of the specific form'.

‡ But a passage much like it appears in Chamberlayne's *Love's Victory*. I owe most of this information on Poe's posings to Stuart & Susan Levine, eds., *The Short Fiction of Edgar Allan Poe: An Annotated Edition* (Champaign, Ill.: University of Illinois Press, 1990).

from Glanvill, this one real but significantly tinkered with
or misremembered; 'The Purloined Letter' with a line from
Seneca that, though it sounds a bit like him, has never
been found in Seneca (*Nil sapientiae odiosius acumine nimio*:
'Nothing is more distasteful to good sense than too much
cunning') . . .

I could go on for pages with this list of gaffes. But, since
poking fun at Poe is too much like mocking the afflicted –
he had a ghastly life, the poor soul – perhaps one should add
a couple of mitigating notes. Some of his epigraphs are
rather haunting, even beautiful. 'The Murders in the Rue
Morgue' is headed by a fine passage from Sir Thomas
Browne's *Urn-Burial*:

> What song the Syrens sang, or what name Achilles
> assumed when he hid himself among women, although
> puzzling questions are not beyond all conjecture.

And 'The Fall of the House of Usher' is tagged with a
(faithfully quoted) couplet from Pierre-Jean de Béranger, a
minor poet quite well known in Poe's day who, at a guess,
deserves to be a little better known in ours:

> Son cœur est un luth suspendu;
> Sitot qu'on le touche il resonne.

Part of the pleasure of reading Poe's stories – if, like me,
you actually do take pleasure in them – is of meeting or re-
meeting these elegant scraps and tags in such unexpectedly
sordid surroundings. Ostentation, then, may not have been
Poe's only motive. A more generous assumption about his
feelings would be that, like many a later epigraphist, he had
taken such a fancy to certain phrases that he simply couldn't

resist sharing them with his public. Moreover, though I've
so far written as if all the vanity in epigraph-mongering were
that of the author, it's fairly clear that Poe was also using his
learned sources to tickle the pride of his readers, and to
strike a sort of contract of mutual reassurance with them.
Safely inoculated by our quick shot of La Bruyère or Servius
at the doorway to Poe's morbid tales, we can snuggle down
for a thoroughly agreeable evening's read about mutilated
cats and dead chicks.

Poe has had many literary offspring in the twentieth
century, not all of them obviously part of his bloodline, and
one diverting way of establishing a family relationship is to
watch out for the ten-cent epigraphs. Today, just as in Poe's
more proper times, a writer of Gothic fiction who wants to
set him- or herself apart from the tribe of mere vulgar gore-
mongers still has to be careful to do as Uncle Edgar did, and
adorn the entrance hall to a presumptuous best-seller with
some improving maxims. Hence, for example, the display put
on in the opening pages of Caleb Carr's enjoyable period
thriller *The Alienist*, whose dedication page bears the words

> 'They who would be young when they are old,
>   must be old when they are young.'
>
> John Ray, 1670

and whose first chapter is attended by two impeccably high-
toned authorities:

> Whilst part of what we perceive comes through our
> senses from the object before us, another part (and it may
> be the larger part) always comes out of our own mind.
>
> William James, *The Principles of Psychology*

> These bloody thoughts,
> from what are they born?

Piave, from Verdi's *Macbeth*

Some other cases are not so easily cracked. I've sometimes wondered, for instance, whether the precedent of Poe's
flashily recondite showmanship might not have been in the
anguished and overeducated mind of another young American, T. S. Eliot, when he set about festooning his earlier
poems with learned epigraphs. Eliot certainly had an eye on
Poe in other respects,* and he certainly wasn't a snob about
spooky tales. (Far from it: Bram Stoker's Dracula creeps face-
downwards into the drafts of *The Waste Land*.) But even if
Poe wasn't a conscious model for Eliot, there's enough of a
similarity between their practices to offer occasions of mild
embarrassment to anyone who has to speak up on behalf of
the modern poet's 'elitism' or snobbery.

Flick through the first thirty-odd pages of *The Complete
Poems and Plays* alone and you will find epigraphs from
Dante (*Purgatorio* xxi, 133–6; *Inferno* xxvii, 61–6) Marlowe (*The
Jew of Malta*, IV, i), Lucian, Shakespeare, Beaumont and
Fletcher, Villon (*En l'an trentiesme de mon aage/ Que toutes*

---

* Sort of. One version of the story would go something like this: Poe, not
always greatly honoured in his own country, was taken up with quasi-
religious fervour by three generations of French Symbolist poets: Baudelaire, Mallarmé, Valéry; Eliot greatly admired and borrowed from all three
Frenchmen; thus, Poe returns to American/English literature greatly
refreshed by his holiday in France. As the critical cribs will tell you, Eliot
grafts a reference to Mallarmé's poem about the tomb of Edgar Poe into
one of the *Four Quartets*. There's probably a Ph.D. thesis there. Someone
has probably written it already.

mes hontes j'ay beues . . .), St Paul's Epistle to the Colossians, another chunk of *The Jew of Malta*, Aeschylus in the original Greek and, for 'Burbank with a Baedeker: Bleistein with a Cigar', a short but bewildering macaronic evocation of Venice compounded of fragments from Théophile Gautier, Mantegna, Henry James, *Othello*, Browning's 'A Toccata of Galuppi's' and Marston's stage directions to the *Noble Lorde and Lady of Huntingdons Entertainement of their right Noble Mother Alice: Countesse Dowager of Darby for the first night of her honors arrivall at the House of Ashby*.* Obviously, sulky undergraduates will be inclined to rubbish this sort of thing in much the same way I've just been cheerfully rubbishing Poe's mannerisms: as rank pseudery, or – in the unlikely event that they possess a vocabulary as *raffiné* as that of the creator of Dame Edna – as the indulgence of a provincial opsimath.

There are a couple of possible responses to such gripes. The first is that, just as Poe's epigraphs, usually archaic, help pump up the general creepiness of his tales – most of them read like extracts from Roderick Usher's library,† and are

---

* Information pillaged, again, from B. C. Southam's invaluable *Guide*. Southam points out that the extravagance of this epigraph may owe something to Tristan Corbière, whose 'Epitaphe' has a joke epigraph, half a page long (attributed to 'Sagesse des Nations' – 'Wisdom of the Nations'), while 'Ça?' has the one-word epigraph, 'What?', mischievously attributed to Shakespeare. I couldn't find the latter in my edition of Corbière, but I did find a notable example of misquoted reference: " 'J'ai scie le sommeil!' ('I've murdered sleep!') (MACBETH)". See Val Warner, *The Centenary Corbière*, pp. 50–51.

† Poe's narrator tells us that this included 'the Vervet et Chartreuse of

thus comparable in their atmospheric effect to the suits of armour, cobwebs, rats, flaming torches and such found in Universal and Hammer horror movies – so Eliot's citations help furnish some of the eerie, or comic-grotesque, or unaccountably unsettling qualities of his own poems. And, rather as Poe's stories would be subtly denatured if one stripped them of their paratextual ornaments, Eliot's poems would be watered down by removing such well-loved appendages as *'Mistah Kurtz – he dead'*, or *'A penny for the Old Guy'* or (in a different register) *'Hence the soul cannot be possessed of the divine union, until it has divested itself of the love of created beings*. St. John of the Cross.'

A second plausible reply to gripers is really a variant of the first. Ask the sulkers in question to concede that Eliot's early poems are partly put together from lots and lots of quotations from other writers; ask them to concede, further, that this is not necessarily a bad thing (here you may have difficulties); then ask them to explain the differences, if any, between putting a quotation inside your poem and putting one at its head. With luck, this might produce an interesting discussion, to which you could give some direction by asking them to consider whether Eliot was right to replace his proposed epigraph for *The Waste Land* (which he described

---

Gresset; the Belphegor of Machiavelli; the Heaven and Hell of Sweden-borg; the Subterranean Voyage of Nicholas Klimm by Holberg; the Chiromancy of Robert Flud, of Jean D'Indagine, and of De La Chambre; the Journey into the Blue Distance of Tieck; and of the City of the Sun of Campanella', as well as the *Directorium Inquisitorium* and the *Vigiliae Mortuorum Secundum Chorum Ecclesiae Maguntinae*. Remarkably similar to my own bedtime reading, now I come to think of it.

to Pound as 'much the most appropriate I can find, and somewhat elucidative'):

> 'Did he live his life again, in every detail of desire, temptation, and surrender during that supreme moment of complete knowledge? He cried out in a whisper at some image, at some vision, – he cried out twice, a cry that was no more than a breath – "The horror! The horror!"'[*]

with the epigraph from the *Satyricon* which has become canonical:

> 'Nam Sibyllam quidem Cumis ego ipse oculis meis vidi in ampulla pendere, et cum illi pueri dicerent: Σίβυλλα τί θέλεις; respondebat illa: ʼαποθανείν θέλω.'

Anyway, whether or not Eliot's quotations are designed to cast light or deepen gloom, elucidation is demonstrably one of the time-honoured functions of the epigraph. Barry Humphries himself goes in for it, just as he goes in for a sly bit of old posh on his title page. Despite his wry observations about the opsimathic nervousness of the high-falutin' quote-drop, the title page of *More Please* bears the words:

> He was always a seeker after something in the world that is there in no satisfying measure, or not at all.
>
> Walter Pater, from *Imaginary Portraits*

---

[*] From Conrad's *Heart of Darkness*.

For the bulk of Mr Humphries's (deservedly) broad readership, Pater is, surely, a pretty exotic source?* Flip over a
couple of pages, though, and you will find a sweeter paraphrase of Pater's sentiments:

'More please'

the author's first coherent utterance

More Please thus belongs to that large, unofficial category of
books which use epigraphs to comment or expand on their
titles, explaining the source of an allusion, illuminating what
might be otherwise be largely, partly or mildly obscure.†

---

* I suspect that Mr Humphries may have derived his fondness for that
ripe term 'opsimath' from Pater's essay on Winckelmann: 'Unhappily',
Pater quotes from the German scholar, 'I am one of those whom the
Greeks call *opsimatheis*. – I have come into the world and into Italy too
late.' (See *The Renaissance*, ed. Adam Phillips, p. 121.) The main epigraph
to *The Renaissance*, for those who may be interested, is *Yet shall ye be as the
wings of a dove*: from Psalms 68: 13: 'Though ye have lain among the pots,
yet shall ye be as the wings of a dove covered with silver, and her feathers
with yellow gold.'

† There is another class of epigraphs, the Epigraph Baffling, which works
in quite the opposite way, and is more perplexing than anything else
in the book. Examples: the epigraph to Edwin Morgan's *Collected
Translations*:

– Habar bar?
– Bar!

or Dai Vaughan's citation of Ernst Toller for his novel *The Cloud Chamber*:

Zirizi Zirizi Zirizi
Zirizi
Urrr

My sentiments precisely.

This category makes some strange bedfellows. If you arranged your book collection according such a system, novels such as F. Scott Fitzgerald's *Tender is the Night* (Keats epigraph), or Hemingway's *For Whom the Bell Tolls* (Donne epigraph)* or John Kennedy Toole's *A Confederacy of Dunces* (Swift epigraph)† would be rubbing covers with – to name a few that I pulled down at random from the bookshelves closest to my keyboard – Robert Junck's history of the Manhattan Project, *Brighter than a Thousand Suns*:‡

> If the radiance of a thousand suns
> were to burst into the sky,
> that would be
> the splendor of the Mighty One –
> *Bhagavad Gita*

or Neil Sheehan's *A Bright Shining Lie: John Paul Vann and America in Vietnam*:

> We had also, to all the visitors who came over there been
> one of the bright shining lies.
>
> John Paul Vann to a U.S. Army historian, July 1963

---

* I can't resist adding here that Donne also furnished an epigraph for a little-known horror film of which I am unhealthily fond, Mark Robson's *The Seventh Victim*. Quite a lot of films have used epigraphs, from *Platoon* to *Wag the Dog*, but I'm willing to bet that there's only one which has used a citation from Henri Michaux: Jim Jarmusch's *Dead Man*.

† Actually, Toole's book has two epigraphs; the other is from A. J. Liebling's *The Earl of Louisiana*.

‡ Which also has the less portentous epigraph: *Why should we always think of what the scientist does and never what he is?* – George N. Shuster, in 'Good, Evil and Beyond', *The Annals*, January 1947.

or J. A. Cuddon's *The Owl's Watchsong: A Study of Istanbul*:

> *Pardedari mikunad dar kasr-i-Kaysar ankebut;*
> *Bum naubat mizanad dar gumbed-i-Afrasiab.*

The spider spins his web in the Palace of the Caesars
And the owl sings her watchsong on the Towers of Afrasiab.

(A verse from Saadi quoted by Mehmet II, 'The Conqueror', when
he walked through the ruined palace of the Byzantine emperors.)

And these four books would, in turn, stand dust-jacket to
dust-jacket with many, many volumes of poetry, especially
collections with slightly cryptic or out-of-the-way titles, such
as Ted Hughes's *Wodwo*, with its justifying extract in period
orthography from *Sir Gawain and the Green Knight*, Thom
Gunn's *Moly*, with its epigraphic paragraph about Circean
transformation (Gunn's own retelling of the myth, I assume),
or Dick Davis's *Touchwood*: 'TOUCHWOOD: *decayed wood
. . . used as tinder.*'*

Thus far, then, we have been wandering around the

---

* Iain Sinclair's *Lights out for the Territory* plays a delicate game with this
explanatory convention, deferring the citation which gives him his grimly
punning title until the last page of text: when I first read it, I wondered
whether this form of epigraph should more exactly be called a postgraph:

> Tom's most well, now, and got his bullet around his neck on a watch-
> guard for a month, and is always seeing what time it is, and so there ain't
> nothing more to write about . . . But I reckon I got to light out for the
> Territory . . . I been there before.
>
> Mark Twain, *The Adventures of Huckleberry Finn*

Naturally, someone else had 'been there before': George Perec, to be
exact, who coined the term 'metagraph' to designate the quotation from
Marx he placed at the end of his debut novel *Les Choses* and the comparable
citations at the end of *La Disparition*.

epigraph as boast, the epigraph as implicit contract, and the epigraph as elucidatory footnote to a title. Anything else? Certainly: the most obvious, and most ancient function of all: the epigraph as declaration of intent, as statement of theme, as promise of topic to be addressed.* When the epigraph first comes into common use in the eighteenth century, it tends to bear almost precisely the same relationship to the work which follows as a short biblical text does to a preacher's Sunday sermon, and the resemblance between the two practices was all the more evident when the work in question was a periodic column, such as Johnson's *Rambler.*† Affixed to longer works, such as novels or poems or works of philosophy, the epigraph is slightly transformed, and becomes not quite so much a sentiment or wisdom to be expounded as a pointer to a big, but not necessarily all-encompassing idea about the work, the author, or both. Hence the epigraphs on the title pages of *Tom Jones*

– Mores hominum multorum vidit. –

(unattributed; it comes from Horace's *Ars poetica*, 'He saw

---

* Sometimes an author will delete an epigraph if it seems to declare a theme too baldly. This may have been Beckett's motive for deleting the Leopardian epigraph *e fangio é il mondo* ('and the world is mud') from his monograph on Proust. See the reminiscence by John Montague in *Or Volge L'Anno/At the Year's Turning*, ed. Marco Sonzogni (Dublin: Dedalus, 1998), p. 254.

† Johnson added greatly to his already considerable misery by issuing the epigraphs for each *Rambler* column to newspapers before he had actually written them, which was tantamount to announcing their subject matter before he quite knew what he had it in mind to write.

the ways of many men'), and of *Tristram Shandy*, which cites Epictetus's *Encheiridion* to the effect that 'it is not things themselves, but opinions concerning things, which disturb men'.*

According to M. Genette, the epigraph, a relatively late arrival on the literary scene, appears as a replacement for the dedicatory epistle. Our theorist says that he can find no examples earlier than the seventeenth century, though he suggests that the epigraph's antecedents may have been the mottoes from coats of arms that were sometimes set in the exergue of an author's works. In Genette's view, the first true epigraph in the modern sense is to be found in La Bruyère's *Caractères* in the year of the Glorious Revolution, 1688: La Bruyère offers his reader an attributed quotation from Erasmus: *Admonere voluimus, non mordere; prodesse, non laedere; consulere moribus hominum, non officere*: roughly: 'We have wanted to warn, not to bite; to be useful, not to wound; to benefit the ways of men, not to degrade them'. Ten years earlier, La Rochefoucauld had opened his *Reflexions, ou Sentences et maximes morales* with the phrase *Nos vertues ne sont, le plus souvent, que des vices deguises* – Our virtues are, most often, only vices in disguise – but Genette disqualifies this because it seems to have been written by La Rochefoucauld himself, and is therefore, in the theorist's terminology, *autographic* rather than *allographic*, and so not strictly kosher.

---

* Genette says, however, that relatively few eighteenth-century novels besides these two deploy epigraphs; writers of the period tend to reserve epigraphs for poems or philosophical treatises. See *Paratexts*, pp. 144–160.

It is not until the rise of the Gothic novel, Genette contends, that the epigraphs start to teem in fiction: Mrs Radcliffe's *The Mysteries of Udolpho* (1794), Lewis's *The Monk* (1795) and Maturin's *Melmoth the Wanderer* (1820) boast epigraphs at the start of every chapter, Walter Scott* generally does the same, and the fad passes over the sea to France in the early nineteenth century. Hugo was a keen epigraphist, as were Stendhal and Balzac. But one of the nineteenth century's master (or mistress) epigraphists passes unremarked by Genette: George Eliot. *Middlemarch*, to confine ourselves to just one work, contains no fewer than eighty-six epigraphs, including quotations from Victor Hugo (in French), Bunyan, Donne (twice), Shakespeare (many times), Goethe (in German), Wordsworth, Blake (twice), Pascal (in French, twice), Tobit, Ecclesiasticus, Samuel Daniel (twice), Chaucer (in Middle English, four times), Goldsmith, Dr Johnson, Sir Henry Wotton, Dante (in Tuscan, twice), Sir Thomas Browne, Spenser, Sir Charles Sedley, Ben Jonson, Burton, Milton, Cervantes (in Spanish, but thoughtfully translated) and Beaumont and Fletcher, among others, not to mention a slew of unsigned pieces of verse and prose generally assumed to be the work of Ms Eliot herself.

---

* As Genette points out, Scott wasn't too particular about the precision of his references, and sometimes couldn't be fagged to check them. The introduction to his *Chronicles of the Canongate* admits that '. . . The scraps of poetry which have been in most cases tacked to the beginnings of chapters in these novels are sometimes quoted either from reading or from memory, but, in the general case, are pure invention. I found it too troublesome to turn to the collection of the British poets to discover apposite mottoes . . .'

Few authors would risk such a copious and traditional anthology of literary plums in our sly and meaner-spirited days, when we more or less expect epigraphs to be coerced into blurting out other things than they seem to be saying. For example, the late Angela Carter was hardly sparing with her indulgences in epigraphs, but where George Eliot's epigraphic statements are mostly plain enough – a quotation from *The Anatomy of Melancholy* about the appalling decrepitude of 'hard students' heads the chapter in which Dorothea receives her proposal from Casaubon – Angela Carter's tend rather to fret and fidget under the gaze. She generally tells you where they come from, but no less generally leaves you pondering, in the idiom of the 1960s, about where they are coming from. *The Passion of New Eve* cites John Locke: 'In the beginning all the world was *America*'. (Huh?) Her slim, post-apocalyptic novel *Heroes and Villains* has no fewer than four epigraphs, from Marvell's 'The Unfortunate Lover', Leslie Fiedler's *Love and Death in the American Novel*, Abbé Prevost's *Manon Lescaut* and – one I have sometimes been tempted to use myself – Godard's *Alphaville*:

> 'There are times when reality becomes too complex for
> Oral Communication. But Legend gives it a form by
> which it pervades the whole world.'*

Her collection of journalism, *Expletives Deleted*, has no overall epigraph, but includes one for each of its five

---

* Walter Abish is another writer who has taken an epigraph from Godard's highly quotable early films: *In the Future Perfect* cites dialogue from *Masculin Féminin*.

thematic sections: 'Death is the sanction of everything the
storyteller can tell. He has borrowed his authority from
death' – Walter Benjamin, for *Tell Me a Story*; 'To eat is to
copulate'* – Claude Lévi-Strauss, for *Tomato Woman*; 'This
precious stone set in the silver sea . . .' – a certain Mr
Shakespeare, for *Home*; '. . . The pure products of America
go crazy . . .' – William Carlos Williams, for *Amerika*; and
'Vive la petite différance!' – Old French Saying, for *La Petite
Différance*. I may be off the mark, but as I read the attitudes
of this quintet, two of them are at least half-sarky or a Little
Bit Political, one is designed to make you jump a bit, two to
make you smile or chuckle, three to declare an intellectual
lineage, and one to make you go off and brood.†

Plenty of other recent authors have been just as fidgety,
and others fidgetier still. Some epigraphists may actually
decide to swipe another's epigraph for their own devious
purposes,‡ as David Lodge does for his novel *Nice Work*:

> Upon the midlands now the industrious muse doth fall,
> The shires which we the heart of England well may call.
>
> Drayton: *Poly-Olbion*

– lines which, as Lodge points out, had previously been used
by George Eliot as her epigraph to *Felix Holt the Radical*.

---

* I have rephrased this one slightly, to spare blushes.

† Even *my* arithmetic isn't that wonky: a single epigraph can serve two or
more functions.

‡ Me, for example. See the top of this piece.

Lodge caps this borrowed, and thus oddly double-exposed, epigraph with a second epigraph cut off in its prime:

> 'Two nations; between whom there is no intercourse and no sympathy; who are as ignorant of each other's thoughts and feelings, as if they were dwellers in different zones, or inhabitants of different planets; who are formed by a different breeding, and fed by different food, and ordered by different manners. . . .'
> 'You speak of—' said Egremont hesitatingly.
>
> Benjamin Disraeli: *Sybil; or, the two Nations*

He was speaking of the rich and the poor, or the RICH and the POOR, of course, but Lodge is nattily reapplying Disraeli's division of the kingdom to the world of the minor industrialist Vic Wilcox and the feminist-theorist academic Robyn Penrose. And in doing so he is being thoroughly modern, since the latter-day epigraphist habitually deals in double-takes, humour, incongruity, bathos, self-satire and general weirdness.

The first section of Thomas Pynchon's *Gravity's Rainbow*, *Beyond the Zero*, opens with what seems to be a wholly solemn, in fact uplifting quotation in the traditional grand style:

> Nature does not know extinction; all it knows is transformation. Everything science has taught me, and continues to teach me, strengthens my belief in the continuity of our spiritual existence after death
>
> Werner von Braun

But Pynchon can't keep such a straight face for long. The

second section of *Gravity's Rainbow*, *Un Perm' au Casino Hermann Goering*, has the epigraph:

> You will have the tallest, darkest leading man in Hollywood.
>
> Merian C. Cooper to Fay Wray

The third, *In the Zone*,

> – Toto, I have a feeling we're not in Kansas any more . . .
>
> Dorothy, arriving in Oz

And the fourth, *The Counterforce*,

> What?
>
> Richard M. Nixon*

Similar epigraphic pranks and jokes, both frank and subtle, are now fairly commonplace. One of the subtler kind is the Epigraph Incongruous. Here are two such epigraphs, one by Samuel Johnson –

> He who makes a beast of himself
> gets rid of the pain of being a man.

the other about him:

> This reminds me of the ludicrous account he gave Mr Langton, of the despicable state of a young gentleman of good family. 'Sir, when I heard of him last, he was running about town shooting cats.' And then in a sort of kindly reverie, he bethought himself of his own favourite

---

* A striking, but probably unconscious echo of Corbière's spoof epigraph; see above.

cat, and said, 'but Hodge shan't be shot: no, no, Hodge
shall not be shot.'

Sources? The latter is the epigraph to Nabokov's *Pale Fire*;
the former to Hunter S. Thompson's *Fear and Loathing in
Las Vegas*, which, I'm ashamed to admit, is where I first
came across that beautifully generous sentiment. (Sometimes
the best thing, sometimes the only thing you take away
from a book is its epigraph.)

Then there is the Epigraph Fraudulent, as in F. Scott
Fitzgerald, *The Great Gatsby*:

> Then wear the gold hat, if that will move her;
>   If you can bounce high, bounce for her too,
> Till she cry 'Lover, gold-hatted, high-bouncing lover,
>   I must have you!'
>
> Thomas Parke D'Invilliers

As the annotated Penguin edition now helpfully informs
readers, Fitzgerald wrote these galumphing verses himself;
Thomas Parke D'Invilliers is a character in Fitzgerald's earlier
book *This Side of Paradise*, based on John Peale Bishop. Some
authors are kinder than Fitzgerald, and tip the wink in a
prefatory note, as Kyril Bonfiglioli does in his blissfully comic
thriller *Don't Point That Thing At Me*: 'The epigraphs are all
by Robert Browning, except one, which is a palpable forgery.' In fact, if one wanted a rule of thumb by which to
distinguish the older kind of epigraph from the newer order,
I'd suggest that it might be just this: the art of the modern
epigraphist resides in some form of provocation to the reader
to look and think twice – though not always, by any means,
just to let a joke sink in. Seamus Deane, for one, confers

new depths of sombre menace to the words of a traditional song by placing them at the head of his painful novel *Reading in the Dark*:

> The people were saying no two were e'er wed
> But one had a sorrow that never was said.
>
> 'She Moved Through the Fair'

while Tony Harrison lent an unwonted dignity to the words of a man who was at the time one of the British media's most constant hate-figures by using them as the epigraph to his poem *V.*:

> 'My father still reads the dictionary every day. He says your life depends on your power to master words.'
>
> Arthur Scargill, *Sunday Times*, 10 January 1982

The effect of this citation is hard to describe, whatever one's views about the rightfulness of the miners' cause or the personal qualities of their leader. Harrison is a man of the Left, and would presumably sympathize with Mr Scargill far more than with the well-paid journalists of a conservative newspaper, and yet the precise bearing of these words on his poem – a reworking of Gray's 'Elegy' which partly concerns an imaginary encounter between the sublimely articulate poet and a ragingly inarticulate skinhead whom he is forced to acknowledge as his *semblable* and *frère* – remains open for pondering even after one has duly brooded on its themes of social inequality and mute ingloriousness. By the mere act of isolating them at the opening of his verses, one could say, Harrison has transformed Mr Scargill's words into a poem in their own right.

I'd contend that the finest and most cherishable epigraphs are those which do just the same, either refining the base matter of prose or speech into brief lyrics by the act of isolating them, as Adam Thorpe does in his novel *Still*,

> The most beautiful thing of all is the complete stillness of an audience so intent that it hardly breathes.
>
> Charles Laughton

or creating a more intricate poem by the weaving together of lines from a variety of sources, noble and unregarded alike. By way of finale, I'd also like to nominate a grand master of this form: the American poet John Berryman. Though I have the impression that Berryman is neither as well known nor as passionately admired by general readers now as he was when I first read him in the early seventies, he still seems to me to be a splendid poet and a brilliant epigraphist. The many epigraphs and sub-epigraphs from *Recovery*, for example, haunted my undergraduate years, not only for what they said but for Berryman's pungent, eccentric decisions as to orthography, typography and attributional style:

> *Oh! I haue suffered*
> *With those that I saw suffer*
>
> Miranda, in Shakespeare's
> second Redemptive work,* I, ii, 5

---

* So what was the first? *A Winter's Tale*? If so, what about *Cymbeline* and *Pericles*? A quarter of a century on, I still don't really see what he was driving at.

'My doctrine is not mine'

John 7 16

Or

Sufficient vnto the day
is the euil thereof.

Matthew 6 34

There are plenty of equally haunting citations in *Recovery*,
and in the *Dream Songs*, but for an example of Berryman's
epigraphizing at the peak of his form, I've chosen the
epigraphs to a relatively neglected work, *Delusions Etc.*, which
boasts a page that is in manner, if not sentiment, reminiscent
of one of the more plangent passages of a poet about whom
Berryman wrote superbly well, Ezra Pound. Let it stand here
as an epitaph on epigraphs:*

We haue piped vnto you, and ye haue not danced:
wee haue mourned vnto you, and ye haue not lamented.

On parle toujours de 'l'art religieux'. L'art est
religieux.

––––––––

* Since some of the mysterious effect of this is due to Berryman's
deliberate omission of names and texts for each citation, it may be crass
to supply them here; still, having recognized only the Chaucer (*Canterbury
Tales*, l. 12), I was happy enough to learn that the lines in question come
from Matthew xi: 17; a text by Claudel; and Tolstoy's story 'The Devil'.
John Haffenden, who supplies this information in his *John Berryman: A
Critical Commentary* (London: Macmillan, 1980), pp. 123–4, is silent on '*Feu!
feu! feu!*'. Any offers?

And indeed if Eugene Irtenev was mentally deranged everyone is in the same case; the most mentally deranged people are certainly those who see in others indications of insanity they do not notice in themselves.

Feu! feu! feu!

Than longen folk to goon on pilgrimages

Prefaces, Introductions, Forewords
and Acknowledgements

> Albert's uncle says I ought to have put this in the preface,
> but I never read prefaces, and it is not much good writing
> things just for people to skip. I wonder other authors
> have never thought of this.
>
> Oswald Bastable*

A. By Way of Preface

One of the murkier by-ways of nineteenth-century cultural
history is, or was, the cult of the Teuton. Fans of all things Ger-
manic would cry up their quaint image of the ancient Teutons
as a pack of magnificently butch warrior-philosophers, and
rain scorn on the products of the warm southern lands
as effeminate, depraved and probably reeking of garlic.
Understandably, this fad – which can claim among its more
palatable fruits the operas of Wagner – was most keenly
pursued in Germany itself, where, the story goes, its adher-
ents helped to purge a fair number of existing Romance
elements from the language and to make sure that when the

---

* In E. Nesbit's *The Story of the Treasure Seekers* (London: Puffin, 1994),
p. 22.

march of science made it necessary for a new word to be coined, it was coined from good honest local ores. As a result, today's Germans buy a *Fahrkarte* rather than a *billet*, watch a *Fernsehen* rather than a television, breath *Sauerstoff* rather than oxygen and so on. A number of eminent Britons looked on the cultural struggle with approving eyes, and felt that Britain would do well to go down the same route – or, rather, the same weg.

One of the local leaders of this movement for purifying the dialect of the Saxo-Celtic tribes was a remarkable Cambridge man, F. J. Furnivall (1825–1910), who among his many accomplishments was a chief promoter and editor of the *New Oxford Dictionary*, prototype of the *Oxford English Dictionary*. Despite Furnivall's heroic energies, the cause made little headway here and has left few visible, audible or legible relics – the prime contender in the last category being William Morris's dismal version of *Beowulf*, written in collaboration with Furnivall's junior colleague A. J. Wyatt. The glossary for Morris's *Beowulf* gives some indication of what a Teutonized form of twentieth-century English might have sounded like: in the hands of Wyatt and Morris, 'disregard' became *forheed*, 'mansion' or 'dwelling place' became *wickstead*, 'curiosity' became *witlust*, 'brave' became *moody*, and 'poured out' became *skinked*.*

As you will no doubt have noticed, the movement was largely forheeded, and only a few twentieth-century oddballs have attempted to take up the Teutonizing baton, most

---

* Oddly enough, I owe most of this opening section to E. M. W. Tillyard's history of the Cambridge English Faculty, *The Muse Unchained* (London: Bowes & Bowes, 1958).

famously the Australian composer Percy Grainger, who did his best to rid scores of their unsightly rashes of Italian and put 'Blue-eyed English' in their place. Yes, yes, all most interesting in its fusty way, you will no doubt be muttering by now, but what in the name of Wotan has all this got to do with the subject of prefaces? Simple: just about the only term that has passed its way out from the archaised word-hoard of Furnivall & Co. and into reasonably common use is our standard synonym for 'preface' or 'introduction': *foreword*.*

Hang on a second, though: is 'foreword' really a precise synonym for those terms, and is a 'preface' really the same as an 'introduction'? The subject is hazier than you might expect. A quick rifle through my bookcases seems to establish that convention nowadays favours 'introduction' for the critical essay that opens a modern edition of a classic work, whereas 'prefaces' are those short pieces that precede the introduction proper and 'forewords' are usually plugs – the work of a well-known author or other celebrity, recommending to the public a book by a rather more obscure author. Furnivall's noblest legacy, the *OED*, is surprisingly unhelpful in clarifying the distinctions between these three forms, so I turned to other authorities.

A passing scholar of the eighteenth-century novel, Profes-

---

* *OED*'s first citation is from 1842 – a translation of the *Prose or Younger Edda*; its second (1868) is from Furnivall himself. 'Preface', by contrast, has been with us at least since the fourteenth century – Chaucer uses it in the *Canterbury Tales* – and the literary sense of 'Introduction' ('the part of a book which leads up to the subject treated, or explains the author's design or purpose') was already current in the first half of the sixteenth century.

sor Robert Mayer of Oklahoma State University, suggested to me that the rule of thumb among about-to-be-published academics these days is that 'If you want people to read your opening essay, call it an introduction, not a preface. If you call it an introduction, it implies that the text is part of the book's general argument, or in some way important for the argument', whereas a preface is taken to be a sort of largely superfluous, throat-clearing exercise. And, yes, Professor Mayer agrees, 'foreword' clearly suggests 'boost'. The publishers I spoke to went along with this party line, more or less, but were often a little vague about the terms. The closest I came to a firm principle of definition was in a guidebook, Peter Finch's *How to Publish Yourself*. Here, again, Mr Finch confirms my hunch that a *foreword* should be an endorsement of the work by some authority or celeb, and that it should come somewhere around page ix of the prelims, a couple of pages before the true *preface* or *introduction* (*c.* p. xi), these being interchangeable terms for the bit explaining what the author was planning to do or how you should read his book;* convention suggests that you should give them a dateline, especially if the place of composition is sufficiently exotic. This seems a pleasingly clear and simple statement of the basic rules of the game.

In the big bad world of mass publishing, however, not everyone seems to be playing by these rules. Thus, T. S. Eliot's urgent commendation of Simone Weil at the front of

---

* 'The preface provides directions for using the book' – Novalis, *Die Enzyklopadie*. It so happens that Tillyard's book (see above, p. 105n) is a case in point, helpfully pointing out to readers with short attention spans the bits they will probably find dull and should skip.

her manifesto *The Need for Roots*, which Finch would class as a *foreword*, is blazoned as a *preface*, and the book's actual foreword is by its translator, A. F. Wills. Eliot begins his brief text with a pregnant critical remark about the nature of introductions: the only kind of introduction, he suggests, that would merit long association with a text as profound as Weil's would be one written by someone who had known her, and that his own preface ought to become superfluous as soon as her work becomes well known.* Conversely, my copy of Byron Farwell's biography of Sir Richard Burton has a *foreword*, written not by some suitable Orientalist big shot but by and about Mr Farwell himself (anecdotes of research, etc.†), followed by a similarly autobiographical *foreword* to the second edition (updated anecdotes), followed by *acknowledgements*, followed by an *introduction*. In a word: chaos. So, for the sake of allowing the following remarks to be made at all, let's abandon any attempt to be pedantic‡ about

---

* Elsewhere, he plunged still deeper into self-effacement: 'The few books worth introducing are exactly those which it is an impertinence to introduce' – the introduction to Djuna Barnes's *Nightwood*.

† I've long been fond of this type of How-I-Did-It anecdote, ever since reading the paragraph in George Thomson's preface to *Aeschylus and Athens* where he thanks the Blasket islanders for showing him what a pre-capitalist social formation looks like. Thomson then concedes that the islanders do nominally fall within the grasp of capitalism, since they are supposed to pay rent to the landowners, but adds that, since none of them ever actually stumps up, this is a mere technicality.

‡ As, say, Jacques Derrida is in his commentary (in *Dissemination*) on the distinction between Hegel's prefaces, which pile up with every new

definitions and use 'preface' and 'introduction' without discrimination as the catch-all words for all kinds of opening salvos, resorting to other formulations only for the sake of avoiding undue tedium.

B. On Prefaces

Prefaces, designed to be read first, are written last. If a book has been a long time in the making, the task can seem horribly arduous. The late Frank Muir, for example, having laboured for some five years at writing and compiling *The Frank Muir Book*, groused that his publisher's demand for a preface was comparable to a circus handler's insistence that his prize female elephant, having strained and groaned to give birth to an outsize calf, should then be asked to complete the performance by balancing a bun on her trunk. Muir was joshing, but only a little. There are other writers, especially historians and literary critics, who will admit that by the time they came to write their introductions, they were so wearied or so heartily sick of their subject that, like a burned-out marathon runner, they could hardly bear to finish the course. Exhaustion can be heard in many learned prefaces, and often accounts for their merciful brevity.

For all this, Paul Fussell is surely on the right track when he observes that the academic preface is by convention a happy form:

---

edition, and his Introduction, which is both unique and far more profoundly joined to the logic of his text. See Genette, pp. 161–2.

The writer of a preface has just finished months or years
of labor: he has finally been sprung from his treadmill, and
he is proud of his book. Relief and pride, even if disguised
with due humility, are the happy emotions we find in
prefaces. A gloomy preface to a learned book is a contradic-
tion in terms.*

Fussell also points out that every good academic preface
contains the same two elements, in the same order: (1) a
statement of the nature of the enquiry, followed by (2) a list
of acknowledgements. (To put it more colloquially, a preface
says 'Good evening' before saying 'Thanks awfully'.) Any
preface which arranged these components in the wrong
order would be considered amateurish.†

Fussell doesn't, though, bother to point out any of the
various well-recognized sub-conventions which govern the
writing of acknowledgements, such as the terminal, humble
or mock-humble confession that 'all remaining mistakes are,
of course, my own'. The art critic Tom Lubbock remarked
to me that he looks forward one day to reading an acknowledgements section which concludes 'All remaining mistakes
are the fault of' – let us say – 'Sid Moron', and then gives

---

* *Samuel Johnson and the Life of Writing*, p. 114. I suspect, as noted above,
that my first reading of this book, some twenty years ago, was the idle
hour in which this present book was unwittingly conceived. So several
tips of the hat are due here, not just for Professor Fussell's observations
on prefaces in general and Johnson's in particular, but for being the
provoker of *Invisible Forms*. Please do not hold this against him.

† Not always, surely? Acknowledgements – as in the present volume –
may be farmed off on their own, and put either before or after the preface,
or even at the end of the book.

Mr Moron's address, phone number and e-mail.* Another convention, which has fallen into understandable disrepute over the last couple of decades, is that of the male author's ritual vote of thanks to his wife for doing the typing, or, slightly more palatably, for putting up with his absences, his absentmindedness or simply with his obsessions: 'Above all, this book owes its life to Doris, who now knows far more about Andalusian grain prices in the 1830s than she ever expected!'†

As to Fussell's first point, the announcement of the scope and nature of the enquiry: the origins of this convention are some three thousand years old, since among the great-great-grandfathers of all modern prefaces must be numbered what Genette calls the 'incorporated prefaces'‡ of the opening

---

* I have tried to oblige. See 'Acknowledgements', p. vii.

† If I read her right, Gillian Beer's acknowledgements for *Darwin's Plots: Evolutionary Narrative in Darwin, George Eliot and Nineteenth-Century Fiction* (London: Routledge & Kegan Paul, 1983) play a quietly naughty feminist joke on the convention: 'Bearing and rearing children', she concludes, 'made me need to understand, first, evolutionary process, and then, the power of Darwin's writing in our culture. So it is to my mother and my sons that I dedicate this book – though without my husband, much would have been impossible.' (p. x).

‡ It's probably worth pointing out here that Genette's three chapters on prefaces form the largest sub-section of *Seuils* – more than 130 pages of the translated text; and I suppose I'd better make a small declaration of originality here by adding that most of the non-classical matter in this essay is mine, all mine: for example, the sole occurrence of Samuel Johnson in Genette's pages is in a quotation from Borges' collection of 'allographic' prefaces, *Prologos*, in which the Argentinian fabulist compares

lines of Homer and Virgil (*Arma virumque cano* . . .), the 'proem' of Herodotus's *Histories* and the introduction to Thucydides' *Peloponnesian War*:

> Thucydides the Athenian wrote the history of the war fought between Athens and Sparta, beginning the account at the very outbreak of the war, in the belief that it was going to be a great war and more worth writing about than any of those which had taken place in the past . . .*

Livy followed this convention of first-person commentary on his enterprise at the beginning of some books of his Roman histories, and it is from the traditional name for these declarations, *praefatio*, that our word is derived. As with so many other IFs, prefaces became rather more complex in the post-Gutenberg era, when they detached themselves from the opening lines of the work itself and set up independent shop in the entrance-way,† whether as addresses to the reader, epistles dedicatory, general prologues and the like or as self-styled prefaces, but a surprising number of the main conventions become established in the classical period. A lot of present-day prefaces, for example, say something about the book's relationship to other books on

---

his reverence for Macedonio Fernandez with that of Boswell for the Great Cham. (*Paratexts*, p. 267).

* Rex Warner's translation, for Penguin Classics, p. 35.

† Or, in the case of the afterword or postface, round the back, next door to the tradesman's entrance. I suspect that there are quite a lot of readers for whom every foreword is really an afterword, since they prefer to plunge straight into the work in question so as not to be swayed in their judgement either by the author or by some dopey critic.

similar matters, thereby hoping to sell the book to a prospective reader* and to forestall anticipated criticisms. Lucian
seems to have been the first to go in for this sort of thing,
since the preface to his *True History* slags off all previous
traveller's tales as mendacious and takes wry credit for at
least being honest enough to admit his own fraudulence.

What else can a preface do? A great number of things,
though most of them can be summed up as an attempt by
the author or editor or translator or plugger to control the
way in which the book should be read or, in the case of a
second or later edition, reread. Fielding's 'Author's Preface'
to his 'comic epic poem in prose', *Joseph Andrews*, can stand
for a thousand thousand similar attempts to lay down the
law:

> As it is possible the mere English reader may have a
> different idea of romance from the author of these little
> volumes, and may consequently expect a kind of entertain-
> ment not to be found, nor which was even intended, in
> the following pages, it may not be improper to premise
> a few words concerning this kind of writing, which I do
> not remember to have seen hitherto attempted in our
> language.

A preface can condescend, bully, cajole, brag, plead, fawn,
whimper, moan and lie. It can tell off stupid critics, or rage
against the stupidity of mankind in general and certain
specimens in particular, as A. E. Housman did in his notorious preface to his edition of Manilius (1903), the twenty-odd

---

* Stevenson entitled the verse preface of *Treasure Island* 'To the hesitating
purchaser'.

pages of which contain some of the most awe-inspiring rudeness in the English language.* Or it can gripe about the tight-fistedness of the reading public, as Lewis Carroll did in his preface to the budget-priced 1896 reprint of *Through the Looking-Glass*, where he snarls:

> I take this opportunity of announcing that the Nursery 'Alice', hitherto priced at four shillings, net, is now to be had on the same terms as the ordinary shilling picture-books – although I feel sure that it is, in every quality (except the *text* itself, on which I am not qualified to pronounce), greatly superior to them. Four shillings was a perfectly reasonably price to charge, considering the very heavy initial outlay I had incurred: still, as the public have practically said 'We will *not* give more than a shilling for a picture-book, however artistically got-up', I am content to reckon my outlay on the book as so much dead loss, and, rather than let the little ones, for whom it is written, go without it, I am selling it at a price which is, to me, much the same as *giving* it away.

The preface can be a sustained exercise in biography, autobiography or confession, especially in the cases where it has been written for a new edition of a book which has either won some notoriety, been recovered from oblivion or had its significance distorted or diminished by the passage of time: Lionel Trilling's retrospective and introspective 'Introduction' of 1977 to the Penguin reissue of *The Middle of the Journey* (1947) is a good example of the autobiographical preface, while Robert Ardrey's plangent essay on Eugene

---

* See Housman, *Selected Prose*, edited by John Carter (Cambridge: Cambridge University Press, 1961), pp. 23–44.

Marais for *The Soul of the Ape*, John Steinbeck's affectionate memoir 'About Ed Ricketts', which is the introduction to his *The Log from the Sea of Cortez*, and Roger Shattuck's preface to René Daumal's *Mount Analogue* are fine examples of the biographical. In the cases where the author has undergone a significant change in the years between the first and the subsequent edition – a change of politics, religion,* sex or simply of talent – the preface may become an act of repentance, or fastidious distancing, or affectionate amusement. In such instances, it would make roughly the same amount of sense to say either that the author has written his or her own foreword, or that someone more mature has been dragged in to write it. Possibly the most masochistic of all such retrospects is Thomas Pynchon's 'Introduction' to *Slow Learner* (1984), a collection of stories he wrote during and just after his college years, from 1958 to 1964.

> You may already know what a blow to the ego it can be to have to read over anything you wrote 20 years ago, even cancelled checks. My first reaction, rereading these stories, was *oh my God*, accompanied by physical symptoms we shouldn't dwell upon ... It is only fair to warn even the most kindly disposed of readers that there are some mighty tiresome passages here, juvenile and delinquent too.

Slangy and rueful, Pynchon's text has the appearance of genuine confession rather than sly fabrication, but you never

---

* For example: Huysmans, as a Catholic convert, writing in 1903 a new and penitent preface to his self-consciously decadent novella about an effete connoisseur of morbid sensations, *À rebours* (1884).

know, since prefaces to works of fiction are notoriously slippery things and are quite often fictions in their own right.* Think of *Gulliver's Travels*, with its prefatory 'Advertisment', its 'Letter from Capt. Gulliver, to his cousin Sympson', and its note, 'The Publisher to the Reader', by 'Richard Sympson': 'Before he [i.e. Gulliver] quitted Redriff, he left the custody of the following papers in my hands, with the liberty to dispose of them as I should think fit . . .' This sort of stunt is what M. Genette would call a 'fictive allographic preface', in which the novel is presented to the reader – 'framing' is a routine name for this trick – as a set of documents that have somehow come into the hands of a fictitious editor, whether anonymous, like the French officer in Potocki's *Manuscript Found in Saragossa*, or identified, like 'John Ray' in *Lolita*, 'Charles Kinbote' in *Pale Fire*, or – tricksier still – 'Umberto Eco' in *The Name of the Rose*. The grand master of its matching convention, the 'fictive autographic preface', in which the imaginary author of the introduction is one and the same as the author of the novel, is Sir Walter Scott, who attributes both his novels and their prefaces to the likes of 'Templeton' for *Ivanhoe*, 'Captain Cutherbert Clutterbuck' for *The Fortunes of Nigel* and 'Jedediah Cleishbotham' for *The Bride of Lammermoor*; I still haven't discovered why Scott was so partial to such prepos-

---

* As, you could argue, are the prefaces to some of the weirder varieties of non-fiction, such as 'Democritus Junior to the Reader', Robert Burton's suitably enormous preface (almost a hundred pages in my edition) to *The Anatomy of Melancholy*. The persona of 'Democritus Junior' both is and is not Burton himself.

terous pseudonyms – pseudonyms which, come to think of it, are pretty well on the cusp of becoming heteronyms.

If Scott's fictional prefaces strive towards independence from their author, there is another class of preface which strives towards independence from the book it introduces. Such works may amount to a manifesto about themes much larger than the work at hand, as in the case of Wilde's brief introduction – or collection of maxims – to *The Picture of Dorian Gray*, which despite its disavowals of personality says next to nothing about the tale and volumes about the teller:

> The artist is the creator of beautiful things.
> To reveal art and conceal the artist is art's aim . . .
> Those who find ugly meanings in beautiful things are
>   corrupt without being charming.
> This is a fault . . .
> All art is quite useless.*

Similarly, Wordsworth's Prefaces to the 1800 and 1802 editions of the *Lyrical Ballads* – which he claimed, implausibly, to have written only to keep Coleridge happy† – aren't merely an attempt to disarm criticism, but a substantial outline for a theory of both poetry and psychology. At around six thousand words, or nine thousand in its revised form, Wordsworth's Preface is, unlike his *Prelude*, rather too short to be published as a book in its own right, but at least a few prefaces have triumphantly seceded from their original covers and made a Unilateral Declaration of Independence:

---

* Wilde, *Plays, Prose Writings and Poems*, pp. 69–70.

† If so, it didn't work: *Biographia Literaria* takes issue with a lot of Wordsworth's contentions.

Jean-Paul Sartre's *Baudelaire* began life as a preface, as did his
Saint Genet, originally composed as an introduction to
Genet's *Œuvres Complètes* and running to 625 pages in the
English-language edition – probably an unbreakable record,
Genette suggests, unless some mad publisher decides to
publish an edition of *Madame Bovary* with the five volumes
of Sartre's *L'Idiot de la famille* as its introduction. (Not so far-
fetched in principle, when you consider how many scholarly
editions have a few elegant slivers of text and acre upon acre
of paratext.)

Such hypertrophied prefaces are, though, relatively rare,
since – as T. S. Eliot's remarks point out – one of the
habitual tones of preface composed for the works of some
other author is that of self-effacement. In his introduction to
the *Complete Poems of Cavafy*, W. H. Auden underlined the
similarity between the social and literary forms of introduction when he proposed that writings of the kind he is
engaged upon are really of interest only to readers who have
not so far read the introducee, and that once a proper
literary acquaintance is made, they will forget the introducer
just as readily as they forget the person at the drinks party
who permits you to strike up a friendship with some
fascinating new person. Auden was being far too modest,
and probably recognized the fact, since he was happy enough
to reproduce his Cavafy piece in a book, *Forewords and
Afterwords*, made up almost entirely of prefatorial essays eked
out with some longer pieces of journalism. There have been
many such volumes – Trilling's *Prefaces to the Experience of
Literature* comes to mind – and at least one of them is an
acknowledged masterpiece: Henry James's *Art of the Novel*, a
major work of aesthetics made simply by gathering together

– R. P. Blackmur was the gleaner – the critical introductions to eighteen of his novels and tales, written for the Scribner's edition of his works in 1907–9.

James's prefaces to the work of others have not always been quite so well received. On reading James's introduction to Rupert Brooke's *Letters from America*, A. C. Benson wrote:

> What nonsense it is, to be sure. H.J. hadn't much to say except that R.B. was a cheerful and high-spirited boy who lived in many ways a normal life, enjoyed himself, was not spoilt, and then wrote some fine bits of poetry. All this is presented in long, vague sentences, very confusing and Johnsonian, with an occasional scrap of slang let in. It *isn't* good writing – of that I am sure. Then come a lot of jolly, ordinary, sensible, wholesome, rather funny letters of travel by R.B. After all H.J.'s pontification, R.B.'s robust letters are almost a shock. It is as if one went up to receive a sacrament in a great, dark church, and were greeted by shouts of laughter and a shower of chocolate creams.

Cruel and funny, though the adjective 'Johnsonian', always dubious when used as an insult,* seems particularly wide of the mark here, for Johnson was, I'd contend, the most accomplished writer of prefaces in English, not to say one of the most prolific. Many of his prefaces were composed anonymously, for others, and almost always for free, simply because he was friendly with or approved of the authors who begged him for such services. When word got out that Johnson was a soft touch in this regard, all sorts of

---

* People seem to regard it as a synonym for 'pompous', 'stilted', 'verbose' and so on. The rumour that Johnson is boring strikes me as one of the most idiotic slanders in the realm of book-chat.

chancers began to pester him, as Boswell reports in his *Life*: Johnson says that:

> 'I remember one Angel, who came to me to write for him
> a Preface or Dedication to a book upon short hand, and he
> professed to write as fast as a man could speak. In order
> to try him, I took down a book, and read while he wrote;
> and I favoured him, for I read more deliberately than usual.
> I had proceeded but a very little way, when he begged I
> would desist, for he could not follow me. Hearing now for
> the first time of this Preface or Dedication, I said, 'What
> an expence, Sir, do you put us to in buying books, to
> which you have written Prefaces or Dedications.'

Boswell wasn't exaggerating. Scholars have identified some fifty prefaces and/or dedications, to such long-forgotten works as William Payne's *The Game of Draughts* (1756) or to John Payne's *New Tables of Interest* (1758), and there may be plenty more still out there. Nor did Johnson always feel obliged to read the work he was recommending to the public. Take the case of Richard Rolt's *Dictionary of Trade and Commerce* (1756):

> I asked him whether he knew much of Rolt and his work.
> 'Sir,' said he, 'I never saw the man, and never read the
> book. The booksellers wanted a preface to a Dictionary of
> Trade and Commerce. I knew very well what such a
> Dictionary should be, and I wrote a preface accordingly.'

What's more, if he had bothered to read the book in question, he felt himself under no obligation to be polite about it:

I was somewhat disappointed in finding that the edition of
the English Poets, for which he was to write Prefaces and
Lives, was not an undertaking directed by him: but that he
was to furnish a Preface and Life to any poet the booksell-
ers pleased. I asked him if he would do this to any dunce's
works, if they should ask him. JOHNSON. 'Yes, Sir, and
say he was a dunce.' My friend seemed now not much to
relish talking of this edition.*

Relish it or not, he wrote the work supremely well. The
book we now know as the *Lives of the Poets* (1779–81) is
seldom (I'd guess) read in its entirety, but is sometimes
spoken of by those who've made the effort as Johnson's
greatest sustained enterprise. The work was originally
entitled *Prefaces, Biographical and Critical, to the Works of the
English Poets*, and Paul Fussell argues that we will misread
these texts if we disregard this exact title and persist, as many
critics have, in regarding them as a set of miniature biogra-
phies rather than a set of prefaces, written according to a
very strict idea of what a preface must do. Fussell cites
Johnson in rare boastful mode:

> There are two things . . . which I am confident I can do
> very well: one is an introduction to any literary work,
> stating what it is to contain, and how it should be executed
> in the most perfect manner; the other is a conclusion
> showing, from various causes, why the execution has not
> been equal to what the author promised to himself and to
> the public.

---

* *Life*, Vol. II, pp. 102–3.

In these *Prefaces* to the lives of fifty-two poets from Cowley to Gray, Johnson applies these two gifts diligently and generally to sombre, not to say harrowing ends, showing how the highest aspirations of his authors tend to come a cropper; how paths of glory lead but to the grave or, at the very least, to toil, envy, want, the patron and the jail. As Fussell sums up, the theme of the Johnsonian preface is 'ironic disappointment: its focus is necessarily on the comic distance between human schemes and human accomplishments. By its very characteristics as genre a Preface is – it must be – about the frailty of man.'*

Johnson did not include himself among the English poets, and he left it to his younger friend to write his life, but there are autobiographical moments scattered throughout every part of his extraordinarily varied work, disguised and overt, and one of the best approximations we have to Samuel Johnson's brief life of Samuel Johnson is in his *Preface to the English Dictionary*.

A modern-day preface, as Fussell has reminded us, should end with thanks, but Johnson was proudly and angrily aware – remember his crushing letter to Chesterfield – that he had nobody to thank for his accomplishment:

> . . . though no book was ever spared out of tenderness to the author, and the world is little solicitous to know whence proceeded the faults of that which it condemns; yet it may gratify curiosity to inform it that the *English Dictionary* was written with little assistance of the learned, and without any patronage of the great; not in the soft

---

* Fussell, p. 256.

obscurities of retirement, or under the shelter of academic
bowers, but amid inconvenience and distraction, in sickness
and in sorrow . . .

And though Johnson was only forty-six when he completed the *Dictionary*, hardly a decrepit greybeard even by
the standards of his century, it suits his rhetorical purposes
to depict himself as an ancient philosopher, the last survivor
of a warmer and more heroic age, too full of years and
sorrows to be anything more than loftily indifferent to the
kinds of critical attention solicited by just about everyone
else who has ever written a preface:

> I have protracted my work till most of those whom I
> wished to please have sunk into the grave, and success and
> miscarriage are empty sounds: I therefore dismiss it with
> frigid tranquility, having little to fear or hope from censure
> or from praise.

Magnificently disingenuous: it is the last word in first
words.

First Lines

The first sentence of *Belphegor* took me years

Julien Benda, *La Jeunesse d'un clerc*

Oi!

That's one way to begin. It's the way *Beowulf* begins (in my as-yet-unpublished 'skinhead' translation, anyway; Victorian gentleman-scholars were inclined to render the Anglo-Saxon attention-grabber *hwæt* as 'Lo!'*), which I suppose means that you could say it's where English literature begins, unless you want to insist that the real kick-off takes place in the seventh century, circa AD 680, with Cædmon's Hymn,† which has much of the formality of ritual:

---

* More recently, translators have opted for 'Hear!' (David Wright, 1957) or 'Listen!' (Kevin Crossley-Holland, 1973; S. A. J. Bradley, 1982); in 1921, Charles Scott Montcrief plumped for 'What!'; a trifle slavish, what? And some scholars deny that the word is an exclamation at all; but hwæt the hell.

† Clive Wilmer points out that you can read the story of Cædmon's Hymn as a fable about overcoming writer's block; and, since Cædmon is the first poet of our language, as a fable about English itself losing its writer's block.

> Nu scylun hergan   hefænricæs uard,
> Metudæs mæcti   end his modgidanc ...*

More plausibly, you could push the starting line forward a few centuries to Chaucer, by which times things have become far more urbane and suave and knowing:

> Whan that Aprille with his shoures soote
> The droghte of March hath perced to the roote ...

The author of *Beowulf* – its *scop*, as they say in the Anglo-Saxon, Norse and Celtic trade – may have suffered, nay, no doubt did suffer from scurvy, lice and an unreliable system of patronage for the arts, but when it came to the choice of overtures and beginners, he had it easy. All he had to do was shut up the drunks – '*Hwæt!*, you beastly philistines' – dodge the flying mutton bones, and then steam ahead with his already familiar story. Allowing for minor local variations, this had been pretty much the standard literary procedure for thousands of years. You shouted for the listeners'/reader's notice, maybe invoked the appropriate muse, explained in a few choice words what the entertainment was all about and who the hero was going to be ('*Arma virumque cano*, everyone OK with that ... ?') and off you went. Piece of cake. Wrote itself. Well, sorry, but you just can't do that any more. Haven't been able to since ... hard to say exactly when, but if you ask me I'd blame that brace of Irish jokers

---

* Clive Wilmer translates: 'Now should we hail heaven's guardian/Praise the Maker, his might and thought ...'

Swift and Sterne,* who both had the bright idea of starting their books with all manner of hummings and hawings that establish just how difficult it can be to get a book properly started. *Tristram Shandy*, whose narrator-hero is conceived on page one but doesn't manage to be born for the first umpteen chapters, opens with a densely rambled sentence evoking his accidental conception – a sentence about primal beginnings that threatens never to end:

> I wish either my father or my mother, or indeed both of them, as they were in duty both equally bound to it, had minded what they were about when they begot me; had they duly consider'd how much depended upon what they were then doing;—that not only the production of a rational Being was concerned in it, but that possibly the happy formation and temperature of his body, perhaps his genius and the very cast of his mind;—and, for aught they knew to the contrary, even the fortunes of his whole house might take their turn from the humours and dispositions which were then uppermost;—Had they duly weighed and considered all this, and proceeded accordingly,—I am verily persuaded I should have made a quite different figure in the world, from that in which the reader is likely to see me . . .

In a different manner but a comparably trouble-making spirit, Swift's *A Tale of a Tub* takes such an inordinate time clearing its throat, enters on such a fatiguing series of prefatory ejaculations – what with the Analytical Table, the Author's Apology, the Bookseller's Dedication (to 'The Right

---

* Soon to be encountered again in the territory of footnotes; see below, pp. 139–60.

Honourable John Lord Somers'), the Bookseller's Address to
the Reader, the Epistle Dedicatory (to 'His Royal Highness
Prince Posterity'), the Author's Preface. . . . that the opening
sentence somehow contrives to feel less like an overture
than an anti-climax:

> Whoever has an ambition to be heard in a crowd, must
> press, and squeeze, and thrust, and climb, with indefatiga-
> ble pains, till he has exalted himself to a certain degree of
> altitude above them . . .

Oh dear. Once you've had it brought to your attention
that there might be some difficulty about the once-humble
chore of beginning your book at the beginning, or even (a
bit more fancily) *in medias res*, all innocence is lost. You can
never quite rid yourself of the nagging worry that there are
dozens, hundreds, an infinity of other ways in which you
could have composed that first line.

*

So let's start again. Denied the fabulist's luxury of simply
saying 'once upon a time',* or 'A long time ago, in a galaxy
far, far away', and lacking any of those other standard
introductory formulae which are so useful in non-literary
modes of address, written or spoken – any handy phrase,
that is, along the lines of 'My Lords, Ladies and Gentlemen',
or 'Dearly Beloved, we are gathered here today' or 'Dear Mr
Jackson, Our final reminder was sent to you two weeks ago
and we are surprised that you still do not seem to have
replied . . .' – the self-aware, self-respecting modern writer

---

* But read on . . .

who stares down at the still unravished whiteness of a page and wonders how best to go about molesting it is obliged to steer between the rock of cuteness and the hard place of mundanity.

Writers of every genre suffer from this self-consciousness, and in some forms cuteness indisputably reigns supreme. Nowadays, any critic who had the crust to begin a piece of literary journalism by saying something as hopelessly old-fashioned and straightforward as 'In this article, I will address the subject of historical novels in the eighteenth century'* would be sneered at, fired and immediately replaced by some sharpy pyrotechnician who realized that the only proper way to launch such a piece is by seizing on some piffling detail about Sir Walter Scott's potato garden or Defoe's nasty case of Tourette's syndrome† and then pulling yards and yards of pert yet swingeing dialectic from this tiny prop like a conjurer whipping Technicolor scarves from an egg.

Elsewhere, the match is rather more equal; quite a few modern novels still adopt, let us call it, option (a), the plain option, by going quietly and dutifully about their tale-telling

---

* And yet plainness can be very fine, in all kinds of expository writing: 'In the second century of the Christian era, the Empire of Rome comprehended the fairest part of the earth, and the most civilised portion of mankind.' My excuse for never having finished reading the *Decline and Fall* is that I don't see how Gibbon could possibly have topped such a triumphant opening.

† Foolish exaggeration? I think not: I recently came across a review of Charles Nicholl's book about Rimbaud which began with an observation about the *poète maudit*'s shoe size.

business, and providing the printed counterpart of what film-makers term an 'establishing shot', informing us as to where we are, who we're about to meet and what's going on. (Many such sentences prove, of course, to be a good deal less naive than they pretend.) In such cases, the novelist is obliged to hope that we'll have the patience to let the story warm up in its own good time without demanding our bon-bons of wit or style or drama, right away. The alternative ploy, which may be logically if unimaginatively labelled (b), is to try to collar the reader from the outset with something fancier: a maxim or *pensée*, a joke, a shock. Category (a) might sound like the soft option – it doesn't obviously require any great powers of wit or invention, and yet it was repeatedly chosen by one of the most masochistically pain-staking of all literary craftsmen, Gustave Flaubert. Thus:

> *Le 15 Septembre 1840, vers six heures du matin,* La Ville-de-Montereau, *pres de partir, fumait a gros tourbillons devant le quai Saint-Bernard.*
>
> > (L'Éducation sentimentale)

> *Comme il faisait une chaleur de trente-trois degres, le Boulevard Bourdon se trouvait absolument desert.*
>
> > (Bouvard et Pécuchet)

> *C'était a Megara, faubourg de Carthage, dans les jardins d'Hamilcar.*
>
> > (Salammbô)

Of that last, apparently self-effacing sentence, an unim-peachable French authority (the novelist Michel Tournier, in his autobiography *The Wind Spirit*) has asserted: 'there can be no doubt . . .' that, 'consciously or unconsciously remembered by so many writers', it 'has had an impact on thousands of subsequent works of every type and description'. Flaubert, it seems, had his reward for agonizing his way towards the perfection of a phrase so unshowy and telling. Henry James, just about the only writer in English to rival Flaubert for fastidiousness, saw fit to set out on that harrowing novel (described by Leavis as one of the two most brilliant in the English language) *The Portrait of a Lady* by presenting his readers with a sentence that appears to have drifted loose from the memoirs of a Staffordshire rector:

> Under certain circumstances there are few hours in life more agreeable than the hour dedicated to the ceremony known as afternoon tea.

Nor did Dickens, who came up with some of the grabbiest of all first-line grabbers ('Marley was dead, to begin with'; 'Now, what I want is, Facts'), disdain some form or other of the establishing shot, presenting either narrator/ hero (*David Copperfield, Great Expectations*)* or location, and the most complex books of his maturity all begin with temporal and geographical directions.

This is *Little Dorrit*:

> Thirty years ago, Marseilles lay burning in the sun, one day.

This is *Our Mutual Friend*:

> In these times of ours, though concerning the exact year there is no need to be precise, a boat of dirty and disre-

---

* Both a bit more complicated than I'm admitting, obviously.

putable appearance, with two figures on it, floated on the Thames, between Southwark Bridge which is of iron, and London Bridge which is of stone, as an autumn evening was closing in.*

And this is *Bleak House*:

London.†

Hemingway, too, is rumoured to have sweated long and hard over the blank inexpressiveness and kindergarten syntax of his opening line of *A Farewell to Arms*:

In the late summer of that year we lived in a house in a village that looked across the river and the plain to the mountains.

Plainly, there's a lot to be said for the simple option, especially since so much is expected from a first line that the attempt to come up with something that cuts the mustard can induce creative paralysis. A well-known story has it that Jean Cocteau – a category (b) opener by nature – was

---

* John Julius Norwich voted this the best of all first lines, and included it in his *Christmas Crackers*. He also commends the opening of Bertrand Russell's *Autobiography*: 'Three passions, simple but overwhelmingly strong, have governed my life: the longing for love, the search for knowledge, and unbearable pity for the suffering of mankind.'

† Much misquoted. 'Michaelmas term lately over', it continues, 'and the Lord Chancellor sitting in Lincoln's Inn Hall . . .' But what people tend to remember is the fog, which doesn't sweep into the prose until the next paragraph: 'Fog everywhere. Fog up the river, where it flows among green aits and meadows; fog down the river, where it rolls defiled along the tiers of shipping, and the waterside pollutions of a great (and dirty) city . . .'

suffering from just such a state of paralysis, until a friend made the helpful suggestion that he should simply write down any old scene-setting phrase like 'It was a dark and stormy night' – the phrase wisely used by Snoopy, the novelist and beagle *de lettres*, whenever he commences a new oeuvre – and carry on from there. Cocteau did just that, and sat down to write *Les Enfants terribles*; it begins:

> That portion of old Paris known as the Cité Monthiers is bounded on the one side by the rue de Clichy, on the other by the rue d'Amsterdam.*

It used to be said that a gentlemen was well dressed when you did not notice his clothes. Similarly, the ideal category (a) sentence would be prose so discreetly crafted that its effect ought to pass unnoticed by the conscious mind. First lines of the (b) class tend towards the ostentatious, sometimes even the gaudy, since they're competing with some of the all-times beaux, belles and swells of the prose racket. If you are literate enough to have read thus far, you are almost certainly literate enough to be able to quote the (b)-category first lines of most, probably all, of these major works with a reasonable degree of accuracy:

> *Pride and Prejudice*
> *Anna Karenina*[†]

---

* The friend was his publisher Jacques Chardonne, who proposed the opening line 'One winter evening . . .'; but Cocteau's biographer has his doubts about the truth of the tale. See Francis Steegmuller, *Cocteau*, p. 395.

† This was Maurice Baring's choice of best first line for a novel, though it tied with *Don Quixote* in his pantheon.

A Tale of Two Cities*
Moby-Dick†
Twelfth Night
Richard III‡
Nineteen Eighty-Four
'The Ancient Mariner'
Genesis

and at least twenty or so more.

Why do these particular examples cut such a figure? Some of the reasons are easy enough to point out. Austen and Tolstoy tend towards the maxim or epigram: 'It is a

---

* Ah, but *can* you really quote it? Any fool can reel off 'It was the best of times, it was the worst of times', but the sentence still has miles to go before it sleeps: '. . . it was the age of wisdom, it was the age of foolishness, it was the epoch of belief, it was the epoch of incredulity, it was the season of Light, it was the season of Darkness, it was the spring of hope, it was the winter of despair, we had everything before us, we had nothing before us, we were all going direct to Heaven, we were all going direct the other way – in short, the period was so far like the present period, that some of its noisiest authorities insisted on its being received, for good or for evil, in the superlative degree of comparison only.'

† All right, Smartiboots: but now tell me which book begins 'Call me, Ishmael'?

‡ Unless you count *Henry V*, I'd say that these are the only two Shakespeare plays which begin with quotable quotes, phrases that have made it into the language. Admittedly, it's not that hard to think of a few others – *Hamlet*, *Macbeth*, *King Lear* (with a bit of fudging), but can you scrape up from memory the first lines even of such much-performed plays as, say, *Love's Labour's Lost*? *Antony and Cleopatra*? *As You Like It*? Let alone *Coriolanus*, or *Timon of Athens*, or *All's Well That Ends Well*?

truth universally acknowledged, that a single man in pos-session of a good fortune, must be in want of a wife'; 'All happy families are alike but an unhappy family is unhappy in its own way'*. Austen's 'universally' and Tolstoy's 'All' are the tip-off words: these openers have the agreeably senten-tious weight of, say, 'The Vanity of Human Wishes':

> Let Observation with extensive view
> Survey mankind from China to Peru

without any distracting hint of the verbal redundancy some low ingrates have complained about in Johnson's great poem. The Dickens is a calculatedly showy piece of rhetoric, and the two Shakespeare overtures are put in the mouths of show-off rhetoricians, Orsino and Richard. It's more typical of Shake-speare to begin his plays with fairly dull lumps of, so to speak, (a)-category prose, usually in the form of minor characters telling each other things they probably already know about some major characters. (*The Tempest*, which contains some of the most piercingly beautiful lines in English, has the almost preposterously unpromising first line: 'Boatswain!') The Orwell has a comic-grotesque sting in the tail: 'It was a bright cold day in April, and the clocks were striking thirteen.' Coleridge's poem, pseudo-archaic, is licensed not to beat about the bush. Genesis is divinely inspired.

Quite a number of more recent first lines have won their memorability by being dramatically abrupt: 'A screaming comes across the sky' (*Gravity's Rainbow*); 'Today Mother

---

* Full marks if you can do *War and Peace*: 'Eh bien, mon prince, so Genoa and Lucca are now no more than private estates of the Bonaparte family . . .'

died' (Camus's *L'Étranger*, translated as *The Outsider* or *The Stranger*); 'Lolita, light of my life, fire of my loins';* 'This is the saddest story I ever heard' (*The Good Soldier*) . . . though when it comes to memorability, few word-slingers can rival Franz Kafka. He isn't usually thought of as a trader in fast-moving action yarns, but the eminently quotable opening sentence of Kafka's *The Trial* is virtually a paradigm of the arresting opening:

> Someone must have been telling lies about Joseph K., for without having done anything wrong he was arrested one fine morning.

And how about *Metamorphosis*?

> As Gregor Samsa awoke one morning from uneasy dreams he found himself transformed in his bed into a gigantic insect.†

Supreme. Try too hard to top something like that and you'll soon find yourself in the business of parody, self-parody or burlesque . . . or, if you're very clever, something less easy to pin down. The first line of Nabokov's *Ada* (full

---

* This is a cheat; the first line of *Lolita* is actually ' "Lolita, or the Confession of a White Widowed Male," such were the two titles under which the writer of the present note received the strange pages it preambulates.'; for the novel begins with a fictional Foreword by one 'John H. Ray, Jr., Ph.D.'.

† Plainly, Kafka wasn't one for beating around the bush. *The Castle*, likewise, pitches you straight in: 'It was late in the evening when K. arrived.'

title: *Ada or Ardor: A Family Chronicle*) offers a double-take on the most inescapable of all Russian first lines:

> 'All happy families are more or less dissimilar; all unhappy ones are more or less alike,' says a great Russian writer in the beginning of a famous novel (*Anna Arkadievitch Karenina*, transfigured into English by R. G. Stonelower, Mount Tabor Ltd., 1880).

And, though her work is seldom mentioned in the same breath as Nabokov's, that noted experimentalist writer Agatha Christie was capable of an intertextual flourish. She chose to begin her novel *The Murder on the Links* (1923) with a joke about literary buttonholing:

> I believe that a well-known anecdote exists to the effect that a young writer, determined to make the commencement of his story forcible and original enough to catch and rivet the attention of the most blasé of editors, penned the following sentence:
>   ' "Hell!" said the Duchess.'*

Anthony Burgess, who hatched probably the most famous stunt-opener of post-war English fiction with *Earthly Powers*'s

> It was the afternoon of my eighty-first birthday, and I was in bed with my catamite when Ali announced that the archbishop had come to see me.

---

* This anecdote exists at least one other form, something like this: a creative writing teacher sends his students off to write a short story, explaining that the key elements of a top-notch yarn are religion, sex, high society and brevity. One of his students duly hands in a piece which reads: 'My God!', said the Duchess, 'Take your hand off my knee!'

is being more sly than you might think. Further down that first page, you find the narrator, a quondam popular novelist something in the Somerset Maugham line, reflecting half-proudly, half-ruefully on his old pro's way with contriving an arresting opening. I'm not sure whether the same is true of the (to say the least) obscure 1940s novel *Sleep Till Noon*, recommended to me by an American physics professor, and I can't make up my mind whether I'd enjoy it more if I were able to convince myself it was penned in earnest; but I reproduce it anyway as my personal nomination for the *ne plus ultra* of the category (b) opener:

> Bang! Bang! Bang!, three shots to the groin and I was off
> on the greatest adventure of my life.

I find it harder to settle on a candidate for the *ne plus ultra* of all first sentences. The author is easy – James Joyce – but my loyalties are torn between three major books. It would have to be either the beginning of *A Portrait of the Artist as a Young Man*, the first words of which look back not only to the author's earliest experience of his life as a story but to the phrase we all heard when we discovered what stories were:

> Once upon a time and a very good time it was there was a
> moocow coming down along the road and this moocow
> that was coming down along the road met a nicens little
> boy named baby tuckoo.

Or that of *Ulysses*, with its deceptively casual, near-category (a) surface and its hermetic depths of allusion (I for one rejoice, no pun premeditated, in my credulous acceptance of the proposition that Joyce arranged for his book's first word, 'Stately' to contain a reversed anagram of its last word, 'yes'):

> Stately, plump Buck Mulligan came from the stairhead, bearing a bowl of lather on which a mirror and a razor lay crossed.

Or that of *Finnegans Wake*, which resolves the question of how to begin a work which denies the ultimate reality of beginnings and endings by evoking Genesis and Giovanni Battista Vico's vision of the circularity of history; by luxuriating in a panoramic establishing shot of Dublin; and by jumping impulsively into the mid-stream of a sentence ('A way a lone a last a loved a long the') that only really begins, again, 626 pages later at the end of the novel's final paragraph:

> rivverun, past Eve and Adam's, from swerve of shore to bend of bay, brings us by a commodious vicus of recirculation back to Howth Castle and Environs.

Footnotes

'Just give me everything you've got by Ibid.'

Harry Belafonte*

At the age of sixteen or seventeen, I settled down one Saturday afternoon to an enthralled reading of Samuel Beckett's second major novel, *Watt*. All was going swimmingly – I giggled, I pondered the Deeper Meaning Of It All with due post-pubescent urgency, I stared at the Void and the Void obligingly stared back, just as Nietzsche had promised. And then I stumbled across a lengthy passage detailing the various branches of the Lynch family, of which one junior member, Kate, is described as 'a fine girl but a bleeder'. That last word 'bleeder' was tagged with the superscript of a number 1. Unaccustomed as I was to scholarly conventions and editorial apparatus (barely eighteen months earlier, my idea of a literary titan had been Ray Bradbury), even I knew the drill. I dutifully jumped my eye to the small print at the bottom of the page, where I was

---

* Cited in 'Belafonte's Balancing Act', by Henry Lewis Gates, Jr (*New Yorker*, 26 August/2 September 1996, p. 135): at the time, Belafonte was a ferocious young autodidact, baffled by the citation codes he found in the works of W. E. B. DuBois.

informed that 'Haemophilia is, like enlargement of the prostate, an exclusively male disorder. But not in this work.'[*]

I giggled again, but felt wrong-footed in a way that was quite novel. Footnotes, I had somehow worked out from my voracious if largely trashy reading, were to proper grown-up books what foundations were to buildings – they made sure that the text was firm and steady. What writers did was to make some claims about reality in the big print on the upper part of the page and then, to show that you weren't just sounding off but actually had some evidence for your various asseverations, you displayed your grounds for such claims in the small print. A reasonable procedure, it seemed to me, familiar as I was with crack-voiced sneers of 'Oh yeah? Prove it!' in playground debates and flytings. Footnotes *proved it*; they put your money where your mouth was. Yet here was Beckett, this author of conspicuous genius, breaking the rules with chilling insouciance.[†] The conclusion was inescapable: footnotes – footnotes in novels by members of the awkward squad like Beckett, anyway – might turn out to be not foundation stones but landmines, exploding upwards into the soft black-and-white underbelly of the main text on contact with the reader's gaze.[‡]

---

[*] *Watt*, Calder and Boyars' 'Jupiter' edition (London: 1970), p. 100.

[†] And breaking it again and again. There are several other comic footnotes in *Watt*, including (a) the po-faced explanation that 'Ego autem' is 'A Latin expression meaning: I (Ego) also (autem)' and (b) the admonition, before the novel's fragmentary final section, that 'The following precious and illuminating material should be carefully studied. Only fatigue and disgust prevented its incorporation.'

[‡] But consider the very different case of, say, Manuel Puig's novel *Kiss of*

My innocence was lost. Within weeks I was seeking more and harder kicks from my footnotes, and I found them in two eighteenth-century Irish wits who, so the books in my public library assured me, might be considered the distant progenitors of Beckett's oeuvre: Swift and Sterne.*
Tristram Shandy, I found, teems with footnotes – some in murky Latin, some in barely less murky French, almost all of them wilfully unhelpful or teasing;† two centuries before my adolescent encounter with *Watt*, Sterne had been playing pretty much the same jokes as Beckett played with his cod-scientific haemophilia reference. Sterne's notes blew a raspberry at the convention that an author should pretend to speak (as the word seemed to imply) authoritatively about his or her created world, or about the big world beyond the page. Thus, when the upper-page narrator of *Shandy* refers to a particular learned tome on childbirth, the lower-page

---

the Spiderwoman, which has a sequence of running notes, mostly from psychiatric and medical sources, about the nature of homosexuality. Here, the footnote seems to be more like the concealed recess in a smuggler's suitcase – it sneaks polemical and clinical matter over to the unsuspecting reader, who expected nothing more than a nice prison yarn.

* The reader will probably be familiar with the old professor's quip that these two writers should have swapped names: Swift was stern, Sterne was swift (that is to say, swift-witted). I am well aware that some purists have disputed the claims of both writers to full or true Irish nationality; but prefer to ignore them. Joyce, at any rate, was happy to regard Sterne as a compatriot, and Yeats was more than pleased to consider Swift an illustrious forebear.

† Take, for example, the note to Vol. V, chapter 25, on the use of the name 'Confucius': 'Mr. Shandy is supposed to mean ***** *** ***, Esq.; member for *******, – and not the Chinese legislator.'

narrator-annotator sniffs that 'The author is here twice
mistaken; for *Lithopaedus* should be wrote thus, *Lithopaedii
Senonensis Icon*. The second mistake is, that this *Lithopaedus*
is not an author but the drawing of a petrified child . . .'*
and so on and on and on. Swift† is somewhat similar. In *A
Tale of a Tub*, a posse of fictitious commentators on the main
text point out the shortcomings not only of what the author
says‡ but what other footnotes say. The more I read this
loony stuff, the more I was confirmed in my suspicion that
there was something faintly unsettling about footnoting, akin
to the sense of mild dismay induced by idly tugging at a
loose thread on a sweater, only to discover that the thread
isn't loose after all, but keeps on unravelling and unravelling
while the garment shrinks . . .

I needed professional help. I found it, or the beginnings
of it, a few months later in Hugh Kenner's tantalizingly brief
volume *The Stoic Comedians*,§ which contains some still

---

* Footnote to Vol. V, chapter 25.

† Like Himmler.

‡ So, in section I, the commentator 'H' notes of an elision, 'Here is
pretended a defect in the manuscript; and this is very frequent with our
author, when he thinks he cannot say anything worth reading, or when
he has no mind to enter on the subject, or when it is a matter of little
moment, or with some satirical intention.' Sound familiar?

§ Full title: *The Stoic Comedians: Flaubert, Joyce and Beckett* (Berkeley:
University of California Press, 1962). Though I read this little book with
pleasure, it struck me that Kenner's arguments were often a bit wide of
the mark – that he exaggerated, for instance, the degree to which *A Tale
of a Tub* is actually a display of Swift's 'ventriloqual' powers: the voices of
the contending commentators are not all that distinctive.

more t.b. remarks on the nature of the footnote – classic
remarks, I'd say, still insufficiently explored. 'The man who
composes a footnote', Kenner writes – unaware from his
innocent, early-sixties vantage point that a shift in sensibilities
is just about to make his goes-without-saying pretence that
authorship is (like enlargement of the prostate) an exclusively
male disorder seem, at best, fogeyish – 'and sends it to the
printer along with his texts has discovered among the devices
of printed language something analogous with counterpoint:
a way of speaking in two voices at once, or of ballasting or
modifying or even bombarding with exceptions* his own
discourse without interrupting it. It is a step in the direction
of discontinuity: of organising blocks of discourse simultaneously in space rather than consecutively in time.'† Yes,
yes, I nodded eagerly, by Jove, I think we're really on to
something here, Prof. . . . and was disappointed to find that
instead of taking off on a long and wild and bracing ramble
through the fells of Footnoteland, Kenner confined his
examples of this architectural use of the footnote to a bare
two: Alexander Pope's *Dunciad Variorum*‡ and Joyce's *Finnegans Wake*§ – rather forbidding works, both of them, which

---

* Here, enacting his own argument rather than merely stating it, Kenner
supplies this footnote: 'Some footnotes of course seem totally unrelated to
the point in the text at which they are appended. They suggest an art
form like the refrains in Yeats' late poems.'

† Kenner, op. cit., p. 40.

‡ In which some literary historians have suspected the hand of Swift.

§ On Joyce's footnotes, and related matters, see Shari Benstock's article
'At the Margin of Discourse: Footnotes in the Fictional Text', *Proceedings*

for all their feats of comic invention tend to be honoured more by citations in lectures or dense critical exegeses than by pleasurable perusal.*

   Still, much of what Kenner says about the great Augustan and the great ·Modern is true of most footnote writers, including those who have no ambitions to explore the spatiality of the printed word, *mise-en-page* or what have you. What's more, something that Kenner very nearly gets around to saying is true of absolutely every pedal annotation: the effect of a footnote cannot be *read out*† – there is no

_____

of the Modern Language Association, March 1983, pp. 204–25. It is customary to use footnotes as the place for acknowledgement of indebtedness to a cited critic's work; but in this case there is, frankly, not that much of a debt to acknowledge. Sorry, Prof. B.

* (a) Lest the tone of this remark be mistaken: this is not a covert sneer at either Pope or Joyce, both of them long-term residents in my literary top twenty. But only a dreamer would seriously maintain that either the *Dunciad* or the *Wake* is much enjoyed nowadays by that noble creature, the common reader.
   (b) And tone can very easily be mistaken: when the *ur*-version of this essay appeared in the *Independent* a few years ago, an otherwise friendly reader remarked that she found my use of the term 'common reader' snobbish and insulting, and remained unmoved by my appeals to authorities from Johnson, S. to Woolf, V. To her, 'common' necessarily implied 'common as muck'.

† When the producer Abigail Appleton and I put together a feature about footnotes for our Radio 3 series *Reading Around* in the summer of 1997, we came up with the convention that every time an actor read out a footnote, it would be signalled as such by the sound effect of a ringing doorbell. Our inspiration for this was a witticism to the effect that 'having to read a footnote resembles having to go downstairs to answer the door while making love'. I'm ashamed to admit that I can no longer remember the

adequate way of vocally reproducing its interplay with the main body of the text, nor any of the leaps of eye, bounds of sense, hesitations in flow of comprehension, backtracking and forward-flipping that are called for in reading an annotated text,* or – in the case of the surly reader who won't play along with the game – of registering the mental effort involved in a stubbornly unscholarly refusal to lower one's gaze. Of all the IFs we have thus far been browsing through, the footnote is the one which is most thoroughly lacking in any real classical or oral precedents,† the one which is most inescapably Gutenbergian.‡

---

author of this remark, though it reminds me a little of Samuel Johnson's less lascivious observation about the chilly effect of notes in editions of Shakespeare: 'The mind is refrigerated by interruption; the thoughts are diverted from the principal subject; the reader is weary, he suspects not why; and at last throws away the book, which he has too diligently studied.'

* To go back to Kenner's hinting word 'counterpoint': you could argue that the peculiar ways in which footnotes interrupt the usual rhythms of reading can also be thought of as allowing the author who is also a composer, such as Anthony Burgess, to introduce an element of something akin to polyphony. See the footnoted chapter in Burgess's theological spy novel *Tremor of Intent*.

† The late Jeremy Maule, of Trinity College, Cambridge, was kind enough to suggest that the first major example of an English poem with built-in footnotes is Spenser's *Shepherd's Calendar*; he believed that it could therefore be described, to warp a phrase, as an 'instant classic', coated with critical moss that Greek and Latin texts had taken centuries to accumulate.

‡ This, apart from a few sketchy asides about Gibbon, John Livingstone Lowe's *Road to Xanadu* (see below) and *Tom Jones* was about as much ground as I covered in the *Independent* version of my essay, unless you

Having misspent a significant portion of my salad days
pottering around such topics, I was of course an absolute
sucker for Nicholson Baker's deliciously footnote-festooned
debut novel *The Mezzanine*, an extended prose aria on such
essential and, as they say, 'strangely neglected' topics as
shoelace abrasion, sock-bunching, the alleged mass death of
brain cells with the passage of years, the motion of straws in
carbonated soft drinks, doorknobs, the diffusion of photo-
copied witticisms from office to office, minutiae of lavatory
and escalator etiquette, milk carton design, the grooves in
long-playing records, perforation (!), vending machines, the
gender specificity of the exclamation 'Oop!', the archaeology
of shampoo brands, traditional insomnia cures and the stoicism of Marcus Aurelius. Though it runs to just 135 pages,
The Mezzanine boasts – by my perhaps sloppy reckoning –
no fewer than forty-eight substantial footnotes, some of

---

count a gratuitous and ill-informed crack about Derrida, appended to or
depended from the final line: 'Western philosophy has sometimes been
described as a series of footnotes to Plato; the time is surely long overdue
for a full-scale philosophy, Platonic or otherwise, of footnotes'. To my
surprise, the article drew a fair amount of correspondence, including a
letter which seemed largely designed to advertise the fact that the writer
had read a book by Nabokov called *Pale Fire* (in which, I feel obliged to
add, the loony commentary takes the form not of footnotes but of
endnotes) and a lovely one from an old chap in Wales who said that he
had largely educated himself by chasing up the footnotes in Joseph
Needham's *Science and Civilization in China*. This seems like a good place
to point out that footnotes are the place where an author can comment
on earlier versions of a text, disagree with the arguments and beliefs of a
younger self, enquire as to the whereabouts of the snows of yesteryear . . .

them running across as many as four sides.* It also boasts a truly splendid footnote on footnotes, which begins with Baker's memory of browsing through the footnotes in William Edward Hartpole Lecky's *History of European Morals*; digresses into anecdotes about Spinoza's fondness for dropping flies into spiders' webs and Hobbes's almost equally eerie penchant for trapping jackdaws with cheese; digresses still further to Wittgenstein's favourite non-philosophical pursuit, gawping at cowboy movies;† starts to manoeuvre gently back towards his main theme by citing Boswell (a notorious, what is the word, podophile? pedestrenotator?) on Johnson's mode of dress for the celebrated Hebridean tour, and a self-justifying mini-memoir of Adam Smith remarking in a lecture that he was glad to know that Milton wore latchets (i.e., proto-laces) in his shoes; and thus rises to a stirring tribute to the great practitioners and connoisseurs of the form:

> They knew that the outer surface of truth is not smooth, welling and gathering from paragraph to shapely paragraph, but is encrusted with a rough protective bark of citations, quotation marks, italics, and foreign languages, a whole variorum crust of 'ibid.'s' and 'compare's' and 'see's' that are the shield for the pure flow of argument as it lives for a moment in one mind. They knew the anticipatory pleasure of sensing with peripheral vision, as they turned

---

* Baker told me that he thinks – or hopes – that the four-pager, to be found on pp. 65–8, is the longest in the history of prose fiction.

† Was it really cowboy movies? I thought Ludwig was more a gangsters and/or Betty Grable man.

the page, a gray silt of further example and qualification waiting in tiny type at the bottom . . .*

And this footnote upon footnotes isn't even halfway done! Baker goes on to revel in the pleasurable smallness of small print,† to digress on digressions, to blast the philistinism of the MLA Style Sheet's warning against 'essay-like' footnotes, to slag off the condescending and babyish annotations in the *Norton Anthology of Poetry* and lastly to return, with a grand rhetorical flourish, to the supplemental, self-correcting footnotes of Gibbon and Boswell and (divine symmetry) Lecky. Punchline: 'Footnotes are the finer-suckered surfaces that allow tentacular paragraphs to hold fast to the wider reality of the library.'‡ *Bravo! Author!*

Obviously, when offered the chance to interview Nicholson Baker for the *Independent* shortly after *The Mezzanine* was published in Britain I took it greedily, but can now remember almost nothing of our agreeable chat save for a confessional discussion about the hauntingly Dantescan flavour of the corporate name 'Beatrice Foods' and for Baker's arresting

---

* Baker, op. cit., p. 122n.

† As he pointed out to me, 'There's a whole hierarchy of type size which is so beautiful with the footnote . . . The footnote type has to be excitingly compact, but there has to be room to have something even more compressed if you quote *within* the footnote . . .'

‡ Ibid., p. 123. Baker tells me that this footnote is all that remains of an earlier project to write a history of footnotes; now that Anthony Grafton has published his history, he feels, he no longer has to fret that the task is undone. But see below.

comparison of the footnote to the bleb.* The better part of
a decade had to pass before I had the opportunity to take
these matters up with him again, for an item about footnotes
– you'll already know all about this, if you've been reading
all the footnotes as you go along instead of skipping them
altogether or saving them up for the end – in the Radio 3
books series *Reading Around*, broadcast in the summer of
1997. One of the minor revelations of our recorded talk was
that Baker's footnote fetishism began in childhood:

> I think the first footnote that impressed me was in a book
> called *How to Attract the Wombat* – I've never seen it again,
> it was on my parents' shelf, but it was a collection of kind
> of jokey essays, and it had those beautiful asterisks and
> daggers and things that have gone out ... Each one of
> those little figures has a history that you can trace in
> manuscripts and find out how their meanings change. I
> didn't know that then, I just loved knowing this rule, that
> you could come to this little machine that looked like
> some kind of a switch in a train track and you would know
> that that meant 'Turn South! You will now go into the real
> rail-yard, where they have all those things in italics and all

---

* Nicholson Baker explained it to me thus: 'As I understand, based on my
comprehensive experience of, I don't know, *Scientific American* or some
popular thing, blebs are these microscopic protuberances in the cell walls
that allow a little bit of the plasmic whatnot that's inside the cell to come
out. And that's what's really happening with a footnote: as you're reading,
you're in the real world of the sentence, and suddenly this secret thing
happens that the sentence doesn't know about. A footnote is there, but
it's not really there as far as the sentence is concerned, it's there as far as
the reader is concerned. It's this little rupture in the propriety of the
sentence, somehow.'

those page numbers and citations and things . . .' In *How to Attract the Wombat* the footnotes were relatively short, but I understood how to do it.*

Baker's condition worsened in college, when he wrote papers on Pope and co.,† and became critical after graduation when he was employed by a law company, where he was given the task of preparing legal briefs, some seventy or eighty pages in length. Since the company didn't have a footnoting program on their software – I think that this idea is horrifying enough to justify the deployment of some Stephen King-style italics – *the footnotes had to be split and recombined manually again and again with each new draft* . . . Plainly, this was intolerable, and Baker was eventually driven to deal with the horror of it all by coming up with a footnote program of his own; but he also became 'hyper-aware' of the importance of footnotes after seeing the lawyers agonizing over whether judges would ever actually read them,

---

* Patricia Duncker points out that there is a certain perversity in footnoting references to conversations like this, though it's quite often done – you look down the page and find the phrase 'personal communication' or some such, generally followed by a date – since, short of turning up on my doorstop and demanding to borrow my tape, there's no way in which any scholar could check the accuracy of my citation. Footnotes to a printed source implicitly promise 'Look, I can prove this'; footnotes to oral sources say 'Sorry, you're going to have to take this one on trust.'

† Which ultimately bore fruit in his long essay on the word 'lumber', published in *The Size of Thoughts*; this essay, he says, was an attempt to show that he could do 'real, sincere, big-boy footnotes' as well as the frisky footnotes of *The Mezzanine*; his whole lumber essay can be considered as an extended footnote to a single couplet of Pope's.

since many cases may hinge on a technicality which is buried far down in the aforementioned-by-Baker typographic silt.

When he came to write *The Mezzanine*,* Baker recalls, he initially resorted to footnotes 'out of desperation' – unsure whether his readers would find observations on the pre-bunching of socks as fascinating as he did, he chose to give them the option of skipping, and 'exiled a lot of the stuff that was most interesting to me to the bottom of the page'. He had firm views on what he would and would not permit himself to do with the notes: there wouldn't, for example, be any footnotes to the footnotes,† which would have been 'too much like Jonathan Swift, too mock-scholarly'; nor any two-columned sets of notes – 'those are so beautiful, so fine, I knew I wasn't up to that, it would have been disrespect-ful . . .'; nor would he yield to the publisher's demand that the footnotes should be numbered consecutively throughout the book, or at least from chapter to chapter: Baker insisted

----

* Having, he adds, already relished the use of footnotes in fiction by the likes of M. R. James and John Updike, and having pondered the status of the footnotes to be found near the end of Proust's big book, apparently put there by conscientious publishers and editors who weren't entirely sure what the ailing Marcel wanted done with them.

† David Foster Wallace, in his collection of journalism and essays *A Supposedly Fun Thing I'll Never Do Again*, uses these meta-footnotes in great profusion. Nicholson Baker observes that if there has been something of a recrudescence of footnoting among novelists, journalists and extra-academic types in the past few years, it may partly be because (a) American magazines such as *Harper's* have allowed writers to use them once more, and (b) because personal computer software now makes it easier to annotate. Or has it been (he was too modest to wonder) because of the success of *The Mezzanine*?

that the only right way to do the thing is 'to start the clock again' on every fresh page. Once having made the decision to indulge in footnotes, though, Baker's acquiescence in their proliferation became inevitable, because *The Mezzanine* has to suggest the variety of reverie and irrelevance which occupy the margins or other zones of the narrator's consciousness as he proceeds through his lunch-hour, and 'footnotes really are a beautiful way of stopping time'.*

And also, of course, because 'it's a lot of fun to pretend to be a scholar, and footnotes are a way of connecting yourself with the rest of scholarship and of thanking people'.†
Yes, I've somehow managed to push this far into the underbrush without spelling out the most obvious of all considerations about footnotes – that they are the invention, the speciality, the particular art form, the home or homeland,‡ the badge of office,§ the *forte*, the signifier, the *sine qua non* and maybe even the *ne plus ultra* or, who knows, the *e pluribus unum* of scholars and scholarship. The contro-

---

* A remark which prompted me to ask whether it had been his long mulling-over of footnotes which prompted Baker's time-stopping novel *The Fermata*? Yes, he said, it had.

† On this point, see *The Mezzanine*, pp. 131–2n, with its references to such publications as *World Textile Abstracts* and the *Proceedings of the Third Japan–Australia Joint Symposium on Objective Measurement: Application to Product Design and Process Control*.

‡ In a newspaper interview I read a few weeks ago, the novelist Amos Oz evoked the bookish nature of his childhood by saying that he grew up in a 'house full of footnotes'.

§ Anthony Grafton rather naughtily compares them to the diplomas on display in dentists' offices.

versial new novelist Steve Doorknob may be as lacking in degrees as the surface of Neptune, but if he uses a footnote, however mockingly, he is bowing in the direction of Harvard Square; and he might be surprised to find that these sneaky little characters lurking below his sightline are starting to take on a life of their own.

Patricia Duncker, an academic who moonlights as a successful novelist, has long been a keen observer of all types of footnoting. She proposes an elementary, alliterative system of classification which covers most types of scholarly footnotes, and is divided, like the *patrie* of Asterix, into three parts:

1) The Footnote Plain and Positive, which simply gives a source and shows the reader how to track it down, offering no comment.

2) The Footnote Paranoid, 'which tries to show that you've read absolutely everything on the subject, that nobody can fault you, that you have the most up-to-date sources, and that, if you haven't mentioned it in the text, it doesn't mean that you haven't read it.' These can also be smokescreens: 'If you're aware that somebody disagrees with you, but you don't want to go into it in the text, you can put at the bottom "But see . . ." and then a list of texts, and it doesn't necessarily mean that you've read them all.' And they can grow so vast – 'like the defences of the Alamo, sandbagging, keeping everybody else out' – that they drive the text to which they are meant to be subservient off the page.* Sometimes, it is true, the

---

* 'Greek texts, like the *Oresteia*, are the worst . . .'

paranoia is fairly discreet, and such footnotes will just give you variants on the texts, or disputes about the interpretation of a line, or corruptions of the text and what it might mean, or bits of the manuscript that are illegible. At the other extreme, this type of footnote will shade off into the final type:

3) The Footnote Perilous and Provocative: 'This is the one which is full of venom. It's usually very understated, and says, "How saddening I find it that a distinguished scholar of this gentleman's eminence should be, in this case, so *inaccurate*, so *corrupt* . . ."' The contrast between the measured sobriety of the upper page and the jeers or lethal asides of the lower page is so striking that 'it can be like having two personalities on the same page some-times. Sometimes the best of the writer is in the foot-notes* . . . I think this is particularly true of Professor Terry Eagleton, who is the master of the Footnote Vicious . . .' It's a persuasive image: *Dr* Jeckyll writes the scholarly thesis in his book-lined study, while *Mr* Hyde lurks and salivates in the cellar; or, as Patricia Duncker puts it less melodramatically, 'The footnote is the uncon-scious of the text.† It's buried there producing all its

---

* Nicholson Baker is of the same mind: 'Writers who are a little stiff and nervous in their main prose can relax in their footnotes . . .'

† As an undergraduate, I was once deeply impressed by someone's carefully-honed throwaway *aperçu* that 'Shakespeare is the unconscious of the eighteenth century'. I think that this was something to do with the way in which the Bard's textual editors would try to tame his native woodnotes wild, not to say demented, into something prosier and more plausible; but your guess is as good as mine, frankly.

dreams because the footnote sometimes contains the text that the author didn't dare to write, and those are the best. It's always the nether regions that give you away.'

It was gratifying to discover that the Princeton historian Anthony Grafton seems to be very much in agreement with this line of thinking: as he says, 'it's always more interesting in the servants' hall, it's where the gossip goes on. Much of the real life in Gibbon is in the footnotes, for example, it's where he's constantly burrowing in, sticking in knives, being irreverent.' Gratifying, because Professor Grafton has a fair claim to knowing more about footnotes than any man living. When I first started to muse about these matters in print, no one had ever thought them worthy of extended study. Grafton, it subsequently emerged, had. He made his findings available to the rest of us in 1997 by publishing *The Footnote: A Curious History,** a book that bursts at the seams with erudition. You can trust a man like Grafton when he makes a flat-out assertion such as 'The longest footnote ever was written in England in 1840 in a history of Northumberland by John Hodsgon, and is almost 200 pages long. Now that's a footnote!', or when he ventures the opinion that

Gibbon is the great master of the footnote,† without peer before or after, the one whose footnotes remain in your

---

* Or, more exactly: *The Footnote* (asterisk; eye drifts down cover page to smaller print): *A Curious History.* This book was originally published in German, and its first title – *Die Tragischen Ursprunge der deutschen Fußnote* – was, Professor Grafton says, 'a bad German joke', alluding to Walter Benjamin's *The Origins of German Tragic Drama.*

† Which is why it's so disconcerting to learn from Grafton's study that

memory when the text has fled, as when he tells the story
of Marcus Aurelius and his wife, who was prostituting
herself to everybody in Rome. He says 'The world accounts
Marcus Aurelius a simpleton', but then in a footnote he
says 'But Madame Dossier assures us, and we may believe
a lady, that the husband will always be deceived if the wife
condescends to deceive him in a serious way.' And I
remember the footnote much better than the text – there's
a silken, bitter irony to these footnotes, especially when his
favourite enemies, Christian theologians for example, are
being discussed.

And in case you might for a second or two be inclined
not to trust Grafton, his whole published argument is – but
of course – massively underpinned with footnotes. His
deployment of the gadget is doubly self-conscious, since one
of his arguments is that footnotes can,

> I'm afraid, be part of the way in which the sclerotic
> establishment fends off novelty . . . When old guard histo-
> rians are confronted by new theses or by new ways of
> doing history, one of their easiest defences is to say, 'Well,
> just look at the footnotes! There are mistakes! This can't
> be any good!' . . . I put a few footnotes in there just for
> fun, to see if I could irritate people, as Simon Schama so
> successfully did when he published a book *without* foot-
> notes,* designed to annoy the pedants.

Gibbon originally objected to having the notes set out at the foot of the
page, and wanted them published at the end of his history.

* *Dead Certainties*. Note also the gathering tendency for historians and
other scholars to publish two versions of their work, a long hardback one

In Grafton's view, the true footnote was born some time around the end of the seventeenth and the beginning of the eighteenth centuries,* though

> it's a point of enormous controversy – no one really knows where the truth is. There's the beginnings of modern science, the beginnings of experimental method, the status of the Bible is in great doubt . . . And it's in that moment, when all forms of knowledge are being called into question, when Newton and Leibniz are inventing a new kind of mathematical reasoning and notation, that historians invent their own new kind of notation, which is the footnote.

Flagrantly learned as it is, however, *The Footnote* isn't really about footnotes in general – it concentrates almost exclusively on the use of footnotes by eighteenth- and nineteenth-century historians, and leaves the vast plains of literary† footnoting from Pope and Fielding via Joyce and

––––––––––

for their colleagues, stiff with footnotes, and a shorter, noteless one for the mass audience.

* You might say that this was when all sort of traditional marginal annotations, etc., flew south for the winter, liked what they found, and decided to settle in the antipodes for good.

† Though it is, again, cheering to learn that Professor Grafton is very keen on *The Mezzanine*; his remarks about the temporal function of the footnoting there corroborate Baker's own:

> Oddly, footnotes – since they come from this belief in verifiability – work very well in post-modernity, as a way of producing a text which is constantly cycling around and subverting itself. I think one sees that wonderfully in . . . *The Mezzanine*, where [Baker] uses footnotes again and again to create a kind of delaying effect in a book which is trying to give you a real-time experience of a narrator over [a lunch hour], and there

Beckett to Baker and David Foster Wallace all but virgin. Why this neglect? 'Sheer ignorance', joshes the Professor.* Nor does he dwell very much on the maddening, almost insane proliferation of footnoting in (particularly) American academic journals, where contributors have to spend so much time demonstrating – cf. Patricia Duncker's Footnote Paranoid – that they have digested every last scrap of pertinent material on their topic, not to mention sucking up to the appropriate authorities, or log-rolling,[†] or micturating on rivals, before minutely inching forward into fresh assertions and hypotheses new . . . that the reader falls down stunned with exhaustion and boredom. Professor Grafton speaks with compassion of his graduate students, who have to master and regurgitate all this mercilessly accumulating print – 'the accredited secondary literature increases every

---

the footnote is both helping him to create an effect of great vividness and hallucinatory clarity, and undercutting that effort at the same time.

On this question of 'circling', see Prof. M. J. Wallen's fascinating article on the labyrinth of cross-referring citations in John Livingstone Lowe's *The Road to Xanadu*, in which, Wallen contends, the study itself becomes like the Ancient Mariner's tale, endlessly repeated: *The Journal of Narrative Technique*, 1987, pp. 259–72.

* Alluding to Samuel Johnson's reply to the woman who asked him why he'd given a wonky definition of, if I recall correctly, the word 'pastern' in his *Dictionary*.

† There used to be a method, no doubt encouraged by bean-counters, whereby the 'objective' worth of an article or book was supposed to be gauged by the number of citations it received in other books or articles. The effect was predictable by anyone who isn't a bean-counter: academics would set up little back-scratching groups or cartels of citation.

year, just as no car nowadays seems to go off the road' –
and with real dismay of the spectacle of footnotes driven 'up
the page higher and higher, like a hideous tide bringing in
more dead jellyfish'.

No, he cheerfully concedes, there remains a great deal of
work yet to be done on footnotes: 'The unwritten history
of the footnote is the unwritten history of the sciences
that don't deal with nature. Thanks to the historians of
science, we now know a great deal about laboratory work,
about astronomical observation and so on; compared with
this, we know almost nothing about the way in which
works of history or anthropology* are actually put together, about the nature of their craft routines.' And when
the unwritten histories of the footnote are eventually written, Grafton has no doubt that, for all his Canute-like
misgivings at the rising tide of small print, it is essential
that they appear in public with their lower limbs properly
covered: 'Publishers nowadays seem to think that footnotes
are some kind of drag on the saleability of a book. But I
think it's important to give some sense of the work that
went into a book. Footnotes are the story of How I Won
The War, how the research was done. If you don't allow
people to see that, you collaborate in a kind of dumbing
down.'

Finally, I am obliged to confess to the ignoble hope –
since, as Patricia Duncker says, it's peculiarly thrilling to find

---

* Though, he also concedes, the anthropologists are starting to investigate
such matters, by examining and publishing the field notes of Malinowski
and so on.

oneself footnoted* – that those scholars yet unborn who come to write and annotate those hypothetical books will be sufficiently painstaking to include at least a passing citation or two of this opuscule somewhere in their works. As it stands, of course, my brief chapter can hardly be considered as anything more than . . . well, a footnote.

---

* Conversely, it's particularly galling to be dismissed in a footnote, as if one were not worthy of attention in the main body of the text.

Marginalia

[handwritten: HAS THIS MAN NEVER HEARD OF JACQUES DERRIDA?]

Mi si tolga lo studio gli amici di lettere e per me sara tutto finito *[handwritten: Pretentious? Io?]* Leopardi*

In the early August of 1992, *Private Eye*'s 'Books and Book-men' column claimed that there was widespread trepidation *[handwritten: 1.]* in literary circles at the news that Graham Greene's personal library would shortly be coming up for sale. Anxiety might seem like an unduly timorous response to such a bland announcement. The alleged object of foreboding, however, was not the words printed in Greene's books but the words scribbled in them – that is to say, Greene's marginalia, which tended (as marginalia so often do) <u>towards the splenetic and contemptuous</u>. For example, the novelist's copy of *Evelyn Waugh and His World* was rumoured to have been slashed over with derisive remarks about Professor Malcolm Bradbury's contribution: 'How E W would have shuddered at the style!'† 'Does this mean anything?' and the like.

[handwritten vertical right margin: ABSOLUTE RUBBISH]

---

* 'Take away from me my studies and my "friends of letters" and everything will be over for me' – a line written by Leopardi in his copy of Annibal Caro's translation of the *Aeneid*.

† Fair comment, I'd guess. In his copy of Cyril Connolly's *The Unquiet Grave*, Waugh wrote 'An Irishman's eschatology. The English Gallows; the

SNOB

Private Eye's gossip served as a useful reminder that the habit of defacing books with handwritten outbursts is not a weakness exclusive to the semi-literate.* True, most of the marginalia one encounters in the course of a lifetime's passage through borrowing libraries have a certain air of pathos, since they are often the only means by which the defacer can ever hope to preserve his or her words between hard covers. Their characteristic notes of thwarted artistry or pedantry, their howls of rage, their inchoate craving for some tiny measure of immortality are a few of the qualities which establish them as blood relatives to that large-scale, public form of marginalia we call 'graffiti'. Yet a fair number of them also have a more charming quality, one to which their more brutal cousins spray-painted on walls and posters can seldom if ever aspire: they can be cosy, affectionate,† domestic, meekly confessional . . . in a word, *chatty*. The wonderful Victoria Wood is as acute on these marginal interjections as she is on the other manifestations of unspectacular Englishness. In her book *Mens Sana in Thingummy Doodah*, she observes that the books in her local library are

---

judgement of Father O'Flynn; the U.S.A.; Hell, a dark place peopled densely with ancestral enemies.' Connolly happened across these jottings years later, and was wounded. See *The Letters of Nancy Mitford & Evelyn Waugh*, ed. Charlotte Mosley (London: Hodder & Stoughton, 1996), pp. 15 and 16n.

* The modern writer who made the most elaborate art of defacing library books is, of course, Joe Orton, in collaboration with his lover Kenneth Halliwell; but the Orton–Halliwell oeuvre so greatly exceeds most marginalia in ambition and range of media that it demands separate treatment.

† 'Dear Mr G.!', W. H. Auden wrote in his copies of Goethe.   NOT TAVE ?

always full of comments such as *Oh, I agree* or *We washed everything by hand, too*: 'I mean,' she concludes, 'it's a bit disconcerting to flick through a copy of *Hamlet* to find "This happened to me" scrawled all over Act Four.'

Amusing, no question, but Ms Wood's 'disconcerting' is surely disingenuous: her joke, or memoir, or joke-memoir is a quiet reminder that chance encounters with marginalia aren't usually anything to gripe about. On the contrary, they're among the distinct, if under-described pleasures of promiscuous reading (and one of the several reasons why browsing in a second-hand book shop is usually so much more absorbing than equivalent time spent in a store selling only new books). Correspondingly, ardent readers everywhere know that the act of taking up a book without simultaneously taking up a pencil or – for the foolhardy and the vain – a pen is not just lazy but a shade bloodless. Though the phrase 'a book to be read with one hand' is commonly an arch euphemism for 'porn', industrious readers, *real* readers will take up their volume with one hand even when the pages in view are as chaste as Diana. At the very least, they will draw lines beneath or beside the words;* more typically, they will annotate. The scrawls they add may be outraged, or learned, or witty, or simply incomprehensible. All of them mark an unresisted urge to make a noise

---

* Once again I am indebted to Nicholson Baker's *The Size of Thoughts*, where he recalls the habit, widespread in the eighteenth century and still not extinct, of marking passages in books by running a sharp fingernail down the margin. Sheridan's *Rivals* alludes to the practice, as does Nabokov's translation of *Eugene Onegin* (which presumably means that Pushkin's original does, too?).

in the white silence* of the page's borderlands. Marginalia
are the handwritten traces of imaginary conversations –
above all, of imaginary arguments.† YES, BUT...

And, should the scribbler have won eminence in more
reputable and substantial literary modes, these jottings may
themselves end up preserved in scholarly editions, ripe
objects for yet further marginalia; some of the canonical
authors of the Western mainstream were also inveterate
writers on the side. Consider Keats, whose beautifully crafted
pen marks in his copy of the *Anatomy of Melancholy* (especially
the 'Love Melancholy' section) speak volumes about his self-
tormenting misogynistic fantasies, and whose annotations
in his copy of *Paradise Lost* have recently inspired a book-
length critical study.‡ Consider Blake, whose annotations to

---

* Since first writing this phrase five years or so ago, I have come across
George Whalley's description of Coleridge's marginalia as being 'often
ringed about with silence in the way poems are': *Marginalia*, Vol. 12, Part
1, p. lx.

† Though they occupy the same spaces on the page that were occupied
by printed marginal notes in the glory days between Gutenberg and the
great southerly migration of the seventeenth century – see the last chapter,
on footnotes – I'd argue that they behave in very different ways. Printed
marginal glosses cited authorities, stressed a particular interpretation of
biblical and other texts and generally acted in a disciplined, disciplining
manner. (On this subject, see, for example, Evelyn B. Tribble's *Margins and
Marginality: The Printed Page in Early Modern England* (Charlottesville and
London: University Press of Virginia, 1993)). Marginalia are far more unruly.

‡ And who wrote of Dr Johnson (in his copy of Shakespeare) the words
'Clamorous owl that hoots at our quaint spirits'. Tennyson was another
memorable annotator of *Paradise Lost*; against the line 'Taste after taste
upheld with kindliest change' (Book V., 336) he wrote: *French cook.*

Lavater's *Aphorisms on Man*, various works by Swedenborg, R. Watson's *An Apology for the Bible*, Bacon's *Essays Moral, Economical and Political*, Boyd's *Historical Notes* on Dante, the *Works* of Sir Joshua Reynolds, Berkeley's *Siris*, Wordsworth's *Poems* and Thornton's *The Lord's Prayer, Newly Translated** can be as pregnant and unforgettable as anything in his lyrics. Actually, some of these marginalia *are* lyrics:

> When Sir Joshua Reynolds died
> All Nature was degraded;
> The King dropd a tear into the Queens Ear;
> And all his Pictures Faded,

jotted Blake in his copy of Reynold's *Works* on 23 February 1792 when he heard that happy news that the academician had been despatched by the 'inordinate growth' of his liver. Just a few of Blake's marginalia are approving ('All

---

* See *The Complete Poetry and Prose of William Blake*, ed. David V. Erdman (Berkeley: University of California Press; revised edition, 1982), pp. 583–670. The American library copy I consulted while writing this chapter turned out – Blake attracts this kind of thing – to be rich in pencil and pen marginalia; e.g., against 'The CLOD & the PEBBLE' on p. 19, someone had pencilled 'Think of/the texture/of the clod/& the Pebble./ One is soft &/easily crushed,/while the other/is hard and course [*sic*]'. Another, smaller hand had inscribed the word 'masturbation' on p. 50, next to lines from 'VISIONS of the Daughters of Albion' (fair comment, really) and, more disturbingly, 'Penis?' on p. 85, against the lines 'an enormous dread Serpent/Scaled and poisonous horned.' (See a doctor immediately, kid.) A third student had smeared 'The Book of Urizen' with barely legible remarks like 'soupy physicality', and filled other margins with utterly illegible clusters of words reminiscent of the mescalin drawings of Henri Michaux. I'm no graphologist, but I for one would think twice about letting the last of these annotators into the US Marines.

Gold' or 'Sweet' or 'Sterling' or 'Noble' he notes against
approved passages in Lavater). The vast bulk are swinge-
ing, with Bacon ('I am astonished how such Contemptible
Knavery & Folly as this book contains can ever have been
call Wisdom by Men of Sense but perhaps this never was
the Case & all Men of Sense have despised the Book as
Much as I do'), Thornton ('I look upon this as a Most
Malignant & Artful attack upon the Kingdom of Jesus By the
Classical Learned thro the Instrumentality of Dr Thornton
The Greek & Roman Classics in the Antichrist I say Is & not
Are as the most expressive & correct too') and above all his
arch-enemy Sir Joshua ('I consider Reynold's Discourses to
the Royal Academy as the Simulations of the Hypocrite who
Smiles particularly where he means to Betray . . .') drawing
his heaviest artillery. Blake's spleen is bracing, as well as
unexpectedly funny in places, and it seems to have inspired
him, too. Fuelled by righteous outrage, but forced by the
limited areas of available blank space to keep his responses
curt, he rose to an aphoristic eloquence depressingly lacking
in his prolix and [all-but-unreadable] visionary epics: 'To
Generalize is to be an Idiot', he generalizes with sublime
self-assurance, 'To Particularize is the Alone Distinction of
Merit – General Knowledges are those Knowledges that
Idiots possess'; '<The Enquiry in England is not whether a
Man has Talents. & Genius? But whether he is Passive &
Polite & a Virtuous Ass: & obedient to Noblemens Opinions
in Art & Science. If he is; he is a Good Man: If Not he must
be Starved>'; 'Christ & his Apostles were Illiterate Men
Caiphas Pilate & Herod were Learned. The Beauty of the
Bible is that the most Ignorant & Simple Minds Understand
it Best . . .' No reputable selection from Blake's writings

come,
now . . .

would be complete without at least a core sampling of such maxims.

Above all, consider Samuel Taylor Coleridge, quite certainly the most prolific of all marginalists, probably the most brilliant: 'There is no body of marginalia – in English or perhaps in any other language – comparable with Coleridge's in range and variety and in the sensitiveness, scope and depth of his reaction to what he is reading'.* Indeed, it was Coleridge who introduced the word 'marginalia' to the English language, in 1832; and it is wholly characteristic of the poet that one of his main autobiographical reflections on marginalizing should itself have been written as a marginalium (on the half-title of Kluge's *Magnetismus*, to be pedantic, probably in 1817 or thereabouts):

AS USUAL

> I am in the habit of making marginal observations on the books I read – a habit indulged by the partiality of my friends. For the past twenty years there is scarce a book so bepenned or bepencilled, but some one or more instances will be found noticed by me of the power of the visual and its substitution for the conceptual . . .†

The history and nature of Coleridge's marginal writings has been brilliantly explored by George Whalley in the long essay‡ which introduces the first book of *Marginalia* in the Bollingen *Collected Works*. Among many other invaluable

---

* The magisterial verdict of George Whalley, editor of Coleridge's *Marginalia* for the Bollingen Series, in his Introduction to *Vol. I (Abbt to Byfield)*, p. lvii.

† Cited in Whalley, p. lxxvi.

‡ To which I am indebted for the following pages on S.T.C.

observations, Whalley points out that if we approach these writings in the expectation that the more important the author, the more copious Coleridge's annotations, we are likely to be disappointed: he wrote nothing on Aristotle, Bacon, Bruno, Augustine or Aquinas, next to nothing on Plato, and the only word to be found in his edition of Dante is 'Pacchiaretti', the misspelled name of a wine he particularly enjoyed tippling. Conversely, his notes on Jakob Böhme run to over 140 pages. Whalley outlines Coleridge's various motives for writing in the margins, from preparing his lectures to educating younger or less erudite acquaintances, but suggests that his most common temptation to pick up his pen was to achieve a form of communion with the distant and the dead.

Whalley also quotes from one of the poet's earliest editors, his nephew Henry Nelson Coleridge (1798–1843), whose sketch of S.T.C. busy at his books may also serve as a fine evocation of many another marginalist's art:

> Although the Author in his will contemplated the publication of some at least of the numerous notes left by him on the margins and blank spaces of books and pamphlets, he most certainly wrote the notes themselves without any purpose beyond that of delivering his mind of the thoughts and aspirations suggested by the text under perusal. His books, that is, any person's books – even those from a circulation library – were to him, whilst reading them, as dear friends; he conversed with them as with their authors, praising, or censuring, or qualifying, as the open page seemed to give him cause . . .*

---

* Henry Nelson Coleridge, in his 'Preface' to S. T. Coleridge's *Literary Remains III* (1838).

S.T.C.'s real-life 'dear friends' knew quite well what they could expect if they agreed to lend him a book, and one of them is well known for having relished the prospect – Charles Lamb, whose essay 'The Two Races of Men' (on the subject of mankind's borrowers and its lenders) concludes with the warm counsel:

> Reader, if haply thou art blessed with a moderate collection, be shy of showing it; or if thy heart overfloweth to lend them, lend thy books; but let it be to such a one as S.T.C. – he will return them (generally anticipating the time appointed) with usury; enriched with annotations, tripling their value.* I have had experience. Many are these precious MSS of his – (in *matter* oftentimes, and in *quantity* not unfrequently, vying with the originals) – in no very clerkly hand – legible in my Daniel; in old Burton; in Sir Thomas Browne; and those abstruser cogitations of the Greville now, alas! wandering in pagan lands. – I counsel thee, shut not thy heart, nor thy library, against S.T.C.†

---

* I take it that Lamb is using the word 'value' in its most general sense here; but to book dealers, of course, annotation by a famous hand will boost up the asking price of any volume.

† Compare De Quincey:

Coleridge often spoiled a book but in the course of doing this, he enriched that book with so many and so valuable notes, tossing about him, with such lavish profusion, from such a cornucopia of discursive reading, and such a fusing intellect, commentaries so many-angled and so many-coloured that I have envied many a man whose luck has placed him in the way of such injuries.

Works, II, p. 314.

Lamb's counsel was heeded. By the end of his life, more
and more of his friends, particularly James and Anne Gillman, were handing books over to Coleridge in the expectation, seldom disappointed, that they would be returned
suitably adorned; and Southey doted on the notes Coleridge
scribbled in his books, even when they were uncomplimen-
tary to him, and took great pains to preserve them. In his
copy of Sedgwick's *Evangelical Preaching*, Volume I, he wrote:
'The marginal notes in this book are S. T. Coleridge's,
written in pencil by him, & traced in ink by me "that
nothing be lost." R. Southey, June 13, 1819.'*

So busy was Coleridge's free hand that his collected
Marginalia will, when the epic work of scholarship is complete, run to five huge tomes† (part one, *Abbt to Byfield*, is
well over a thousand pages) of the Bollingen edition, of
which the *Marginalia* is classed as volume 12 of 16. This
gigantic labour will complete a process which began in
Coleridge's own lifetime, since his marginal comments began
to find their way into print from as early as November 1819,
when *Blackwood's Edinburgh Magazine* published extracts from
the marginalia he had written in March 1804, for the benefit

---

* Whalley, p. xciii.

† In his *Church and State* (1830) Coleridge printed three of the notes he
had written in his copy of Isaac Taylor's *Natural History of Enthusiasm*
(1829), and said that they were examples of the 'Marginalia, which, if
brought together from the various books, my own and those of a score
others, would go near to form as bulky a volume as most of those old
folios, through which the larger portion of them are dispersed.' Whalley
comments that even Coleridge's best friends might have thought that this
was pushing it a bit, but we now know better.

of Sara Hutchinson,* in a copy of Sir Thomas Browne's
Works. 'Much more nearly than any of his printed works',
the anonymous editor 'G.J.'† assured readers, these remarks
conveyed 'the style of Coleridge's conversation'. Here are a
couple of samples. The first is from the Hutchinson mark-
up:

> So compleatly does he [i.e., Browne] see every thing in a
> light of his own, reading Nature neither by Sun, Moon, or
> Candle-Light, but by the Light of the Faery Glory around
> his own Head, that you might say, that Nature had granted
> to him in perpetuity a Patent and Monopoly for all his
> Thoughts. – Read his Hydrotaphia above all – & in addition
> to the peculiarity, the exclusive *Sir Thomas Brown-ness* of all
> the Fancies & modes of Illustration wonder at and admire
> his *entireness* in every subject, which is before him – he is
> totus in illo – he follows it, he never wanders from it – and
> he has no occasion to wander – for whatever happens to
> be his Subject, he metamorphoses all Nature into it.

The second is from a later perusal of Browne – or, at any
rate, it can be found in one of Coleridge's copies of Browne's
Works:

> The difference between a great mind's and a little mind's
> Use of History – The Latter would consider, for instance,

---

* He included an extraordinary series of symbols to indicate what he
thought – or more exactly what he thought she was meant to think – of
various passages: the simplest of these are the letters Q and F: 'Q signifies
characteristic Quaintness; and F, that it contains an *error* in fact or
philosophy'. Whalley, p. 765.

† Possibly James Gillman.

what Luther did, taught, or sanctioned: the former, what
Luther, *a* Luther, would *now* do, teach, and sanction.

Occurred to me Midnight, Tuesday 16 March 1824, as I
was slipping into bed, my eye having glanced on Luther's
Table Talk.

As the former example shows, some of Coleridge's marginalia were in the nature not of imaginary conversations
with his authors, but of real written intercourse with a
specific addressee; as the latter shows, he would sometimes
recognize that he was basically talking to himself, and merely
exploiting the nearest half-inch of unsullied paper as if it
were one of those many notebooks in which he would write
in a state approaching trance.*

Less serenely unselfconscious scribblers than Coleridge
may address their comments in quite other directions –
sending them off to unknown subsequent readers of the
same volume, say, in accordance with much the same
impulse that makes people put messages in bottles. Occasionally, these annotations will be offered in genuinely helpful
spirit. When I enquired about the matter at the London
Library, I was told by its Librarian of the time, Mr Douglas
Matthews, that it is this category of scribblings which pose
his colleagues their most ticklish ethical question: should
they apply their erasers if the correction is just? More
commonly, such defacers set out to solicit agreement, to
provoke, to impress readers of a future day.

It was this last consideration which inspired Flann

c.f. Fermat's Last Theorem

1806

* May, 1908: 'I write more unconscious that I am writing, than in my
most earnest modes I *talk* . . .' etc. See Whalley, p. lix.

O'Brien, writing in the *Irish Times* as Myles na Gopaleen, to
concoct his ingenious scheme for a book-handling service,
aimed at those rich enough to have accumulated a private
library but too busy, idle or stupid actually to read it. Any
such citizen who wanted to make a favourable impression
on those who took down a volume or so from the shelves
would simply have to call in Myles's team of expert book-
maulers, who would not merely crease, dog-ear, crumple
and stain them, but, for those willing to fork out for Class
Four treatment ('the Superb Handling, or the Traitement
Superbe, as we lads who spent our honeymoon in Paris
prefer to call it') make apposite and erudite annotations:

> suitable passages in not less than fifty per cent of the books
> to be underlined in good-quality red ink and an appropriate
> phrase from the following list inserted in the margin, viz:
>
> Rubbish!
> Yes, indeed!
> How true, how true!
> I don't agree at all.
> Why?
> Yes, but cf. Homer, Od., iii, 151   — *sic in Myles*
> Well, well, well.
>
> Quite, but Boussuet in his Discours sur l'histoire Univ-
> erselle has already established the same point and given
> much more forceful explanations.
>
> Nonsense, nonsense!
> A point well taken!
> But *why* in heaven's name?
> I remember poor Joyce saying the very same thing to
> me.
>
> Need I say that a special quotation may be obtained at any

time for the supply of Special and Exclusive Phrases? The extra charge is not very much, really.*

Caveat scriptor, however: even when such personal comments have not been commissioned from Myles's specialists in *Buchhandlung*, but are wholly original to the scribbler, they may give quite the wrong impression, or backfire in unforeseen ways. The poet Peter Robinson once told me the story of coming across a paperback of (I think) W. H. Auden's selected poems in a friend's bookcase: next to one of the verses was written, in a juvenile version of that friend's all-too-recognizable handwriting, the guileless exclamation 'At last I understand this poem!'; Robinson's chum was so mortified at being shown up by his younger self in this way that he tore out and then tore up the incriminating page. My own increasing reluctance to lend out books that I have owned for more than twenty years has less to do with the fear of never seeing them again, or of seeing them defaced,† than with the misgiving that they may contain some shudder-inducing spoor of my painfully earnest, appallingly ignorant teenage sensibilities, of which the mildest cases would be

---

* Myles na gCopaleen (a.k.a. Myles na Gopaleen, a.k.a. Flann O'Brien, a.k.a. Brian O'Nolan), *The Best of Myles: A Selection from 'Cruiskeen Lawn'*, ed. Kevin O'Nolan (London: Macgibbon & Kee, 1968), pp. 20–21.

† Slightly to my own surprise, I can only recall one occasion on which I lent out a book which came back augmented as Lamb expected his lendings to S.T.C. to be augmented. Against a passage in *The Unquiet Grave* where Cyril Connolly moans that one usually wishes to be taken away from a business lunch in a coffin, my loanee had written, in indelible blue ink, the single word 'True.' He was at the time a recent graduate, not too happy with the world of commerce.

sombre, self-instructing annotations along the lines of 'irony', 'motif', 'Wasn't it Chuang Tsu?' or 'cf Gamini Salgado on the crisis in Renaissance self-confidence' while the worst . . . simply do not bear thinking about.

In the pages of library books, ill-judged observations are likely to draw rebuttals, and every snide or angry expostula- tion will draw an angry or snide reply, which will then provoke another reply, and another, until there is no white space left and the beleaguered librarians have to either labour for hours with the rubber or fork out for a virgin copy. (Mr Matthews asked me to remind all readers of the obvious fact that wanton scribbling in library books is an act of selfish vandalism, and that would-be offenders should curb their nibs; if the urge to deface is irresistible, go and buy your own copy.) On rarer and more unsettling occasions, one blunders across a reader's arguments with him- or herself. Take this outburst, found by a friend of mine several years ago in the pages of a library copy of T. S. Eliot's *After Strange Gods*,* next to his notorious remarks about 'free-thinking Jews': '*YOU BASTARD*. (Control yourself, remember you are dealing with a very sick mind.)' Well, yes; but the schizophrenic address to 'you' hints that the very sick mind haunting this page may not be Eliot's. While the first two words, five times underlined – though unaccountably lacking exclamation marks – scream at Eliot in impotent rage, those in brackets are more like the angry muttering of that loony

TYPICALLY IGNORANT MISUSE

---

* This book is always a happy hunting ground for marginalia, partly because of the sentiments Eliot expresses, partly because he never reissued the book and most of us can only read it in much-annotated library copies.

on the far side of the underground carriage – a kind of neo-Jacobethan aside or truncated soliloquy from a mad scene.

It was Eliot who occasioned some of the best-known marginalia of the twentieth century – comments which belong to the particular sub-sub-genre of marginal notation found on manuscript drafts and page proofs: Ezra Pound's impatient yelps of disapproval or gruff praise accompanying his surgical strikings-out on Eliot's early versions of *The Waste Land*. Since the publication of the facsimile edition in 1971, a handful of Pound's commands and nudges have become virtual shibboleths for modernists: 'make up yr mind you Tiresias if you dont know damn well or else you dont [*sic*]' or, against the word 'perhaps', 'damn per'apsez'. And the same documents contain what must be the eeriest marginal addition in literary history. The drafts of a section entitled 'In The Cage' incorporate a sketch version of that creepy portrait of a modern marriage in Book Two of *The Waste Land*, 'A Game of Chess' – a portrait generally agreed *By* to be based on Eliot's own harrowing evenings with his mentally ill wife Vivien. Next to it, Vivien Eliot has written a single word: '*WONDERFUL*'.

That trisyllabic tick of approval seems to me more flesh-crawling than the most sustained flight of invective ever found in margins; a great deal more horrible even than, say, the long thin stream of bile left* by William Beckford on the endpapers of his copy of *The Decline and Fall of the Roman Empire*:

---

* Compare this tasteless image with Whalley, again, who remarks that Coleridge's marginalia were 'an essential physical deposit or secretion in the process of self-knowing, self-realisation, "self-production".', op. cit., p. lxi.

The time is not far distant, Mr Gibbon, when your almost ludicrous self-complacency, your numerous, and sometimes apparently wilful mistakes, your frequent distortion of historical Truth to provoke a gibe, or excite a sneer at everything most sacred and vulnerable, your ignorance of the oriental languages, your limited and far from acutely critical knowledge of the Latin and Greek, and in the midst of all the prurient and obscene gossip of your notes – your affected moral purity perking up every now and then from the corrupt mass like artificial roses shaken off in the dark by some Prostitute on a heap of manure, your heartless scepticism, your unclassical fondness for meretricious ornament, your tumid diction, your monotonous jingle of periods, will be still more exposed and scouted than they have been. Once fairly kicked off from your lofty, bedizened stilts, you will be reduced to your just level and true standard.

(Come on, man, get off the fence and tell us what you really think of him.) While Beckford's venom seems deliberated, I imagine that most marginalia of such a high order of savage indignation are prompted by first readings; subsequent perusals are almost always calmer, less likely to call for the spontaneous overflow of graphite or ink – though Saul Bellow has recorded one terrible occasion on which John Berryman picked up a copy of one of his own collections of poetry and went through it wildly scrawling 'crap!' and other self-lacerating judgements. Berryman's scatology is suggestive. All abusive forms of marginalia – and anecdotal evidence suggests that abusiveness is the tone most commonly heard on the margins – bear a whiff of the same ribaldry found in the scrawlings on lavatory walls. These marginalia

Fool

You

have affinities, it seems to me, with the leering, vomiting, defecating clowns and monsters which flock and mock around the edges of manuscripts in the Middle Ages;* if and when literary critics start to address marginal annotation properly as an IF, they would do well to cross-refer to such studies.

But it would be unjust to quit the subject with the implication that marginalia are chiefly interesting because they are in some way – as carpet-slipper literary revolution-ists are fond of putting it – 'subversive'.† The form is much more supple and various than that, or at any rate can be in the hands of a virtuoso or wit; a wit such as Max Beerbohm, for example, who was such a compulsive marginalist that his biographer, David Cecil, decided to open his biography *Max* with an anecdote of the Incomparable One busy with his pencil. True, Beerbohm's annotations were often caustic enough. In a copy of Vernon Lee he wrote:

> Poor dear dreadful little lady! Always having a crow to pick, ever so coyly, with Nietzsche, or a wee lance to break with Mr Carlyle, or a sweet but sharp little word of warning to whisper in the ear of Mr H. G. Wells or Strindberg . . . What a dreadful little bore and busybody!‡

---

* But compare the delighted marginal note of an anonymous eighth-century Irish scribe: 'Pleasant to me is the light on these margins, because it flickers so.'

† Which is why I have studiedly avoided any use of the cant word 'marginality'.

‡ David Cecil, *Max* (New York: Houghton Mifflin, 1965), p. 367. Beerbohm was also a dab hand at bogus dedications and inscriptions; see pp. 366–75

And in Kipling's *A Diversity of Creatures* he wrote the mock-inscription:

> By R.K. the
> Apocalyptic Bounder
> who
> can do such fine things
> but
> mostly prefers to stand
> (on tip-toe and stridently)
> for all that is
> <u>cheap</u>
> <u>and nasty</u>.   *TOO TRUE*

A fair number of his marginalia, though, were considerably more measured and reflective. Against the description of himself as 'the wittiest mind in England' in William Rothenstein's *Twenty-Four Portraits*, Beerbohm wrote:

> No! I am not nearly so witty as Chesterton for one. But certainly I have not prostituted and cheapened my wit as he has. How about Lytton Strachey? There's the wittiest mind of the age – and the virtue of it guarded even more strictly and puritanically than I have guarded the virtue of mine.
>
> And I am forgetting G.B.S. He has prostituted his wit certainly and made a drudge of her too. But she can stand it! She's gigantic.

---

passim. Cecil points out that Beerbohm, no misogynist in most other respects, had a terrible thing about lady authors.

And when he found, in a volume of contemporary memoirs, the sentiment 'Posterity will be puzzled what to think about Sir Edmund Gosse', Max was moved to reply:

> Posterity, I hope, will be puzzled what to think about anybody. How baffling and contradictory are our most intimate and contemporary friends! And how many of us can gauge even himself!

Not the most searching of *pensées*, perhaps, but it would not look at all uneasy in a dictionary of quotations or an anthology of ponderable ponderings. Like many of Blake's marginalia, this is an example of a note which can thrive perfectly well out of context – a note which is no longer subordinate to some other writer's main text, and is able, if it so desires, to go and settle inside other covers. When this happens, the marginalium has ceased to be an IF and has evolved into a major form. A marginalium by Beerbohm's frequent target, Rudyard Kipling, did just this: his poem 'The Coin Speaks' first saw life in June 1907, when Kipling wrote it on the fly-leaf of Sir Charles Oman's copy of *Puck of Pook's Hill*.* And we have it on the authority of Ford Madox Ford that Joseph Conrad, bored one night as his ship was in port, began to scratch some notes in the margins and endpapers of his copy of *Madame Bovary*. These notes eventually developed into Conrad's first novel, *Almayer's Folly*. One could, in other words, say that not only Conrad's novel but his whole literary career began as marginalia to Flaubert.

— SHAMELESS PLUG!

* It is reprinted in *The Oxford Book of Money*, pp. 100–101.

Stage Directions

Enter Prine, Leonato, Claudio and Jacke Wilson

Much Ado About Nothing (First Folio)*

Apocalypse then:

> *The flames immediately flare up so that the fire fills the entire space in front of the hall and appears to seize on the building itself. Horrified, the men and women press to the very front of the stage. When the whole stage seems to be engulfed in flames, the glow suddenly subsides, so that soon all that remains is a cloud of smoke which drifts away to the back of the stage, settling on the horizon as a layer of dark cloud. At the same time the Rhine overflows its banks in a mighty flood, surging over the conflagration . . .*†

After Wagner, the deluge. The composer's terminal instructions for *Götterdämmerung*, first staged in 1876, would appear to mark the extreme limit of what any dramatist or music-dramatist can reasonably hope to put on the boards: short of wiring up the auditorium with dynamite and blast-

---

* The point? 'Jacke Wilson' doesn't appear in the scene, or anywhere else in the play.

† Translation by Stewart Spencer, in *Wagner's Ring of the Nibelung: A Companion* (London: Thames and Hudson, 1993), p. 351.

ing the pit, the stalls and the circle to smithereens, how can you top the end of Valhalla and earth? Yet from the Rhine-sodden ashes of Wagner's mythic world rose not only new styles of drama, but new ways of putting dramatic writing onto the page. All the standard reference books will tell you that the period of the late nineteenth century to the early twentieth was a golden age for drama, jewelled with the names of Ibsen, Chekhov, Strindberg, Wilde and Shaw. Few, if any, take the trouble to point out that this was also the golden age for the stage direction. A strange oversight: the rise of this paratextual element of play scripts in this period was, so to speak, dramatic. Egged on by a revolutionist like Shaw, the stage direction suddenly declines to serve its traditional role – a more or less anonymous, self-effacing flunky of the play's real meat, its dialogue. It starts to throw its weight around. It shows that it can dish out the polemic as though it were a muck-raking pamphlet or, more exactly, a Shavian preface (the first few pages of a Shaw play tend to be crammed with the author's opinions, as if his preface had burst its banks, Rhine-wise, and flooded onto the stage), wax didactic like a lecturer, rhapsodize over scenery like a nature poet and anatomize character like a novelist, or like one of those new Viennese mind-doctors. And, though Shaw is mostly valued as a realistic writer today, he was also happy to write stage directions of Wagnerian scope, using them as a gateway to the infinite, as he did in *Back to Methuselah** (1921):

---

* Justice demands mention of a much funnier direction from *Methuselah*: '*The Garden of Eden. Afternoon.*' The Monty Python team used a similar gag in *The Life of Brian*, sixty-odd years later.

> *They contemplate the void with awe. Organ music of the kind*
> *called sacred in the nineteenth century begins. Their awe deepens.*
> *The violet ray, now a diffused mist, rises again from the*
> *abyss . . .*

The author of *The Perfect Wagnerite* had plainly learned a thing or two about stage directions from Bayreuth; the author of *The Quintessence of Ibsenism* also bowed respectfully towards Norway, where Ibsen had been showing other ways of putting pictures on the stage for years,* and dreamed up catastrophic finales – not quite as universal as Wagner's Teutonized Ragnarök but, in a good production, every bit as emotionally intense:

> *The ladies on the veranda wave their pocket-handkerchiefs, and*
> *the shouts of 'Hurrah' are taken up in the streets below. Then*
> *they are suddenly silenced, and the crowd bursts out into a*
> *shriek of horror. A human body, with planks and fragments of*
> *wood, is vaguely perceived crashing down behind the trees.*

A shattering moment, and, if one turns a deaf ear to those shouts of 'hurrah', all achieved without any character uttering a single word. Ibsen's plummeting form in *The Master Builder* (1892) is a feat of dramaturgy which anticipates some of the defining, dialogue-free coups of twentieth-century drama, from the silent scream of Brecht's Mother Courage to the terrifying hoovering-in-the-dark of Pinter's *Caretaker* to the camp Annunciation (very Stephen Spielberg) at the end of Tony Kushner's *Millennium Approaches*. And yet . . . all right, I'd better own up to puerility, philistinism and

---

* *Brand*, Ibsen's first success, was staged in 1866, though it took him another twenty years to establish his reputation in Britain.

probably worse by confessing that I find it hard to read this scene from *The Master Builder* without smirking. Not, I nervously add, because the image is silly in itself, but because it's all too easy to imagine the disasters of a less than perfect production, in which the plummeting body is either an obvious dummy, or an intrepid stunt man who ricochets back from his trampoline into the audience's view (isn't this supposed to have happened once at a performance of *Tosca*?), or in which the whole set, battered by flying planks, falls inexorably to pieces while the stage manager commits *seppuku* in the wings. The more spectacular the stage action, the greater the potential for a really superlative cock-up: the great innovators – the Wagner of *Götterdämmerung*, the Ibsen of *The Master Builder* and the Shaw of *Back to Methuselah* – were all 'daring' in more than the once familiar sense. They were willing to risk the bathos that lurks, grinning evilly, in all-too-fallible props and sets.

It's easy to see, though, why they were willing to take the risk. As the theatre critic Michael Billington was good enough to explain to me, the rise of the stage direction at the end of the nineteenth century is in large measure a consequence of the rise of naturalism, and of the author's wish to control not only what was spoken on stage, but the shapes, the sounds and the look of the play.* The composi-

---

* Or even, on rare occasions, its smell. I recall the enthusiasm with which a friend of mind responded to the Royal Court production of Michael Hastings's play about T. S. Eliot's ghastly first marriage, *Tom and Viv*. The moment at which Eliot is received into the Anglican communion is rendered sensuous by the burning of incense. How refreshing, my friend

tion of highly specific directions was, Mr Billington suggests, a way for the writer to seize back control from the director – witness Chekhov's row with Stanislavki on the occasion when the director took it into his head to introduce the noise of croaking frogs into a passage which was wholly free of batrachians in Chekhov's text. It is hard for audiences made blasé by a century of cinema to appreciate quite how remarkable it was for playwrights to conceive a school of drama in which the play's emotional force might be brought to focus in its italicized and parenthesized passages: the slamming of the door in *A Doll's House*, say, or, most terrible and haunting of all, the finale of *The Cherry Orchard* (1904):

> *(A sound is heard that seems to come from the sky, like a breaking harp-string, dying away mournfully. All is still again, and there is nothing heard but the strokes of the axe far away in the orchard.)*

I am, of course, exaggerating the radical novelty of such effects just a hair. Many if not most playwrights from Aeschylus onwards had written with a view to the kinds of emotional effect particular sights or actions or noises or groupings of characters would have on the audience; and, after all, the most famous stage direction in literary and theatrical history comes not from Ibsen or Chekhov or Shaw but from Shaw's *bête noire**, one William Shakespeare: *The Winter's Tale*, Act III, sc. iii:

------

thought, to let that unintellectual organ the nose be the first to apprehend Eliot's conversion.

* 'With the single exception of Homer, there is no eminent writer, not even Sir Walter Scott, whom I can despise so entirely as I despise

Exit, pursued by a bear.

The scholarly consensus seems to be that it is quite OK to laugh at that one, because Jacobean and Elizabethan audiences always considered bear scenes a great hoot. It's also quite possible that the Bard would have been happy to hear laughter, albeit horrid laughter,* at his early anticipation of *The Texas Chainsaw Massacre* in *Titus Andronicus*, Act II, sc. iv:

Enter the empress' sons, with LAVINIA, *her hands cut off, and her tongue cut out, and ravish'd.*

As one of my schoolteachers remarked, the problem of how to make Lavinia's state of ravishment visible to the audience has always taxed the taste and intelligence of directors. My favourite Shakespearean stage direction is rather more deli-cate, and comes at the end of an unusually copious note in *Timon of Athens*, Act I, sc. ii:

Hautboys playing loud music. A great banquet serv'd in; and then enter LORD TIMON, *Athenian Lords and Senators,* VENTI-DIUS *which Timon redeem'd from prison;* LUCULLUS *and* ALCIBIADES. *Stewards and others in attendance. Then comes, dropping after all,* APEMANTUS, *discontentedly, like himself.*

'Excellent examples', comments *Timon*'s Arden editor H. J. Oliver, 'of the "descriptive" stage directions which show

---

Shakespeare when I measure my mind against his.' – Shaw in the *Saturday Review*, 1896.

* For which unsettling noise, see Nicholas Brooke's *Horrid Laughter in Jacobean Tragedy* (London: Open Books, 1979).

that the author's draft (or a transcript of it) was "copy" for
the printed text.' Possibly, maybe probably; but, reluctant as
I am to take so much as the smallest issue with a genuine
scholar, the sorry fact is that we have no way of determining
which if any of the stage directions we have received from
the First Folio and other early editions are direct from
Shakespeare's pen, and which are lifted from prompt books
and the like.* True, it does seem likely that, as Shakespeare
distanced himself more and more from London and the
practical world of the theatre, he made some attempt to
control his productions from a distance by writing his ideas
and wishes into his scripts, which is why Shakespearean
directions start to wax more eloquent from, roughly, *Corio-*
lanus onwards. Yet even this much is conjectural, and,
barring some miraculous recovery of manuscripts or the
intervention of spiritualists, we will never be certain that
Shakespeare wrote any of the stage directions, with or
without bears, that our most sober editions continue to
reprint. Shaw, you may recall, liked to set himself up against
the Swan of Avon in *Shakes. v. Shav.* matches. Usually Shav.
ends up looking fairly preposterous, but when it comes to
the Stage Directions heat, we're obliged to concede that
Shakes. isn't even a starter, let alone a contender.

Concessions duly made, I resume my untroubled dog-
matism. The theatrical revolution known as 'naturalism' was
triumphant, so much so that the formerly downtrodden
script-paratext not only took a real measure of equality with

---

* To make sure I wasn't talking out of my hat here, I consulted Professor
Anne Barton, who kindly confirmed the first point and introduced me to
the second.

the dialogue, but in some cases – such as the plays of J. M. Barrie – actually became the dominant part. Or, as one theatrical historian* wrote of Barrie in a rather less excitable metaphor: 'His plays in printed form are often a trickle of dialogue through a forest of commentary.' Quite so: take the opening of Barrie's greatest hit *Peter Pan* (1904):

> *The night nursery of the Darling family, which is the scene of our opening Act, is at the top of a rather depressed street in Bloomsbury. We have a right to place it where we will, and the reason Bloomsbury is chosen is that Mr Roget once lived there. So did we in days when his Thesaurus was our only companion in London; and we whom he has helped to wend our way through life have always wanted to pay him a little compliment. The Darlings therefore lived in Bloomsbury . . .†*

Now this jolly verbosity, and the rolling acres of agreeably rambling prose which follow it, has absolutely zero to do with naturalism and just about everything to do with the other historical cause of the s.d. revolution: more and more publishers were finding it attractive to publish editions of works by popular playwrights, which meant that playwrights could feel free, indeed were encouraged, to think in terms of

---

* J. C. Trewin, *The Theatre Since 1900* (London: Andrew Dakers, 1951), p. 52.

† Michael Billington tells me that, in the last decade or so, directors of *Peter Pan* have taken to salvaging some of this material from the page by casting an actor as a Barrie-Narrator figure, and having him speak chunks of it out from the stage or the stalls.

a readership as well as an audience.* (And when the play-wright was a novelist, failed novelist, or novelist manqué, categories which embrace both Shaw and Barrie, the stage direction was the ideal place to flex the old fiction-writing muscles: *Peter Pan* began life as a novel.) The development had a number of interesting consequences. It led, for example, to the writing of a type of play which could never be staged, and was intended solely for the mental prosce-nium of the reader, such as Sadakichi Hartmann's† mystical play *Confucius*, which ends with the italicized words

The New Era of Mankind Begins to Sense Its Way‡

Somewhat closer to the mainstream, there is Hardy's *The Dynasts* (1904–8; eventual full title: *The Dynasts: An Epic-Drama of the War with Napoleon, in three parts, nineteen acts, and one hundred and thirty scenes, the time covered by the action being about ten years*). Hardy's 1903 Preface to the work frankly describes it as 'presented to the mind's eye in the likeness of a drama', insisting that it is 'intended simply for mental performance, and not for the stage'. This was a

---

* William Archer's translations of Ibsen sold handsomely from the 1880s onwards, and many of the playwright's admirers – including Shaw – first encountered his works on the page.

† 1869–1944; no, I haven't made him up: he was an American poet and man of letters, a connoisseur of photography and the visual arts of Japan, and, if I recall correctly, he knew both Whitman and Mallarmé. Ezra Pound gives him a favourable name-check in *The Pisan Cantos*.

‡ *Buddha, Confucius, Christ: Three Prophetic Plays*, edited by Harry Lawton and George Knox (New York: Herder and Herder, 1971).

sensible emphasis, as substantial parts of *The Dynasts* are literally unstageable:*

> *At once, as earlier, a preternatural clearness possesses the atmosphere of the battle-field, in which the scene becomes anatomised and the living masses of humanity transparent. The controlling Immanent Will appears therein, as a brain-like network of currents and ejections, twitching, interpenetrating, entangling, and thrusting hither and thither the human forms.*[†]

Vile cynics might add that it is also literally unstageable since Hardy's ear for dialogue is less than completely felicitous in this work:

> SPIRIT SINISTER: Come, Sprite, don't carry your ironies too far, or you may wake up the Unconscious Itself, and tempt It to let all the gory clock-work of the show run down to spite me![‡]

– a line which makes me, for one, think more kindly of the sort of dialogue like what Ernie Wise wrote. Surprisingly, plenty of otherwise talented people thought that *The Dynasts* was tip-top stuff, including Siegfried Sassoon, Ford Madox Ford and Walter de la Mare. Astoundingly, one of the admiring crowd was Max Beerbohm. For those who have not yet had the good luck to encounter Beerbohm's *Seven Men* (1919), let me try to justify that little spasm of incredulity in the last sentence by recommending one of the stories in

---

* In its definitive form, that is. A chopped-down version was performed some years ago at Chichester, reputedly with some success.

[†] Hardy, *The Dynasts*, p. 172.

[‡] Ibid., p. 336.

Seven Men, ' "Savonarola" Brown', which ends with a lengthy parody of rubbishy historical drama in general and the idiocies of stage directions in particular. Its most sublimely hilarious moment is the stage direction for the end of Act III:

> (*Re-enter Guelfs and Ghibellines fighting.* SAV. *and* LUC. *are arrested by Papal officers. Enter* MICHAEL ANGELO. ANDREA DEL SARTO *appears for a moment at a window.* PIPPA *passes. Brothers of the Misericordia go by, singing a Requiem for Francesca da Rimini. Enter* BOCCACCIO, BENVENUTO CELLINI, *and many others, making remarks highly characteristic of themselves* but scarcely audible through the terrific thunderstorm which now bursts over Florence and is at its loudest and darkest crisis as the Curtain falls.†*)

In the decades since Beerbohm's glorious parody appeared, playwrights have tended to become more tight-lipped and rigorous in their approach to directions;‡ if you wanted to suggest a paradigmatic stage direction for the drama of the later twentieth century, you could hardly do better than Harold Pinter's legendary: '(*Pause.*)' It would be

---

* Blissful joke; but was Beerbohm perhaps half-remembering Shakespeare's 'APEMANTUS, *discontentedly, like himself* '?

† Note, again, the hint of Wagnerian Armageddon.

‡ There are exceptions.

> *The apartment faces an alley and is entered by a fire escape, a structure whose name is a touch of accidental poetic truth, for all of these large buildings are always burning with the slow and implacable fires of human desperation . . .*
>
> Tennessee Williams, *The Glass Menagerie* (1944)

Believe me, I could have chosen something far worse.

lovely to say that the return to modesty was a direct result of Beerbohm's spoof; the real reasons are doubtless to be found elsewhere, and above all in the newly thriving cults of the director and designer. Plenty of playwrights are now happy either to collaborate with their creative partners or simply to stand back and let them get on with the squalid task of presenting their text to the public. In quite a few contemporary playscripts* you will find that the printed directions are less an indication of the playwright's ideal vision than a straightforward record of how the play was staged in its first or most profitable run. Which, of course, may be exactly what has been handed down with us between the lines of Shakespeare's plays.

This is not to say, however, that the history of stage directions has come full circle – centuries of functional scribbles, fifty-odd years of unwonted eloquence, a gradual return to the utilitarian. Slightly closer to the mark would be Marx's old thigh-slapper about the tendency of history to repeat itself, the first time as tragedy, the second time as farce. Writers continued to lavish the greatest care and ingenuity on footnotes well after the heyday of GBS, Harley Granville-Barker and company, but they increasingly did so in search of a laugh, and in the spirit of parody. Beerbohm is one star of this movement, and another is Ring Lardner, who wrote eight or nine so-called 'Dada' (though he was no Dadaist) or nonsense plays, ripe with demented stage directions. These included *The Tridget of Greva*, *Dinner Bridge* (much admired by Edmund Wilson, who published it in the

---

* Such as some of Peter Shaffer's plays (Michael Billington's example).

New Republic), *Clemo Uti – The Water Lillies* (whose first act curtain rises on 'the outskirts of a parchesi board'), *Cora, or Fun at a Spa* (subtitled *An Expressionist Drama of Love, Death and Sex*), *Taxidea Americana* and a parody of Eugene O'Neill's *Mourning Becomes Electra*,* consisting in large measure of menus for the ample lunches and dinners to be served between acts, entitled *Quadroon – A Play in Four Pelts Which May All Be Attended in One Day or Missed in a Group*.† His three-act drama *I Gaspiri* (*The Upholsterers*), 'Adapted from the Bukovinian of Casper Redmonda', gives a fair idea of the genre. We join the proceedings at the end of Act I:

(Three outsiders named Klein go across the stage three times. They think they are in a public library. A woman's cough is heard offstage left.)

A NEW CHARACTER: Who is that cough?

TWO MOORS: That is my mother. She died a little while ago in a haphazard way.

A GREEK: And what a woman she was!

(The curtain is lowered for seven days to denote the lapse of a week.)

ACT II

(Deleted by the censor.)

---

* O'Neill's stage directions are, as Lardner might have said, a whole other ball game. Mercy forbids extensive quotation.

† See Donald Elder, *Ring Lardner* (New York: Doubleday, 1956), pp. 283–8; and Jonathan Yardley, *Ring* (New York: Random House, 1977), pp. 270–72.

ACT III

*(The Lincoln Highway. Two bearded glue lifters are seated at
one side of the road. . . .)*

One or two critics made fairly large claims for the
philosophical dimensions of Lardner's work, though the best
theory is that he was just mucking about. Still, it's odd that
he isn't cited more frequently as a Yankee precursor of the
Theatre of the Absurd, especially since that movement's
most enduring genius, Samuel Beckett, has one or two
faintly *Gaspiri*-ish touches in his work, and was fond of
making some genuinely philosophical jokes in his stage
directions: look at his 'Three Dialogues with Georges
Duthuit',* or at the make-up suggestions for *Rockaby*, or at
the set description for his television play *Ghost Trio* (in which
a window is described as 'imperceptibly ajar'; *imperceptibly*?),
or at the sly note about Hodge the Cat in his uncompleted
first play, *Human Wishes*.† Beckett is also, surely, the only
great playwright ever to have written plays which consist
wholly of brief stage directions – *Act Without Words*, and
Breath, which lasts well under a minute and is peopled by
motionless actors strewn around a landscape more devas-
tated than anything dreamed of by Wagner.

To put it mildly. Beckett's spare and scrupulous and
astringently witty notations are so far removed from Wagner's gigantism that they might be the product of an entirely

---

* 'D.—One moment. Are you suggesting that the painting of van Velde is
   inexpressive?
   B.—(*A fortnight later*) Yes.'

† Published in *Disjecta*.

different civilization, yet there is at least one bridge between them, and his name is James Joyce. Beckett worked as a sort of secretary for Joyce, learning a great deal from him about what the art of writing was and might be; Joyce, having idolized Ibsen in his youth* but failed to emulate his Norwegian master in *Exiles*, went on to write the most sustained and searching parody of elaborate stage notations in the 'Circe' episode of *Ulysses*; and, here's the pay-off, one of the targets he has most frequently before him is the megalomaniacal grandiloquence of Wagner. My guess is that there's at least one passage in 'Circe' which simultaneously makes fun both of *The Ring* and of *The Master Builder*:

STEPHEN: *Nothung!*

(He lifts his ashplant high with both hands and smashes the chandelier. Time's livid final flame leaps and, in the following darkness, ruin of all space, shattered glass and toppling masonry.)

Wagner and Ibsen aren't the only big guns Joyce has in mind. 'Circe' makes exuberant mock of every visionary playwright who has ever chafed against the limitations of the stage, yearned to encompass continents and epochs, lay waste the earth, storm the heavens, and generally try it on a bit:

(Bloom walks on a net, covers his left eye with his left ear, passes through several walls, climbs Nelson's Pillar, hangs from the top ledge by his eyelids, eats twelve dozen oysters (shells included),

---

* At the age of eighteen, he wrote an enthusiastic review of *When We Dead Awaken* (1899) for the *Fortnightly Review*.

heals several sufferers from king's evil, contracts his face so as to resemble many historical personages, Lord Beaconsfield, Lord Byron, Wat Tyler, Moses of Egypt, Moses Maimonides, Moses Mendelssohn, Henry Irving, Rip van Winkle, Kossuth, Jean Jacques Rousseau, Baron Leopold Rothschild, Robinson Crusoe, Sherlock Holmes, Pasteur, turns each foot simultaneously in different directions, bids the tide turn back, eclipses the sun by extending his little finger.)

And there's plenty more where that came from; more than a hundred pages of hallucinatory fun and games, which makes 'Circe' longer than *Hamlet*. Massively influential as it was, *Ulysses* alone was not potent enough to put paid to the lavish stage direction, although anyone who wanted to draw a line across the chronological chart at the exact point when the triumphant half-century of the s.d. came to an end could do a lot worse than plump for the novel's publication date, 1922. What Joyce did achieve, among so many other things, was the most brilliantly sustained demonstration of all the effects that prose writers might steal or liberate from the brackets and italics of their more successful cousins the playwrights. But that is a different story, and it is time to lower the curtain.

(JACKSON groans, leans back in his chair and massages the small of his back, which is giving him gyp. Can he knock off for the day? No, for his editor has no mercy. JACKSON groans again, scuttles to the fridge for a glass of cheap white wine, returns to his chair, opens a new file and types out three new words.)

Lectures: A Lecture

I spoke to them of the early Florentines, and they slept as though no crime had ever stained the ravines of their mountain home.

Oscar Wilde, on his lecture to the miners of Leadville

'LADIES AND GENTLEMEN,

'It is customary for a lecturer to open his or her address with some throwaway observation about the particular circumstances of her or his lecture: to allude, perhaps, to the dismal or glorious state of the weather – though not, nowadays, quite so floridly as Emerson did in 1838 when he prefaced his lecture to the Divinity College in Cambridge with the words "In this refulgent summer, it has been a luxury to draw the breath of life. . . ."

'More typically, the lecturer might begin by paying respects to previous lecturers in the same series, or making some flimsy quip to win the audience's goodwill, or otherwise ingratiating himself – or, of course I must rapidly add, *her*self – with the company; but, in an august and erudite gathering such as this, I would obviously be foolish to try to warm things up with some vulgar ploy such as . . . such as, perhaps, recalling some famous comic lectures in fiction – Jim Dixon's disastrous "Merrie England" address in *Lucky*

Jim, perhaps, or Morris Zapp's pyrotechnical discourse on interpretation as striptease in David Lodge's *Small World* or – a less flagrantly caricatural, but no less telling study – Robyn Penrose's brisk and knowing dissection of ideology in the Industrial Novel in the same author's *Nice Work*. You may rest assured that I shall not be presumptuous enough to refer to these, or any other fictional works too well known to warrant discussion.

'There is another prefatorial convention, however – and, by the way, a radio producer once told me that one should never use words like "however" or "moreover" in a broadcast script –; another convention, I suggest, which most lecturers can benefit from following, and that is to proffer some show of appropriately becoming modesty. At times, the tone of these throat-clearing exercises may be close to apologetic. Such was the tone adopted by the great American psychologist and philosopher William James when, in 1901, he travelled to Edinburgh to give the Gifford Lectures on Natural Religion: "It is with no small amount of trepidation", he began, "that I take my place behind this desk, and face this learned audience." By referring to his "trepidation", the psychologist might easily have been about to launch into a discussion of that strange mental affliction, the fear of public speaking – an affliction so widespread that, I am reliably informed, it comes second only to the fear of heights in the top ten chart of phobias; it has certainly brought agonies to the most celebrated of lecturers, including the otherwise dauntless William Morris. On that particular day, though, James was not directly concerned with morbid mental symptoms: he was performing a ritual act of humility. He went on to explain that, while Americans were very much in the habit of sitting quietly and listening to Europeans talking, "the contrary habit, of talking while the Europeans listen, we have not yet acquired; and in him who first makes the adventure it begets a certain sense of apology being due for so presumptuous an act". Since the lectures James was about to give were the first version of his masterpiece *The Varieties of Religious Experience* – a wonderful book I heartily commend to anyone here today who has not yet had the pleasure of reading it – it is hard not to feel that his avowed diffidence was a bit overstated . . . though, for all its conventionality, it does not seem to have been at all insincere. Well! There's seldom much profit to be had from ignoring a tried and trusted formula – or come to that, a tried and trusted phrase like "tried and trusted": in oral presentations, a certain indulgence in cliché is not so much permissible as mandatory, if you want the audience to follow you without too much strain. (Lectures are almost by definition a sloppier medium than essays for print, which is one reason why James, despite the extraordinary success of, among other talks, *Pragmatism*, which drew well over a thousand listeners, dreamed of "abandoning the squashy popular-lecture style": I owe this point to Margaret Knight's old collection of James's writings.) And so, I've decided to begin my remarks with a double apology: first for the necessarily cursory nature of this hop, skip and jump through the lecture genre in the short time available to us, and second – a far more important expression of regret – I'd like to apologize directly to the audience for the fact that they, which is to say *you*, do not exist.

'The only justification I can offer for this act of ontological discourtesy is, again, the justification of precedent – the precedent of a psychologist who we must surely continue to regard, despite the assaults on his reputation, as a writer and thinker quite as great as William James. I refer, of course, to Sigmund Freud. If you consult the volume entitled *New Introductory Lectures on Psychoanalysis*, which was written in 1932 and translated by James Strachey (Penguin issued it in paperback in 1973), you will find that chapter one – which is to say, Lecture 29 – begins like this:

> "LADIES AND GENTLEMEN, – If, after an interval of more than fifteen years, I have brought you together again to discuss with you what novelties, and what improvements, it may be the intervening time has introduced into psychoanalyis . . ."

Freud's "If . . ." was a pretty major "If . . ."; for, as a matter of fact, he had not brought together any such collection of auditors, and the male and female faces he addressed existed wholly in his active fantasy life. I shall be returning to the topic of Freud the lecturer in a short while (every lecturer should provide clear signposts to the road ahead); first, I'd like to provide something of the literary and cultural context of his public talks.

'Freud, we are often reminded by his detractors and supporters alike, was very much a man of the nineteenth century, and it is significant that the most widely distributed and translated of all Freud's books in his own lifetime (their only close rival is *The Psychopathology of Everyday Life*) should have taken the form of lectures, for the lecture was as characteristic a literary product of that century as – for reasons I'd like to hear explained by a professional Victorianist – a vaguely related form, the dramatic monologue.

Obviously, this isn't to say that the nineteenth century invented lecturing, which has an exceptionally noble ancestry going back, in Europe, to classical oratory, to sermons, and to medieval courses of instruction in universities – many if not all of these utterances being delivered from memory, and constructed, if we are to believe Dame Frances Yates, in accordance with occult mnemonic systems. Some of the most imposing pillars of the Western canon are cast in the form: the works of Aristotle, for example, are essentially a vast and incomplete set of lecture notes; and some modern critics have contended that all literature may be regarded as a development of certain principles of public speaking. But it was not until some way into the eighteenth century that the public lecture became a well-recognized form of secular entertainment and improvement, and not until the nineteenth century that a writer could reasonably expect to win riches and influence people by reading out homilies, digressions or rants to paying crowds.

'Consider the masters of the form in some emblematic moments: at the start of the century, Coleridge, eking out his pitiful income with rambling, idiosyncratic, fitfully sublime, mostly extemporaneous talks on Shakespeare at £140 a series that, in scraps and tatters and mangled reports, have become classics of Romantic criticism; then Emerson, talking his solemn way painfully to glory around the young republic; then Carlyle, suffering agonies of emotional stress as he spoke of *Heroes and Hero-Worship* to glittering audiences, with such resounding success that he promptly gave up this blend of "prophecy and play-acting", and never spoke in public again; then Ruskin, declaring open war time and again on the commercial spirit of his age, and fulminating like a hell-fire preacher at the Bradford merchants who had asked him to chat to them about their proposed Exchange building; then Pater, mumbling of beauty to the ardent young men of Oxford ("I hope you heard me," Pater said to Wilde after a talk on Merimée; "We overheard you," Wilde replied); and then, best remembered of all, Wilde himself, the young disciple of Ruskin and Pater, single-handedly invading the United States with a rather different doctrine of beauty, but none the less deploying a mannerism – the interjection "Well!" – that he had stolen directly from Pater. (The sharper-eared among you may have noticed that I had resort to this interjection myself a few minutes ago.)

'Great moments, and, as the century grew older, great rewards. Wilde's lecture tour took some $18,000 at the box office, of which Wilde pocketed $5,000. (Matthew Arnold, who lectured in America the year after Wilde, was indiscreet enough to admit that he only did it for the money – he needed to bail out his spendthrift son.) Even after the advent of television, which closed down so many lecture halls, swallowed up the lecture genre whole and regurgitated it in the form of the "authored series" such as Lord Clark's *Civilization* or Simon Schama's *Landscape and Memory* or Robert Hughes's *American Visions* (to mention only three modern-day successors to Ruskin's pulpit) – even after this, the American lecture tour continued to be a reliable money-spinner for the gifted (think of W. H. Auden's cheerful poem "On The Circuit") or the merely famous, though no professional writer has so far matched the fee Ronald Reagan took from his hosts in Japan: a cool $12,000,000 for just eight days.

'In the epoch before television, public speaking was so

reputable a diversion that even the talentless and the obscure could make a comfortable living at it, provided they were well supplied with glibness and dimples. If you'd like to see a scathing portrait of the ghastly, genteel middle-brow climate which made careers of the latter type possible, simply consult Edith Wharton's sardonic tale "The Pelican", first published in 1899.

' "The next time I saw her", says the male narrator of the story's heroine, or villainess, Mrs Amyot, "was in New York, when she had become so fashionable that it was part of the whole duty of woman to be seen at her lectures ... The subject of her discourse (I think it was Ruskin) was clearly of minor importance, not only to my friend, but to the throng of well-dressed and absent-minded ladies who rustled in late, dropped their muffs, and pocketbooks, and undisguisedly lost themselves in a study of each other's apparel."

'Thank heavens things have changed in the last hundred years! But, before we preen ourselves on our superiority, it would be worth recalling that other accounts of nineteenth-century novelists offer perspectives that are rather less flattering to us. If the lecture is one of the vital genres of that time, then the report or memoir of a given lecture is one of its livelier sub-genres. Mrs Amyot's remarks on Ruskin may have been anodyne, but the man himself could be electrifying. There's a splendid passage in one of A. E. Housman's letters, written in 1877 when he was an undergraduate at Oxford, describing the afternoon when Ruskin brought in a framed and glassed picture by Turner, depicting the landscape near Leicester. To dramatize the horrors that industrialism had inflicted on earth, sky and water, Ruskin took up a paintbrush and slapped an indigo factory, a soap factory, an iron bridge and other horrors onto the glass:

> '". . . A puff and a cloud of smoke all over Turner's sky; and then the brush thrown down, and Ruskin confronting modern civilization amid a tempest of applause, which he always elicits now, as he has this term become immensely popular, his lectures being crowded, whereas of old he used to prophesy to empty benches . . ."

'Ralph Waldo Emerson, as I've already suggested, made first his living and then his name with tireless lecture tours – sweltering in cheap hotels and a Great Lakes steamer, freezing in blizzards, having his pocket picked, almost catching cholera and, as Mark Van Doren summed up, "in general suffer[ing] the exhaustions incident to 'a puppet show of Eleusinian mysteries', as he once called his trade." Though he was not always successful in holding attention – Emerson's great failing, which he lamented himself, was that he had no sense of humour, and it pained him to see frontier audiences walking out on him because he wasn't cracking jokes – he could, at his best, be quite magnificent. James Russell Lowell remembered him in these words:

> '"I have heard some great speakers and some accomplished orators, but never any that so moved and persuaded men as he. There is a kind of undertow in that rich baritone of his that sweeps our minds from their deeper waters with a drift we cannot and would not resist. And how artfully (for Emerson is a long-studied artist in these things) does the deliberate utterance, that seems waiting for the fit word, seem to admit us partners in the labor of thought, and make us feel as if the glance of humour were a sudden

suggestion, as if the perfect phrase lying there were as unexpected to him as to us."

'Lowell's account is better than a tribute: it's a sharp, if appetizingly brief analysis of the high skill Emerson brought to his lecturing – an art which involves many of the ploys of the actor as well as those of the writer. (In case I've not made this point plainly enough already, let me spell it out: *a good writer isn't always a good lecturer*. Melville, for one, was such a terrible public speaker that one newspaper in Rockford, Illinois protested that "It has rarely been our lot to witness a more painful infliction upon an audience", while another declared that "No man has a right to set himself up as a lecturer at $50 per night, who cannot for one minute take his eyes from his manuscript.") In many cases, we have word-perfect versions of the texts of great lectures, but unless these texts are supplemented by anecdotes such as Housman's and Lowell's, or by technical annotations, such as the minutely annotated map of Oscar Wilde's speech mannerisms drawn up by Helen Potter for her book *Impersonations* (1891), we can have only an etiolated and impoverished notion of what a given talk was actually like. "Oh, to be reading greats at B[rasenose] C[ollege]", wrote the *fin de siècle* poet Lionel Johnson in his review of Walter Pater's *Plato and Platonists*, ruefully acknowledging how greatly these writings, full though they are of agreeably chatty allusions to Oxford life, would have been enriched by being there to hear Pater mumble them.

'Fortunately for us, we have both the definitive texts and a fair number of biographical supplements in the case of the man who might be regarded as the last great Victorian lecturer – for, as I promised, we have now come full circle and returned to Sigmund Freud, to whom I will devote the majority of the scant, and rapidly diminishing time now available to us.

'As Freud points out in the preface to his *New Introductory Lectures on Psychoanalysis*, two major events had taken place between the delivery of his original *Introductory Lectures* in the Winter Terms of 1915–16 and 1916–17 in the lecture rooms of the Vienna Psychiatric Clinic: he had grown too old to be a full-time member of the University, and he had endured surgery which made public speaking impossible for him.

> '"If, therefore," Freud sums up, "I once more take my place in the lecture room during the remarks that follow, it is only by an artifice of the imagination; it may help me not to forget to bear the reader in mind as I enter more deeply into my subject."

'It is a fascinating sentence, and Freud himself has given us some of the means to look at it a little more closely. Is Freud's suggestion that he needs to fantasize about *listeners* so as to pay due attention to *the reader* really so plausible? After all, one of Freud's most consistent strengths as a writer is the exemplary lucidity with which he can expound ideas of unusual, indeed poetic complexity. And even if he found the imagining of an audience a useful expository discipline, did he really need to keep jogging his own memory at the begging of each new chapter, as he does, by writing out a ritual repetition of the greeting "LADIES AND GENTLE-MEN"? Was there perhaps something about the precise nature of his illness that called out for a wish-fulfilling fantasy about engaging in sustained and fluent speech? Was Freud fully aware – as the father of, precisely, the *talking* cure, he can scarcely have been wholly unaware – of the role-reversal involved in standing up for an hour and talking about dreams and suchlike to people who mostly stay silent, when the psychoanalyst's usual practice is to sit more or less silently for fifty minutes and listen to a patient talking about dreams and suchlike?

'I don't presume even to begin to answer such questions here; they're the proper study of intellectual historians and psychoanalysts themselves, rather than a *flâneur* through the winding alleys of the paratext and surrounding neighbourhoods. What I will venture is that Freud's awareness of the conventions of lecturing not only colours the manner in which he expresses his ideas, but plays a considerable part in determining their content. And, as you might expect from my earlier remarks, I'd also suggest that this is also the case with many lecturers other than Freud; my reason for dwelling on him at length today is that I believe his individual practices can point us to some general principles.

'We shouldn't be surprised, Freud once remarked, if "the influence of a work is determined not by the strength of its arguments but by its affective tone." Some people, including some people of genius, won't admit the force of such arguments: Samuel Johnson, for example, once denied that it was possible for a student to derive any benefit from a lecture that he could not just as satisfactorily dig out of a book, except, perhaps, when the subject demanded a certain amount of demonstration, as in a chemistry experiment. A similar thought must have struck every student who has snoozed or shuffled buttocks through a tedious, meandering exposition by some ignorant, witless pedagogue; but I'm going to be patricidal towards Johnson for a change, and suggest that Freud came closer to the truth: the personality of the speaker (more exactly, the speaker's *persona*) may do more than any rigorous display of logic or erudition alone to persuade or educate an audience. (As Richard Ellmann writes of Wilde, he "had lectured to [Americans] as much through rhythm and manner as through argument, heaping up cadences to make them imagine the beauty he did not define . . .") We can see a number of ways in which Freud played on and played up the "affective tone" of his lectures. From the very outset, he engages in a sly set of rhetorical games with them, urging them not to "be annoyed, then, if I begin by treating you in the same way as . . . neurotic patients", and pretending to do everything in his power to dissuade them from attending a series of talks which will only enrage them: "I seriously advise you not to join my audience a second time". And then there was his general demeanour; quiet, but compelling. He was a bold, almost reckless improviser. Just before one of his talks, Ernest Jones asked him what the subject would be, and Freud replied, "If I only knew! I must leave it to my unconscious." This was an extreme case, but it was typical of Freud to deliver talks extempore from notes rather than script every word; roughly the first half of the original *Introductory Lectures* were improvised on his feet, and only written down immediately afterwards. His lectures, one is tempted to say, leapt straight from his unconscious to the grouped unconscious of his audience. Even when he had prepared a full script, Freud would often improvise, digress, and welcome remarks from the floor. One of his followers recalled that "Freud was fond of using the Socratic method. He would break off his formal exposition to ask question or invite criticism. When objections were forthcoming, he would deal with them wittily and forcibly." (The follower in question was F. Wittells, in his *Sigmund Freud: His Personality, His Teaching, and His School*, published in 1924.) Consistent with this preference, Freud made it a rule that papers delivered to the Vienna Psychoanalytic Society be improvised from notes or from memory, believing that the delivery of a script hampered intimacy.

'The sense of being privy both to the calculated and to the unbidden movements of Freud's mind was intensified for his audiences by the strikingly intimate tone he adopted; and this tone seems to have been as much a help to Freud as it was to his listeners. Theodor Reik recalls that Freud

'"once wrote to me that when he lectured he chose one sympathetic person from among the audience and imagined that he was addressing this person alone. If this person was absent from among his listeners, he would not feel at ease until he had found someone to understudy, so to speak. This attitude explains the direct address form of his lectures and the manner in which he anticipated objections, formulating the doubts and questions of his audience as he could their minds."

'In his valuable book *Freud as a Writer*, to which I am indebted for many of these facts, Patrick J. Mahony argues convincingly that in 1912 and 1913 it was Lou Andreas-Salomé who provided Freud with his target audience and source of confidence; when she didn't show up, he complained of speaking "uncertainly", and of staring fixedly at the empty place where she usually sat. Mahony also points out the way in which Freud contrives an air of earnestness and propriety in his lectures – an important defensive measure, in the days when psychoanalysis was first a scandal – by his insistent recourse to terms such as "right", "correct" and their cognates in German: in the first two lectures alone, we find: *berichtigt* (justified), *Anrecht* (right, claim), *Richtung* (direction), *Unterricht* (training), *Richtigkeit* (correctness), *Verrichtungen* (procedures), *mit Recht* (rightly) and many others: Mahony describes their frequency as "amazing".

'As to the question of how the content of Freud's arguments could be determined by their context, perhaps the clearest example comes from the talks he gave at Clark University in 1909. Freud attempted to make the concept of repression and resistance vivid to his audience by asking them to imagine that one of their number has turned into an oafish heckler; then to imagine that he has the man evicted from the hall. Freud returns to his abstract discussion, and then interrupts himself by suggesting that the heckler is now making such an intolerable racket outside the door that no one can concentrate. At this point in the visionary proceedings, the President of Clark University, Dr Stanley Hall, intervenes. He permits the heckler to be allowed back into the room; pacified, the man now becomes docile and the lecture is continued; as is Freud's previous line of thought . . .

'Now, I can plainly see that, although you are just as much of a rhetorical fiction as Freud's repressed hooligan, many of you are already bursting to interrupt me and bombard me with objections and, no doubt, abuse. I shall, of course, be only to happy to answer your imaginary questions in a few moments, but as the clock on the wall informs me that our hour has almost come, I shall have to break off here with the traditional expression of thanks for your kind attention; and since my own powers of eloquence are scarcely adequate to the non-existent courtesy you have shown me today, I have chosen to end by borrowing some words of Carlyle – the very last words he ever spoke as a lecturer, on Friday 22 May, 1840, and which we can now read as the final paragraph of *On Heroes and Hero-Worship*:

> ' "Often enough, with these abrupt utterances thrown-out, isolated, unexplained, has your tolerance been put to the trial. Tolerance, patient candour, all-hoping favour and kindness, which I will not speak of at present. The accomplished and distinguished, the beautiful, the wise, something of what is best in England, have listened patiently to my rude words. With many feelings, I heartily thank you all; and say, Good be with you all!" '

Follies*

Rats who construct the maze from which they must escape

Commonly cited description of the Oulipians

A *Void*, the English translation (1994) by Gilbert Adair of Georges Perec's novel *La Disparition* (1968), boasts many gloriously ingenious qualities, far and away the most ingenious of which is its triumphant execution of a feat quite unrivalled (for its only plausible competitor, *Gadsby*, published in 1939 by the American author Ernest Vincent Wright, and dedicated 'To Youth', is a piffling fifty thousand words long and, by all accounts – I must admit I have not gone to the trouble of reading it – of negligible literary worth) in our literature: in the entire course of its 280-odd pages, which recount a detective story of sorts about a search for two kidnapped men, *A Void*, in punctilious emulation of its French original, never once uses the letter 'e'.

B ut what, you may well ask in exasperated or wondering tones, is the point of such a bizarre literary stunt, how-

---

* My heading is not intended pejoratively; it's an allusion to Isaac D'Israeli's chapter on lipograms and such in *Curiosities of Literature*; see below, pp. 235–46.

ever dazzling, funny and – unlikely as it may seem to anyone who has not made a foray into its 'e'-less thickets – ultimately moving (for the book proves to be about a far greater loss than that of a mere unit of the alphabet, and it aches with that loss: Perec's parents were 'disappeared' in the Second World War) its execution?

C ertainly, the exercise must appear perverse to the point of lunacy in Britain, where the prevailing fictional mode, notwithstanding the best efforts of our experimentalists, Goths, SF writers, psychogeographers, magic realists and others, remains steeped in the well-mannered conventions of nineteenth-century realism; in France, the traditional home of all manner of artistic experiment, works such as *La Disparition* tend to find a much more sympathetic and informed reception.

D espite, that is to say, occasional lofty dismissals by the stuffier members of Paris's cultural *arrière garde*, the work of Georges Perec (1936–1982) – and one should hasten to add that *La Disparition* is far from being either the best-known or the most awe-provoking work of a remarkably fecund career, which began in triumph with his prize-winning, if widely misunderstood novel *Les Choses*, and attained its capstone in 1978 with another prize-winner, *La Vie mode d'emploi* (*Life: A User's Manual*) – is not only widely admired by the literate French, but also widely understood as a product, if that word is not too glumly industrial or basely biological in connotation, of the curious post-war literary movement to which Perec belonged: Oulipo, or OuLiPo, the *Ouvroir de littérature potentielle* ('workshop', or, as Harry Mathews once translated it, 'sewing circle for potential literature'),

an elite group of writers, mathematicians and writer-
mathematicians, founded by the novelist Raymond
Queneau and the chess master François Le Lionnais in
1960 (or, as Harry Mathews's version has it, in 1961) at
a conference in Cerisy-la-Salle and dedicated to the composition of works in accordance with rigorous formal
constraints: some of them already well known, such as
anagrams, pangrams, palindromes (Perec wrote what
has already been acknowledged by the *Guinness Book of
Records* as the longest palindrome in any language – it
is, one suspects, the longest that the mind of man will
ever conceive – which runs some five hundred words in
each direction, and includes the words 'palindrome' and
'Perec' in both its opening and, inescapably, its closing
lines) and the rules of the Japanese game of Go (the
basis for a selection of poems by Jacques Roubaud;
Perec, as one might expect, excelled at this game); some
of them revived from antiquity, such as the lipogram, in
which a single letter of the alphabet (or, sometimes,
more than one letter) is strictly excluded, as in *La
Disparition*; and some wholly novel ones which Oulipo
members invent for themselves and present to each
other at the group's reputedly lively and bibulous
monthly meetings.

E ven those British readers to whom the name 'Oulipo' is
unfamiliar will probably have heard of *Life: A User's
Manual* (the English translation is by David Bellos), a
tome of quite staggering complexity which, among many
other Oulipian constraints, describes its way in 99 chapters (it is crucial, for reasons too complex to explain here,
that there should not be 100) round the apartments in an

imaginary French house, 11 rue Simon Crubellier, following what chess players know as a 'knight's tour' around
a 10 x 10 grid; incidentally, the one other Oulipian (except,
maybe, Raymond Queneau) with a fairly sizeable reputation in Britain, Italo Calvino, used the rules of the tarot
pack to give order to his novel *The Castle of Crossed
Destinies*, and a far more complex scheme – idiosyncrati-
cally adapted, in Calvino's own words, from 'the formulations of structural semiology of A. J. Greimas' – to
discipline the giddying *mis-en-abîme* of *If on a Winter's
Night a Traveller*; interested readers should consult the
intricate diagrams in his article 'How I Wrote One of My
Books' (the article's title, like that of Marcel Benabou's
Why I Have Not Written Any of My Books, alludes to
Raymond Roussel's *Comment j'ai écrit certains de mes livres*,
1935 – 'Roussel's book possesses what is surely one of the
most misleading titles in literary history', writes Warren
Motte, an American scholar of the Oulipo and its works),
which can be found translated in *Oulipo Laboratory* (edited
by Alastair Brotchie, London: Atlas, 1995).

F or anyone who would like to find out more about the
Oulipo, that modest volume is one of the best starting
points, since it includes, besides Calvino's essay, the
Oulipo manifestos by François Le Lionnais; Raymond
Queneau's set of quasi-Euclidean axioms 'The Foundations of Literature'; some funny and beguiling eye-rhyme
sonnets and limericks by Harry Mathews; and the complete text of a work which, had the French author not
got there first, I would have been profoundly tempted to
try myself – Paul Fournel's *Suburbia*, a spoof 'novel' (it's
partly a joke about the humourless pedantry of the

annotated editions of contemporary fiction given to
French schoolchildren) made up exclusively of paratexts:
a title, a disclaimer ('This is a work of pure fiction . . .'), a
copyright statement, two epigraphs, a dedication, a Table
of Contents, a 'Word from the Publisher', a Foreword by
Marguerite Duras, an Introductory Note by the Author,
a set of running footnotes, an Afterword by François
Caradec, a 'Supplement for School Use', including a
(mendacious) note on the Author and questions about
Suburbia's subject and form, an Index of place names, a
list of Errata ('52 for: he pisses through the door of the
lift read: he passes through the door of the lift'), a rear-
cover-style author's blurb, plus bar code and prices; the
novel's 'text', allegedly a couple of hundred pages long,
is completely blank; *Suburbia* is thus, as Alastair Brotchie
points out, a lipogram in a, b, c, d, e, f, g, h, i, j, k, l, m,
n, o, p, q, r, s, t, u, v, w, x, y and z.

G iven the apparent perversity – at times, one might think,
well-nigh impossibility – of some of the hoops which
Perec, Calvino, Queneau, Benabou, Fournel and company have lovingly constructed for themselves to jump
through, however, perhaps the most remarkable aspect
of Oulipian writing is its capacity to delight, to instruct
and to move, whether to giggles or to more sombre
manifestations of feeling.

H arry Mathews's novel *Tlooth*, for example, contains a droll
'blue movie' scene in which the initial consonants of its
drooling words are swapped around – I believe 'metath-
esized' is the technical word – much as the Reverend
Spooner might have jumbled them had he made an
improbable career move into pornography: '. . . I found

myself facing the swerving eeks of her chass, molded by muthing but their own nuscles under the elasticated skitted nirt . . .'; while Mathews's intermittently harrowing love story 'Their Words, For You', from his book *Selected Declarations of Dependence* is made up wholly of 'preverbs', which is to say twisted or cross-bred proverbs, which is to say that it has a vocabulary of fewer than two hundred words, lifted from forty-four well-known phrases or sayings such as 'red sky at night, shepherd's delight' or 'every cloud has a silver lining' or 'a stitch in time saves nine'; its final sentence is, I find, unaccountably haunting: 'Red clouds dispose the night.'

I t makes sound Oulipian sense that Perec should have been the one to translate *Tlooth* and other works by Mathews into French (they were close friends, and Mathews wrote an affectionate memoir of Perec, *The Orchard*, which borrowed the form of Perec's *Je me souviens*), since, regarded from a certain angle, translation – the attempt to construct in one language a precise counterpart of a work originally written in another – is itself the kind of formal constraint that Oulipo would have had to invent had it not already been a routine literary practice for centuries; by the way, the Oulipian term for any form which can in some way or another be seen as a precursor of their methods, such as the lipogram or the sestina, is 'anticipatory plagiarism', and their roll call of anticipatory plagiarists includes the Mallorcan philosopher Ramon Lull, whose *Ars Magna* (much admired by Giordano Bruno), with its figure of a permutatory and combinatory language system based on as many as fourteen concentric circles of words, has been

      proposed as a forerunner of Queneau's inexhaustible
      work *100,000,000,000,000 Poems* (see below, under 'Q').

J   okes, as many writers have observed, can be among the
      hardest things to translate, which means that Perec –
      whose own jokes very often depend on cunning allusions
      to his favourite (or least favourite) authors, including
      Herman Melville and Thomas Mann – often had to
      abandon strict fidelity to come up with suitable French
      counterparts to Mathews's word-play, and which also
      means that Gilbert Adair was obliged, in similar fashion,
      radically to rework a section of *La Disparition* where
      Perec strips the 'e's from six well-known French poems
      by reworking, instead, half-a-dozen equally familiar
      English poems (faithfully maintaining metre, general
      sense and, where appropriate, a comparable rhyme
      scheme), 'all of which', as he explained to me, 'hover
      over the theme of negativity in some way, so that Edgar
      Allan Poe's "The Raven" becomes "Blackbird" by Arthur
      Gordon Pym and Milton's "On His Blindness" becomes
      "On His Glaucoma"; "Ozymandias", for obvious reasons,
      can keep its title, though Shelley has to become P.B.S." . . .'

(K   afka, one should add by way of parenthesis to that remark
      about 'favourite authors', seems to have been the writer
      Perec most revered – he once wrote to Jacques Roubaud
      that the three writers who had provided him with his
      self-image were 'Kafka, Kafka and Franz Kafka' – and one
      of Perec's unrealized (as far as I know) projects was a
      drama about Kafka's use of language, entitled *Wie ein
      Hund* (an allusion to the last line of *The Trial*, 'Like a
      dog . . .'); though Kafka can't be regarded as one of
      Oulipo's anticipatory plagiarists, the two did have certain

things in common – their condition as European Jews, a marked facial similarity (or so Perec liked to believe), and so on – and Perec would surely have been alive to the fact that the letter 'K', which has come to be emblematic of the Czech writer's work, is something of an underdog (*'wie ein Hund'*), almost a *Gastarbeiter*, in the French language.)

'L iberating' is the paradoxical adjective some commentators have applied to the Oulipian constraint, recalling that Perec first turned to the lipogram when he was suffering from writer's block, and discovered that in the service of a self-imposed rule one may find an unexpected kind of freedom.

M oreover, Gilbert Adair says that he found an unforeseen freedom of his own in the later stages of transforming *La Disparition* into *A Void*, since he 'managed to formulate a language which did perfectly well without the letter "e", in which I eventually became able to write as fluently as I could write in conventional English, and which produced effects that I could never have achieved otherwise – in much the same way that disabled people can live full, rich, interesting lives, so e-less English is not a *crippled* language, but, so to speak, a *differently abled* language.'

N o doubt this bold claim will sound exaggerated to sceptics, but when Adair illustrates his point by reading out a brief extract from *A Void* – the aforementioned 'Blackbird' – his assertion seems rather more plausible, not least because the laughter it provokes is largely due to what one might call its acrobatic quality, meaning the impression it can convey of being something like a circus

performer who teeters agonizingly close to a disastrous
fall (in this case, into a glaring indulgence in the letter
'e'); no wonder Perec sometimes compared himself to a
trapeze artist.

O n the other hand, it has to be admitted that a lot of
Oulipian productions can be a bit rarefied, even for a
specialist audience, and even in Perec's *patrie*.

P erec's books, with the exception of his pre-Oulipian *Les
Choses*, sold in pitiful numbers until the sudden success of
La Vie mode d'emploi in 1978 brought him national fame –
the kind of fame which involves waiters and taxi drivers
saying, 'Here, aren't you that Perec geezer?' several times
a week – though, to be scrupulously honest about it, a
good part of this notoriety came from the little portrait
which accompanied his weekly crossword puzzles in
every issue of *Le Point*, from his increasingly frequent
appearances on television, and from the fact that his
unfeasibly large goatee, huge sunburst of hair (in the
fashionably expansive style that sardonic Americans used
to call a 'Jewfro') and general appearance of a benign
gremlin made him hard to forget.

(Q ueneau, on the other hand, was well known and well
respected in France for several decades, as a philosopher,
pataphysician, psychologist, polymath and publisher – in
1941, he was made General Secretary of the distinguished
house Gallimard, for which he went on to direct the
Encyclopédie de la Pléiade – and became internationally
famous for his *Exercices de style* (1947, trans. 1958) and
Zazie dans le métro (1959, trans. 1960), especially after the
latter was filmed by Louis Malle; Queneau's most
astounding work, *Cent mille milliard de poèmes* (1961) is a

collection of ten sonnets, each line of which is sliced (with a cut that runs from the edge of the page back towards the spine, but not quite reaching it) away from the ones which precede and/or succeed it, so that it offers the possibility, according to how one chooses to flip the book open, of being read in a total of 10^{14}, or 100,000,000,000,000 ways; Queneau calculated that if one read a 'potential' sonnet every minute for eight hours a day, two hundred days a year, it would take more than a million centuries to exhaust the text.)

R emarkably, Perec stuck to his resolutely uncommercial guns throughout years of neglect, supporting himself with a day job as a scientific archivist and never succumbing to the temptation of churning out more conventional writings with an eye to the best-seller market – though he had no objections at all to being paid a decent retainer for that notoriously difficult weekly crossword in *Le Point*.

S ome of his fellow writers have wondered whether Perec really put his prodigious talents to the best possible use; Anthony Burgess, a writer generally supportive of literature composed in the playful (he would perhaps have opted for the more recondite 'ludic') mode, complained that *La Vie mode d'emploi*, for all its manifest genius, was a cold, heartless book.

T here are times, certainly, when at least some Oulipian writings start to seem less like a charming game and more like the symptoms of an obsessiveness that borders on the frightening; what on earth can have been going through Perec's mind when he was writing *Les Revenentes*, a formal retort to *La Disparition* (it uses no vowels *except* 'e', though not without inflicting torture on the French language) which, uniquely in an otherwise somewhat chaste *œuvre*, answers to old-fashioned British notions of a typically French *feelthy book*?

U nless a handful of gifted British obsessives club together and form an Anglo-Saxon counterpart to Oulipo, it is unlikely that we can expect many home-grown successors to such doubly driven works (though Richard Beard, a young British novelist who is not, or anyway isn't yet, a member of Oulipo, has written *X20*, a fiction about giving up smoking which observes some typically Oulipian constraints – every chapter has the same number of words, and there are the same number of chapters as there are cigarettes in a standard pack).

V oluntary self-limitation of the Oulipian kind requires a singular kind of talent, in some ways closer to the mathematical than the poetic – for all that the vast majority of poems (in English, anyway) have been written in rhyme as well as (before the rise of *vers libre* in the early twentieth century) in reasonably strict metre; constraints that might themselves seem eccentric or pathological to a visitor from another culture.

W hat, then, are we finally to make of the whole Oulipian business?

X enophobic critics of the old school will probably continue to write it off as yet another horrible and fraudulent manifestation of Gallic pseudo- or hyper-intellectualism, and further good reason for blocking up the Channel Tunnel with barriers constructed from the collected works of F. R. Leavis.

Y ounger and more open-minded readers, though, may well start to realize that they have little to lose except their 'e's, since even the most cursory acquaintance with Oulipo's many and occasionally glorious productions can show that rule-bound works can be as cherishable as they are stimulating; Perec, too, is the sort of writer, as he was the kind of man (see David Bellos's huge, erudite and endlessly re-readable *Georges Perec: A Life in Words*, the one twentieth-century literary biography I can think of to rival Ellmann's *Joyce*), who inspires deep affection – an affection which can spill over and engulf all the people who collaborated with Perec, or helped make his 'potential' works actual: Queneau, Roubaud, Zingg.

Z ingg – Gerard Zingg, to give his full name, a professional tennis player and sometime political scientist turned film-maker – drew a touching portrait of Perec at the time of his death in March 1982; Perec, whose career gave an entirely new resonance to the phrase 'man of letters', would surely have smiled at the knowledge that the final moments of his life should be commemorated in this way by a man whose first name begins, like his own, with a 'G', and whose surname begins with the letter with which the alphabet ends; who knows, he might even have smiled at a piece about his work which ends with the word 'ends'.

Imaginary Books, Imaginary Authors

It is necessary to understand
That a poet may not exist, that his writings
Are the incomplete circle and straight drop
Of a question mark . . .

Ern Malley, 'Sybilline'

I was once witness to the embarrassing spectacle of a teenage Goth attempting to purchase a copy of the *Necronomicon* – a grimoire which existed only in the feverish imagination of the American horror writer H. P. Lovecraft. The lad went away thwarted, but his quest set me to pondering. Evidently, books such as the *Necronomicon* and authors such as Abdul Alhazred, the mad poet of Sanna (alleged to have written that accursed tome, *c.* AD 700), do not need to exist in order to cast a spell; and there have been times when imaginary books and imaginary authors have enjoyed a career far more vexed and strange than anything their primary creators ever had in mind. For those who've heard of him – a contingent which includes a fairly large slice of the Australian population – the posthumous fame of 'Ern Malley' is the classic proof of this assertion. It's a glum fact that though Australian poetry buffs are the only people who can confidently reel off the names of his sly creators, James McAuley and Harold Stewart, there must be literally thousands of readers who know a thing or two about Ern.

Before spiralling around to the ineluctable Yarn of Ern, however, a word or two of taxonomic clarification. My headings 'imaginary authors' and 'imaginary books' aren't meant to refer to the squadrons of poets, novelists, dramatists and other scribblers who populate umpteen novels and dramas and poems, juicy as that topic would obviously be. Without taxing more than a random synapse or two, I can come up with the examples of Casaubon and his 'Key to all Mythologies' in *Middlemarch*, the doomed, indeed dead hero (based on Delmore Schwartz) of *Humboldt's Gift*, Stephen Dedalus and his vilanelle of the temptress, Henry Bech in the Updike novels, Baal in Brecht's *Baal*, Samuel Cramer, the poet-hero of Baudelaire's singleton novel *Le Fanfarlo*, Jo in *Little Women*, Edwin Reardon and Jasper Milvain and Harold Biffen in *New Grub Street*, Gordon Comstock, author of *Mice*, in *Keep the Aspidistra Flying* . . .

No, not those. The kind of phantom-mongering I'm after here is more the work of pranksters, hoaxers, spinners of conceits and, sometimes, dabblers in metaphysics. The recent past has yielded some rich examples of cultural hoaxing in and around the tradition I'm browsing:

a) the notorious *affaire Sokal*, in which an American physicist cobbled together an assortment of standard-issue postmodernist flannel, GCSE-level scientific solecisms and howling non-sequiturs into an article entitled 'Transgressing the Boundaries: Toward a Transformative Hermeneutics of Quantum Gravity', duly published by the allegedly rigorous journal *Social Text*;

b) the praise heaped by the likes of Ron Sillman, a poet (existent, if gullible) of the Language Poetry persuasion, on a poet of the 'Hiroshima school', 'Araki Yasusada' (1907–1972), who turned out to be the spoof creation of an American academic, Kent Johnson; and

c) the novelist William Boyd's slender biography of the American painter 'Nat Tate', and the accompanying launch party which, so the British papers said, left those New York art-world Johnnies with an omelette or two on their stubbly faces.

Various as their motives and methods have been, all of these hoaxers might legitimately claim some illustrious ancestry. Stretching it a tad, the clan of imaginary-writer-writers could probably lay claim to descent from Homer or 'Homer', on the grounds that he (or, for those who buy Samuel Butler's line in *Authoress of the Odyssey*, she) has always enjoyed a somewhat tenuous grasp on existence. Rather more plausibly, they could roll out a family tree which goes back at least as far as the early sixteenth century on the imaginary book side and to the eighteenth century on the imaginary author side.

Four centuries before H. P. Lovecraft codded up a textual history of the *Necronomicon* in the interests of making the flesh creep, Rabelais spewed out a copious list of patently bogus volumes in the pursuit of a more agreeable physical response. Among the 140 barmy volumes he lists as being in the possession of the Library of St Victor's (*Pantagruel*, Book 2, Chapter 7) are:

Bragueta juris (The Codpiece of the Law).
The Elephantine Testicle of the Valiant.
The Apparition of St Geltrude to a Nun of Poissy in labour.
Ars honeste petandi in societate, by M. Ortuinum (The Art of
    farting decently in public, by Hardouin de Graetz).

Tartaretus, de modo cacandi (Tartaret, on methods of shitting).

The Tripe-pod of Big Thoughts.

The Body-odours of the Spaniards, supercockcrowed by Brother Inigo (de Loyola).

and (shades of H. P. Lovecraft),

Ingeniositas invocandi diabolos et diabolas, per M. Guingolfum (The Method of Invoking Demons, male and female, by Master Gingulf).

Not all that funny? Maybe you had to be there. Contemporaries, at any rate, seem to have found Rabelais's imaginary booklist a proper caution, and it inspired any number of successors, imitations and epigones across the centuries, from Johann Fischart's *Catalogus Catalogorum perpetuo durabilis* (1590) and Sir Thomas Browne's *Musaeum Clausum* or *Bibliotheca Abscondita: containing some remarkable Books, Antiquities, Pictures and Rarities of several kinds, scarce or never seen by any man now living* to dozens of similar mock catalogues, most of which were political squibs.

One of them, which was quite explicitly modelled on the Librairie de L'Abbaye de Sainct-Victor, is a comparatively little-known *jeu d'esprit* by John Donne, the *Catalogus Librorum Aulicorum incomparabilium et non vendibilium*, probably written *c.* 1603–11, but first published in 1650. In this short Latin work, generally referred to as *The Courtier's Library*,* Donne furnishes a list of thirty-four imaginary books ascribed, with varying degrees of malice aforethought, to real authors. Even

---

* I'm referring to the Nonesuch edition of 1930, edited by Evelyn Mary Simpson, to which I am in debt here.

the form of the book is a kind of satire, since Donne purports to offer it in helpful spirit as what his age would have called an epitome and our age would call a bluffer's guide: '. . . with these books at your elbow,' he assures the reader, 'you may in almost every branch of knowledge suddenly emerge as an authority, if not with deeper learning than the rest, at least with a learning differing from theirs . . .' Donne's debt to Rabelais isn't hard to tease out:

10. John Harington's *Hercules, or the method of purging Noah's Ark of excrement.**

13. Martin Luther, *On shortening the Lord's Prayer.*†

20. *On the Navigableness of the Waters above Heaven; and whether a ship in the firmament will in the Day of Judgment land there or in our harbours,* by John Dee.‡

23. Cardan, *On the nullibiety of breaking wind.*§

26. *Of an animate Pessary, and the manner of giving every disease to women,* by Master Butler, of Cambridge.¶

It's about time for me to advance another sweeping generalization: from Rabelais's and Donne's catalogues of

-----

* Harington's *Metamorphosis of Ajax* (1596) – the classical name is yet another botty joke, cf. 'Jacques' in *As You Like It* – was a satire on Elizabethan loos.

† Because Luther lengthened the *pater noster* in his 1521 translation of the Bible by adding the 'power and glory clause' – Donne, *Satires* – on the authority of Erasmus, who found it in the Greek codices.

‡ Shades of Lovecraft, again.

§ Knowing who Girolamo Cardano (1501–76) was doesn't really do much to make this funnier; in fact, he was an Italian physician.

¶ Ditto for this one: William Butler (1535–1618) was another famous doctor, apparently notorious for boozing rather than wenching.

imaginary books to the poems of 'Araki Yasusa', the central
tradition of imaginary books is comic and satirical, whether of
specific authors, modes of writing and belief, or human
credulity in general. The two most important groups of
exceptions to this literary rule are to be found

i)   in this century, in the work of writers such as Jorge Luis
     Borges,* Fernando Pessoa[†] and Max Aub,[‡] none of whom
     I plan to discuss here, and

ii) in the eighteenth century, a time when lengthy prose
     narratives apparently written by 'Lemuel Gulliver' and
     'Robinson Crusoe' were sent to market, and when some
     of the choicest verses a discerning reader could latch onto
     were the medieval poems of 'Thomas Rowley' (actually
     by Thomas Chatterton); *Fingal, an ancient epic poem in six
     books* (1762), otherwise known as the 'Ossian' poems,
     worshipped by Goethe and Hölderlin and Napoleon and
     others[§] (actually by James Macpherson, 1736–96); and a
     rediscovered play by 'Shakespeare', *Vortigern: a Tragedy*,

---

* *Locus classicus*: 'Pierre Menard, Author of the Quixote': *Labyrinths*
(London: Penguin, 1970), pp. 62–71.

[†] See, if you're reading this book in non-linear order, the piece about
'heteronyms', above.

[‡] My excuse for not having read this author is that he doesn't appear to
have been translated into English yet. According to Alaistair Reid, Señor
Aub '. . . was forever inventing imaginary writers, writing their works, and
then entering into controversy with them': *Oases*, p. 37.

[§] 'I am not ashamed to own that I think this rude bard of the North the
greatest poet that has ever existed': Thomas Jefferson, 1773.

worshipped by James Boswell, who, on seeing the forgeries, went down on his knees and declared 'I shall now die contented . . .' (William Henry Ireland was the guilty man). Anyone interested in pursuing some of the metaphysical, aesthetic and literary-historical dimensions of this latter group could do worse than start with Hugh Kenner's slim and jaunty book *The Counterfeiters* and Gwyneth Lewis's essay 'The Three Faces of Forgery'.*

These two dissenting tendencies aside, the comic-satirical tradition goes smirking on from generation to generation. In the 1880s comes 'Adoré Floupette', author of *Les Deliquescences*, a slender garland of decadent verses by a poet whose properties and techniques owe much to Mallarmé, Rimbaud and Verlaine, but more to Gabriel Vicaire and Henri Beauclair, who wrote them as a smack at the *Symboliste* school. Their invention – who was fleshed out in a biography written by Vicaire, writing as 'Marius Tapora', a humble pharmacist – is like a Gallic cousin to Max Beerbohm's immortal or amortal creation Enoch Soames, whose precise degree of non-existence continues to wax ever more debatable.† In the teens of the twentieth century come 'Anne Knish' and 'Emanuel Morgan', leading lights of the 'Spectra' group, fabricated by Arthur Davison Ficke and Witter Bynner as a squib directed at Ezra Pound and his imagist acolytes. In the early 1930s comes the *Concentriste* school, and its founder, the Toulouse poet Jean du Chas, invented by Samuel Beckett for a paper

---

* In the 'Hoax' issue of *Poetry Review*, Volume 87, No. 2, Summer 1997.

† See the appendix: 'Enoch's Castle'.

delivered to a Modern Languages society in Dublin.* And at the height of the Second World War comes the greatest non-existent poet of all time: Ern Malley.

The saga of Ern Malley is so rich in novelistic detail that it deserves treatment at book length, and, fortunately, has received it in Michael Heyward's elegant and searching study *The Ern Malley Affair*.† Stripped to the bones, the story runs thus: one day in 1943, the very young editor of a self-consciously wild and crazy Australian literary journal, *Angry Penguins* (I'm not making this up), received a precariously literate letter from a young woman called Ethel Malley, who had, she explained, recently lost her twenty-four-year-old brother to Graves' disease.‡ Ern, for such was her brother's name, had written a few poems before his death. Ethel was no judge of such things, but did the editor think they were up to anything? Harris turned to the poems, began to read them –

> I had often, cowled in the slumberous heavy air,
> Closed my inanimate lids to find it real,
> As I knew it would be . . .

– and flipped. He wrote back a condescending but feverishly excited letter to 'Ethel', and, ignoring wiser counsellors who smelled a *raton*, if not a *canard*, rushed the complete works of Malley§ into print. Only a tiny fraction of what happened

---

* It's been republished in *Disjecta*.

† London: Faber and Faber, 1993.

‡ Which isn't fatal: clue number one missed.

§ Title: *The Darkening Ecliptic*: delicious! Connoisseurs of the paratext will like to know that the book also has an epigraph ('Do not speak of secret

next was predictable. The foreseeable part was that the hoaxers came forward, and the Australian press gleefully reported that Lieutenant James McAuley and Corporal Harold Stewart, poets hostile to the *Penguins'* brand of avant-gardism, had created Malley in a single underemployed afternoon of their war service at the Directorate of Research and Civil Affairs. McAuley and Stewart had done their best to produce verses that gave the polish of a superficial technical competence to matter that was at best flatulent bombast and at worst mere word salad, utterly devoid of paraphraseable sense. The unforeseeable bits included a vast ripple of publicity throughout the United States and Britain as well as Australia, a vicious obscenity trial against Harris (sincerely regretted by the hoaxers), and a series of rows and thoughtful discussions of principle which have still not completely died away.

The Ern Malley fraud was welcomed by many in the same way that a lot of exasperated Anglo-Saxon empiricists welcomed the *affaire Sokal*, as a healthy exercise in exposing one species of fraud by means of another. Others were less sanguine: the triumph of Ern gave comfort not only to enemies of a particular school of modernism but to enemies of art as a whole. Australia's most celebrated contemporary poet Les Murray, no great fan of modernism himself, has

---

matters in a field full of little hills' – Old Proverb), two internal epigraphs (one from *Pericles*, one from the inexistent Odes of Solomon 24: 8), and a swaggering preface ('These poems are complete. There are no scoriae or unfulfilled intentions . . .'). And, of course, there is the magnificent comic-ponderous name itself, abbreviated from 'Ernest Lalor Malley', alluding to Mallarmé, the *Fleurs du Mal*, Max Ernst ('St Ern'?) . . .

said that the whole business brought about a 'narrowing and deadening of the arts in Australia', and prolonged 'some pretty lousy anti-artistic attitudes here'. Perhaps the oddest fallout from Ern's blast, however, was a critical-cum-philosophical debate about intentionality, the role of the unconscious, surrealist method and the like. In less polysyllabic words, there are a fair few people who hold to some version of the defence Max Harris put forward when the mess first blew up – that, whatever their wicked plans, Stewart and McAuley unwittingly created a body of work that was not merely good, but a great deal better than anything they had so far achieved or would go on to achieve in their own, 'authentic' work. Ern Malley may not have been a real man, but he was a real poet – more real than his creators.

This is cruel and unfair to the memories of Stewart and McAuley, and yet it's not without a sliver of sense. Ern's fans, including John Ashbery, have a point: some of the poems *are* surprisingly readable, verging at times on impressive ('I have split the infinitive. Beyond is anything', runs the prophetic final line of his final poem), and must have seemed all the more so in March 1988, when Max Harris hosted a launch party for the new edition of *The Darkening Ecliptic*, at which the poems were declaimed by a bespectacled man in a red bow tie: Ern Malley himself, it seemed, who was watched with approval by his befrocked sister Ethel.* For there is a curious final truth about imaginary authors and imaginary books: sometimes, they take on new forms of substance. In the 1950s, a broadcaster in New York used to

---

* See Heyward, p. 219.

go on and on about a book called *I, Libertine*, inflaming the curiosity of his listeners to such a point that the book was forced to appear in bookshops. Reasonably reliable report has it that a copy of the *Necronomicon* has shown up in the library of Brown University, Providence, Rhode Island. Enoch Soames, the diabolist poet, who complained in his final hour before damnation that history would remember him only as a character in a laboured satire by Max Beerbohm, manifested himself in the British Library in the summer of 1997.* And even this book you are now perusing with such intelligence and sympathy, dear reader ... well, by way of a Parthian shot, let me simply quote from the final chapter of Alberto Manguel's *A History of Reading*, in which he entertains a reverie about a vast imaginary book that exists in a Borgesian library somewhere in this universe or another – a book which offers not *A* history of reading, but *The* history of reading, written by an author of omnivorous habits:

> Reading fiction is not our author's only preoccupation. The reading of scientific tracts, dictionaries, *parts of a book such as indexes, footnotes and dedications* ... each merits (and receives) its own chapter.

Italics, of course, mine. And people say that H. P. Lovecraft is spooky. Hah!

---

* See appendix, as before.

I.D.: Homage to Isaac D'Israeli

'The struggle for knowledge hath a pleasure in it, like that of wrestling with a fine woman.'

Marquis of Halifax* (attrib.)

You can't choose your ancestors but you're at liberty, if so inclined, to pick your predecessors. Mind you, it can be risky. Others may carp at your choice, or ridicule it, and the poet who declares himself the rightful heir of Virgil, Dante and Milton had better be braced for the sarky reviews which point out that his true precursors are Ella Wheeler Wilcox and Eric Jarvis Thribb. But to claim that one is trying to work in a genre established or brought to perfection by an earlier and better writer isn't necessarily immodest. Just as the Sunday painter who adores Cézanne will know quite well that his own renditions of apples or mountains aren't remotely in the same league as the master's, yet will still cherish some warming sense of lineage, so the most unassuming books page hack can legitimately comfort himself with the thought that when he hastily bashes out his five

---

* I'd better hasten to point out that this tasteless remark was used by Isaac D'Israeli as the epigraph for the third volume of *Curiosities of Literature*, 1817.

hundred word review or twelve hundred word Think Piece he is (as a hugely gifted literary journalist of our day put it) touching the grubby paw of Samuel Johnson. I hope, then, that I won't be attracting more enmity than I've already occasioned by admitting that I had, and have, a particular precedent in mind when I was writing some of *Invisible Forms*, especially since the volume in question isn't particularly exalted ... in fact, let's admit it, is now all but forgotten by the average reader:* *Curiosities of Literature*, by Isaac D'Israeli.

Tales of lost celebrity are all too common in literary history, but Isaac D'Israeli's slump into oblivion is more unaccountable than many. If for nothing else, he ought surely to be remembered for having sired the (apostrophe-free) novelist and Prime Minister Benjamin Disraeli, and for having been the associate of such hardy favourites as Lord Byron, who said affectionately of him that he was 'the Bayle† of literary speculation, who puts together more amusing information than anybody'. He was also a good deal more than simply a father, and a friend, to the illustrious. *Curiosities of Literature* was, in the words of his biographer‡ 'almost embarrassingly successful' in D'Israeli's long lifetime, and

---

* And, at an informed guess, by most students of English literature, too. The English Faculty Library at Cambridge doesn't have a single copy of any work by Isaac D'Israeli.

† Pierre Bayle, that is, the author of a *Dictionnaire* of French literature, much admired by D'Israeli.

‡ James Ogden, to whose invaluable *Isaac D'Israeli* (Oxford: Clarendon Press, 1969) I am indebted for all the biographical detail in this piece.

became a standard text, pirated by several publishing houses, after his painless death in 1848. (He was eighty-one.) D'Israeli published the first edition in 1791, when he was twenty-five, and it made him a celebrity – if not literally overnight, then within a few weeks. In response to an unflagging public appetite for the work, which overshadowed almost all his other productions, he kept tinkering with and adding to *Curiosities* for the next half-century, until, twenty-five reprints and fourteen editions later, it had grown to three weighty volumes of about five hundred pages of close type, filled with 276 essays.

The publisher's 'Advertisment' to the 1881 edition offers a fair summary of these 'volumes that have been always delightful to the young and ardent enquirer after knowledge':

> They offer as a whole a diversified miscellany of literary, artistic, and political history, of critical disquisition and biographic anecdote, such as it is believed cannot be elsewhere found gathered together in a form so agreeable and so attainable.*

In less wooing terms, D'Israeli's book of assorted essays looks to the innocent eye as if it's a bit of an *omnium gatherum, olla podrida*, medley or plain old ragbag, into which he threw just about anything that took his fancy. The 'Literature' of his title means not, or not simply, what it signifies to us, but refers to anything that the diligent researcher might happen to truffle out from old works of biography, folklore, natural philosophy, travels and the like.

---

* 'Attainable' seems to have been the late Victorian equivalent of our own cant term 'accessible'.

Consequently, sketches from history such as 'James the First as a Father and a Husband', a 'Secret History of the Death of Queen Elizabeth' and 'General Monk and His Wife' were allowed by D'Israeli to mingle promiscuously with an enquiry 'Whether Allowable to Ruin Oneself?', a disquisition on 'Perpetual Lamps of the Ancients', and entries on topics as diverse as 'Cicero's Puns', 'Cervantes', 'Introducers of Exotic Flowers, Fruits etc', 'On the Custom of Kissing Hands', 'Wax-work', 'Virginity', 'Names of our Streets', 'Solitude', 'Political Nicknames' and 'Fire and the Origin of Fireworks'. It probably sounds like the kind of book that should be studied by elitist players of *Trivial Pursuits*, or by any spiritual son of Caine who enjoys throwing a chunk of recondite knowledge into the conversation and suffixing it with the words 'Not a lot of people know that.'

But D'Israeli was more than a trivia buff. As James Ogden has shown, his plans for the book were, if not rigid, a good deal less arbitrary than they may appear. Its immediate success was due in large part to a popular demand for collections of anecdotes. The vogue had begun in France in the seventeenth century, but Britain was slow to catch up, and until *Curiosities* stepped in to supply the need, the average English reader was hungry ('famished'*) for anything much in the way of biographical literary history, let alone

---

* D'Israeli's word for the condition of Johnson: 'Dr JOHNSON was a famished man for anecdotical [sic] literature, and sorely complained of the penury of our literary history.' – 'Preface' to *Curiosities of Literature*, second volume, second edition. For the purposes of this piece, I've used the 1881 edition of three volumes, published by Frederick Warne and Co.; all page references are to this edition, and this quotation is from II, p. xli.

book-chat as we now enjoy it. Among the few competitors for *Curiosities* were Horace Walpole's *Anecdotes of Painting in England*, James Pettit Andrews's *Anecdotes Ancient and Modern* and – the only one still thriving today – Boswell's *Life of Samuel Johnson*. D'Israeli, who at the time was rather more keen to be known as a poet or novelist than as an *homme de lettres*, said that the first edition of his book was intended to be nothing much more presumptuous than a collection of translations and paraphrases of the best bits from well-known *ana* – French anecdote-books.

As the work grew and blossomed with revision, however, D'Israeli's ideas began to change. He seems gradually to have come to regard his labours as stepping stones towards more substantial works – a critical history of English writers and writing (a project partly realized in his *Amenities of Literature*, 1841, which covers the ground from *Beowulf* and Cædmon to the Commonwealth) and a study of the psychology of exceptionally gifted artists, particularly authors (a project partly realized in *The Literary Character . . . of Men of Genius*, 1818). The tone of the essays grew more generalizing and philosophical, and the anecdotes, though still entertaining in their own right, were increasingly put to service as illustrations of some theme: 'An induction from a variety of particulars seemed to me to combine that delight, which Johnson derived from anecdotes, with that philosophy which Bolingbroke founded on examples . . .'* D'Israeli also began to develop a clearer idea of the kind of person for whom he was writing:

---

* Ibid., p. xliii.

This first volume had reminded the learned of much which it is grateful to remember, and those who were restricted by their classical studies, or lounged only in perishable novelties, were in modern literature but dry wells, for which I had opened clear waters from a fresh spring. The work had effected its design in stimulating the literary curiosity of those, who, with a taste for its tranquil pursuits, are impeded in their acquirement.*

Exactly: when Horace Walpole turned up his nose at *Curiosities* and its paucity of original research, sneering that 'these compilers seem to forget that people have libraries', he had evidently forgotten that most of the middle-class people eagerly buying the book weren't anything like wealthy enough to have their own libraries, and that a good number of the happy few who did have private libraries lacked either the leisure or the incentive to use them well. D'Israeli may have glanced nervously over his shoulder at the scholars now and again, particularly in the earlier part of his career, but he recognized that the true audience for his work was made up of those non-aristocratic readers who had little time, energy or training for the pursuit of literary scholarship, yet who were intelligent and lively enough to enjoy some of its fruits. He took a justifiable pride in asserting that the *Curiosities* 'have diffused a delight in critical and philosophical speculation among circles of readers who were not accustomed to literary topics'.†

No need to labour the attractiveness of this precedent, I

---

* Ibid, p. xlii.

† Ibid., p. xliv.

trust. There is, though, another, more direct way in which *Curiosities* is an example for *Invisible Forms*. To the best of my knowledge, D'Israeli was the first English writer ever to apply himself vigorously and directly to the kind of paratextual and quasi-paratextual matters that are the subject of this book, and as well as devoting chapters to such rewarding invisible (or dim) forms as 'Errata', 'Diaries', 'Quotation', 'Parodies', 'Neologisms', 'Pamphlets', 'Blunders' and 'Lost Works',* he discourses on 'Literary Forgeries' (cf. 'Imaginary Authors'), 'Literary Follies' (cf. 'Follies'), and on 'Titles', 'Dedications' and 'Prefaces'. Delightful and instructive in their own right, these shortish digressions also furnish a number of tantalizing glimpses into D'Israeli's tastes, opinions and loyalties. For example, 'Titles of Books' begins in straightforward literary style, discussing the difficulty of coming up with a decent name ('Were it inquired of an ingenious writer what page of his work had occasioned him most perplexity, he would often point to the *title page* . . .'), and then awarding marks for good titles and bad (first class honours for the *Tatler* and *Spectator*, at best a bare pass for the *Idler* and the *Rambler*, fails or aegrotats for the *Lounger* and the *World*). It ends by advancing a broad recommendation of caution:

> It is too often with the Titles of Books, as with those painted representations exhibited by the keepers of wild beasts; where, in general, the picture itself is made more

---

* *Invisible Forms* was once going to include a piece on lost books, but, fearing that this was pushing the notion of invisibility to the point of the absurd, I decided to lose it.

striking and inviting to the eye, than the inclosed animal is
always found to be.*

But between these resolutely bookish starting and finish-
ing lines, D'Israeli's mind has wandered gently yet unstop-
pably towards the subject of religion. To be exact, it drifts
towards the topics of religious obfuscation and intolerance
as these unseemly things are made manifest in titles.
D'Israeli, who fell out badly with his local synagogue and
was pragmatic enough to have his own children baptized by
the Church of England, thus removing a major stumbling
block from the career track of his energetic son, is unsparing
of his ancestors' holy men:

> A rabbin published a catalogue of rabbinical writers, and
> called it *Labia Dormientium*, from Cantic. vii 9. 'Like the
> best wine of my beloved that goeth down sweetly, causing
> *the lips of those that are asleep to speak.*' It hath a double
> meaning, of which he was not aware, for most of his
> rabbinical brethren talk very much like *men in their sleep.*†

Naughty, naughty. Not much comfort for the Gentiles
here, though: D'Israeli then goes on to disparage the Puri-
tans, or 'modern fanatics', who displayed a 'most barbarous
taste for titles', from *The Gun of Penitence* to *The Sixpenny-
worth of Divine Spirit* to, most outlandish of all, *Some fine
Biscuits baked in the Oven of Charity, carefully conserved for the
Chickens of the Church, the Sparrows of the Spirit, and the sweet
Swallows of Salvation.* Amusingly dismal as his examples are,

---

* D'Israeli, op. cit., p. 292.

† Ibid., p. 289.

I suspect that D'Israeli's sensibilities were ruffled as much by the wild-eyed provenance of these titles as by their gaucheness. Sceptical of religious extremism, D'Israeli also had his doubts about ardent political passions. In his youth he had, like so many other literary types, been inflamed by the French Revolution, and some residue of this youthful radicalism is plain to see in the disgusted terms with which he describes the practice of dedication. He finds little to applaud save mere ingenuity and a great deal of sycophancy to deplore: 'Never was a gigantic baby of adulation so crammed with the soft pap of *Dedications* as Cardinal Richelieu', he shudders. He's also dismayed at what he regards as the shameful curtsying of 'our great poet Spenser', who

> in compliance with this disgraceful custom, or rather in obedience to the established tyranny of patronage, has prefixed to the Faery Queen fifteen of these adulatory pieces, which in every respect are the meanest of his compositions. At this period all men, as well as writers, looked up to the peers as if they were beings on whose smiles or frowns all sublunary good and evil depended.*

A bit of a pinko, then? Not exactly: D'Israeli's fondness for the French regicides didn't last long, and in his forgotten novel *Vaurien* (1797) he launched one of the earliest attacks on the fellow-travelling English 'Jacobins', Godwin, Thomas Holcroft and company, much to the delight of conservative reviewers.† Accordingly, his article on dedication proceeds from tales of writers sucking up to the nobility to equally

---

* Ibid., p339.

† See Ogden, pp. 17–18.

displeasing accounts of writers toadying to Cromwell: '*Serenissimus*, *Illustrissimus*, and *Honoratissimus*, were epithets that dared not shew themselves under the *levelling* influence of the great fanatic republican.'*

Wary in spiritual matters, warier still in political matters, D'Israeli was immoderate in just one respect: his passionate love of books and the life spent among books. His essay on 'Prefaces', more a string of aphoristic prescriptions than a sequential argument, is plump with that vocabulary of eating and drinking which seems to have come to readily to him – remember Richelieu, 'crammed' with 'soft pap' . The prose smacks of his sense of literature as a succulent feast:

> The Italians call the preface *La salsa del libro*, the sauce of the book, and if well seasoned it creates an appetite in the reader to devour the book itself.†

Devour: books made him greedy, and he accumulated some twenty-five thousand volumes for his own library by the time of his death, as well as swelling the world's libraries by writing more than twenty books of his own, including three novels, a highly successful collection of Oriental 'Romances',‡ *Commentaries on the Life and Reign of Charles I* and the deliciously named *Calamities of Authors*.§ None of them seriously challenged *Curiosities* in the marketplace. It's

---

* *Curiosities*, I, p. 340.

† Ibid., p. 71.

‡ One of which, 'Mejnoun and Leila' has been described as having 'influenced' Poe's 'Ligeia'; see Ogden, p. 56.

§ See below, p. 293.

all but impossible to browse for long in *Curiosities*, which remains one of the most enjoyable of all browsing books, without feeling the stirrings of affection for this amiable cove. Ogden, his most recent biographer, has gently pointed out the ways in which Benjamin Disraeli, his earliest biographer, piously exaggerated the extent of Isaac's saintly good temper and distance from the more squalid aspects of literary life: 'The philosophic sweetness of his disposition,' wrote Benjamin, 'the serenity of his lot, and the elevating nature of his pursuits, combined to enable him to pass through life without an evil act, almost without an evil thought.'* No, certainly not 'evil'; some of his actions and sentiments, however, were less than supremely elevated. Isaac went in for all the standard dust-ups, vendettas and eager angling for sales of the life of writing, and Ogden is at one point exasperated enough with his subject to describe his grovelling poetic response to a satire on him as 'disgraceful'.

Still, when a literary career of getting on for six decades is marred by nothing more damaging than a touch of self-abasement here and self-satisfaction there, talk of canonization is, however unorthodox, forgivable. It would be a fine thing if Isaac D'Israeli's many virtues† became better known, because his son wasn't too wildly far of the mark in claiming

---

* 'On the Life and Writings of Mr. Disraeli [sic] by his Son', in *Curiosities*, I, p. xxxvi.

† Here's a small but pregnant instance: outside the small circle of the poet-artist's intimates, D'Israeli was the first connoisseur ever to buy Blake's illuminated works; he built his purchases into the largest contemporary Blake collection in England, and delighted in it. See Ogden, pp. 43–4.

that he was 'the first writer who vindicated the position of the great artist in the history of genius', or in finding 'a vital spirit in his page, kindred with the souls of a Bayle and a Montaigne', or in concluding that:

> . . . for sixty years, he largely contributed to form the taste, charm the leisure, and direct the studious dispositions of the great body of the public.*

If we're disbarred from elevating him to the status of a patron saint, then let's think of him as a kind of usefully avuncular tutelary spirit for all of us who have long since graduated from schools and universities (or who, like Isaac, never went to college; private income, you see) but who still take pleasure in literature; and particularly for those of us who occasionally try our hand at writing about literature – not for the attention of specialists, but for anyone, as the man said, 'with a taste for its tranquil pursuits'. Isaac D'Israeli deserves a glass or two raised in his memory, and – since he 'was wont to say that the best monument to an author was a good edition of his works'† – he definitely deserves another crack at the only kind of afterlife in which he expressed much interest, a literary afterlife, in the shape of a new edition of *Curiosities*. Who knows, maybe the twenty-first century will find unexpected delights in the cheerfully informative pages of old I.D.

---

* Ibid., p. xxxvii.

† Ibid., p. xxxv.

Last Words (Famous and Otherwise)

> . . . so there ain't nothing more to write about, and I am
> rotten glad of it, because if I'd a knowed what a trouble
> it was to make a book I wouldn't a tackled it . . .*
>
> *Adventures of Huckleberry Finn*

Last lines are not quite the same thing as last words, but
students of Italian literature could be forgiven for thinking
otherwise. There is a legend,† which I hanker to credit, that
Dante expired within less than an hour of composing the
final line of the final stanza of the final canto of the final
book of his *Commedia*, viz., the *Paradiso*:

> *l'amor che move il sole e l'altre stelle.*
> (the love which moves the sun and other stars.)

---

* Not precisely Huck's final utterance, but close. The novel actually ends
two sentences later: for the text, see above: 'Epigraphs', note to p. 91.

† Cited, for example, in Robert Hendrickson's *The Literary Life* (San Diego,
New York, etc.: Harcourt Brace, 1991): fun, but not 100 per cent reliable.
Another legend has it that the last thirteen cantos of the *Paradiso* went
missing, and were only found several months after the poet's death: he
appeared to one of his sons in a dream and showed him where the lost
drafts were stashed. On waking, the son went to the room he'd dreamed
about, and, sure enough . . .

If this fanciful tale is true – and it's gratifying to note that the generally sober editor of the Oxford *Paradiso* asserts that 'these are Dante's last recorded words'* – we can assume that, having brought the hundredth canto of his epic to its numerologically perfect conclusion with these deceptively commonplace words, the poet then set off on his real-life, real-death journey into the next world glowing with writerly satisfaction as well as his vision of divine radiance. For there's no more deathless a line than this one anywhere in Western literature, not even in the *Inferno*:

> *e quindi uscimmo a riverder le stelle.*
> (came out from there to see again the stars.)

nor in the *Purgatorio*:

> *puro e disposto a salire alle stelle.*
> (pure and primed to climb up to the stars.)†

Consult the scholarly editions for further commentary on Dante's penchant for bringing down his curtains on the word *stelle*.

Sadly, stories of such immaculately timed departures from this life tend to sound a little too picturesque to be true, and in Dante's case are many miles or kilometres too picturesque. So many of his scribbling fellow-countrymen are reputed to have ended their lives with the ink barely dry on the page before them that, had Dante not died with such

---

* *Paradiso* (Oxford and New York: Oxford University Press, 1971), p. 492: the editor and translator is John D. Sinclair.

† Renderings into spavined English iambs all mine; the permission fees on this book are already way too high.

consummately dramatic timing, some hagiographer would have had to contrive it. (Which means that some hagiographer probably did.) The obituaries column is quite impressive. Petrarch, the story goes, died on 18 July 1374 while scratching away at the final pages of a manuscript. The historian Giovanni Villani wrote the words '. . . in the midst of this pestilence there came to an end . . .', and came to his own end, struck down by a pestilence. Giacomo Leopardi, closest runner-up to Dante and Petrarch in the pantheon of Italian poets, was also *proxime accesit* in the last words stakes: according to one account, he wheezed out a dictation of the final lines of his poem 'The Setting of the Moon'* no more than a few hours before his death in Naples on 14 June 1837, though literalists would poop the party by adding that the last words he actually spoke – to his friend Antonio Ranieri – were quite prosaic, if sad: 'I can't see you any more.'

Spoilsports of that grouchy order, to digress for a moment, would no doubt point out that Keats similarly failed to oblige sentimentalists by promptly breathing his last as he scrawled a signature to his final note from Rome, seventeen years before Leopardi's demise. Still, that note – it is the one that speaks of 'leading a posthumous existence' – provides a magnificent ending for the masterpiece Keats may not have been aware he was writing, his *Letters*, and was composed so soon before his death that any fair-minded observer would surely see it as grounds for granting him honorary citizenship in the Italian *repubblica* of letters. The

---

* A nasty pedantic itch compels me to add that some editions date this poem to several months before Leopardi's death.

note was written to his friend Charles Armitage Brown, and is dated 30 November 1820.

> I can scarcely bid you good bye even in a letter. I always made an awkward bow.
> God bless you!
> John Keats.*

Keats's last spoken words, according to Severn's account, came on 23 February 1821, and also invoked the deity, and were also heroically considerate of the feelings of others:

> Severn – I – lift me up – I am dying – I shall die easy – don't be frightened – be firm, and thank God it has come!†

But if you visit Keats's grave in the Protestant – or 'Acatholic' – cemetery in Rome, just a short stroll from Gramsci's tomb, you will find the assertion that the poet composed his epitaph ('Here lies one whose name was writ in water') on his deathbed, so he may be closer to the Italian way of death than Severn's account suggests.

To return to our perishing Italians. The Baroque architect Francesco Borromini (1599–1667) succumbed to an attack of melancholia and committed suicide in the antique Roman style, by falling on a sword. The wound did not kill him at

---

* Cited in Walter Jackson Bate, *John Keats* (Cambridge, Mass.: The Belknap Press of Harvard University Press, 1963; fourth printing, 1978), p. 680; and in Christopher Ricks's *Keats and Embarrassment* (Oxford: Oxford University Press, 1976), pp. 217–18. Prof. Ricks: 'It must be the least awkward bow ever made, and this for the saddest, fearful final bow. There is no more to say of it than that it brings tears to the eyes.'

† Bate, p. 696.

once, so Borromini dragged himself over to a desk and, as his blood ebbed away, wrote a detailed account of his dying sensations.* Finally, for the time being, there is a much more recent suicide, that of the novelist and poet Cesare Pavese, who concluded his diary entry for 26 August 1950 with words that have become as notorious as they are agonizing:

> All it takes is a little courage.
> The more the pain grows clear and definite, the more the
>   instinct for life asserts itself and the thought of
>   suicide recedes.
> It seemed easy when I thought of it. Weak women have
>   done it. It takes humility, not pride.
> All this is sickening.
> Not words. An act. I won't write any more.†

(Appalling. Although it's highly unlikely that Samuel Beckett might somehow have read them, and had them in mind, when he composed the final lines of *Malone Dies* – one of the handful of fictions‡ in which the narrator perishes in the

---

* I owe this story to Alan Warner's introduction to the Rebel Inc. edition (Edinburgh, 1997) of Sadegh Hedayat's *The Blind Owl*: '. . . every work of art worth its salt is a suicide note as well', Warner says, '. . . we're all of us writing our suicide notes, us scribblers.' The final line of *The Blind Owl*: 'And on my chest I felt the weight of a woman's dead body . . .'; the ellipsis belongs to Hedayat.

† *This Business of Living: Diaries 1985–1950*, trans. A. E. Murch and Jeanne Molli (London: Quartet, 1980), p. 350. Pavese's diaries contain a number of references to both Dante and Leopardi – a detail that I won't labour.

‡ Another one that comes to mind is Poe's 'MS. Found in a Bottle'.

midst of trying to give utterance to his moribund thoughts –
the English versions of Beckett's novel and Pavese's diary
manage to rhyme eerily with each other.

> or light light I Mean
> never there he will never
> never anything
> there
> any more

No full stop.)*

Now, the fact that these increasingly gloomy anecdotes
all issue from Italy says nothing, as far as I'm aware, about a
dark strain in Italian culture. Like those in the heavens, this
saturnine constellation of literary stars is a product of nothing
more than the wishful – or diseased – habit of seeing patterns
where there is only happenstance. The mere fact, or rumour,
that a few Italian writers seem to have died on the job
plainly says nothing of the least significance about the
aesthetics of last lines.

Still, I'm not about to let that stop me, because at this
point I'm going to bang my fist on the table and revise my
opening sentence thus:

---

* I could easily have filled this chapter with Beckett's last lines; but will
indulge myself with just one more, the last he ever wrote, for his
contribution to *The Great Book of Ireland* – a revised version of a poem
about his father, 'Da Tagte Es':

> and the glass unmisted above your eyes

No full stop. See Anthony Cronin, *Samuel Beckett: The Last Modernist*
(London: HarperCollins, 1996), pp. 589–90.

Last lines are not quite the same thing as last words, but every last line is a *memento mori*.

Yes, every last line, not just those written with the Grim Reaper hovering over the far side of the desk as he did in the final hours of Dante, Petrarch, Leopardi, Borromini and Pavese. No matter with what sentiments of joy and relief an author puts down that last full stop – or, in the case of Beckett, abstains from it; no matter if that last line is as howlingly funny as the best gag you've ever heard ... No matter all of that: the completion of any literary work will always carry a whiff of mortality, if not its good old hearty stench. In his critical book *The Sense of an Ending* (which, disappointingly, has nothing overt to say on the subject of last lines) Frank Kermode, contemplating fictions of the Apocalypse, proposes that 'The End they [i.e., humankind] imagine will reflect their irreducibly intermediary preoccupations. They fear it, and as far as we can see have always done so; the End is a figure for their own deaths.'*

The End is a figure for their own deaths. Once the wormy thought that the end of a book is emblematic of the end of life has wriggled its slimy way into your mind, it permanently changes the way you look at last lines. Obviously, I'm not quite barmy enough to suggest that *memento mori* quality of such writings is always translated into literal references to coffins and tombs and epigraphs: *The Importance of Being*

---

* *The Sense of an Ending* (Oxford: Oxford University Press, 1967), p. 7.

Earnest refutes me,* as do a couple of Flaubert's sublime pay-offs,† those for *Madame Bovary*:

> *Il vient de recevoir la croix d'honneur.*

and for *L'Éducation sentimentale*:

> '*Oui, peut-être bien? C'est la ce que nous avons eu de meilleur!*'
> *dit Deslauriers.*

And yet, and yet . . . If you go off in search of death, like the crooks in Chaucer's 'Pardoner's Tale', you'll find it in the most unexpected finales – at the end of fairy stories, say, where the immemorial sign-off phrase *happily ever after* begins to grin back at you less like a good fairy than like a Jack O'Lantern (there's only one kind of *after* that is truly for *ever* . . .). Or reverberating deep beneath the final thundering chords of Johnson's first and most fascinating biography, the *Life of Savage*, which is at once an epitaph and a terrible admonition:

> This Relation will not be wholly without its Use, if those, who languish under any part of his Sufferings, shall be enabled to fortify their Patience by reflecting that they feel only those Afflictions from which the Abilities of *Savage* did not exempt him; or if those, who, in confidence of superior Capabilities or Attainments, disregard the common Maxims of Life, shall be reminded that nothing will supply the Want of Prudence, and that Negligence and Irregularity, long continued, will make Knowledge useless, Wit ridiculous, and Genius contemptible.

---

* Or does it?

† Or do they?

When I tried to be a good empiricist and put my *memento mori* principle to the test, a random-ish trawl through my shelves for examples of particularly well-known last lines yielded the following:

a) It was the devious-cruising Rachel, that in her retracing search after her missing children, only found another orphan.

b) 'Like a dog!' he said: it was as if he meant the shame of it to outlive him.

c) *Das Ewigweibliche*
    Ziegt uns hinan.

d) The offing was barred by a black bank of clouds, and the tranquil waterway leading to the uttermost ends of the earth flowed sombre under an overcast sky – seemed to lead into the heart of an immense darkness.

e) shantih shantih shantih

f)   So they performed
    the funeral rites of Hector, tamer of horses.

g) Go, bid the soldiers shoot.

and

h) Whereof one cannot speak, thereof one must be silent.*

Am I being unduly morbid? Wilfully seeking out tragedies and books by notorious gloombags? Possibly, but give it a try yourself. Have you ever noticed, for example, how many

---

* Sources: *Moby-Dick*; *The Trial*; *Faust* (admittedly, not everyone finds this one suggestive of death as I do); *Heart of Darkness*; *The Waste Land* (ditto); *The Iliad*; *Hamlet*; *Tractatus Logico-Philosophicus* (ditto). A classicist once pointed out to me how ominous the phrase 'tamer of horses' is, for the Trojan side – if Hector had lived, maybe he could have tamed the wooden kind.

of the classic nineteenth-century novels end in graveyards, or among ruins, or in ruined graveyards? Here's a typical example:

> I lingered round them, under the benign sky; watched the moths fluttering among the heath, and hare-bells; listened to the soft wind breathing through the grass; and wondered how any one could ever imagine unquiet slumbers, for the sleepers in that quiet earth. I took her hand in mine, and we went out of the ruined place; and, as the morning mists had risen long ago when I first left the forge, so, the evening mists were rising now, and in all the broad shadows of tranquil light they showed to me, I saw the shadow of no parting from her. But the effect of her being on those around her was incalculably diffusive: for the growing good of the world is partly dependent on unhistoric acts; and that things are not so ill with you and me as they might have been, is half owing to the number who have lived faithfully a hidden life, and rest in unvisited tombs.

All right, so I cheated; I meant well. The first sentence is the last sentence of *Wuthering Heights*, cited in the second volume of John Julius Norwich's *Christmas Crackers* as a conclusion worthy to stand alongside such gems as those from Zola's *La Fortune des Rougon* and Flaubert's *Herodias*;* the second is the last sentence of *Great Expectations*, which echoes the ending of *Paradise Lost* (Book XII, 628–32) – the poem which explains how Death was brought into the world – and was revised as many as six times by Dickens, after Bulwer-Lytton told him that the version he'd written in 1861

---

* Op. cit., p. 48, if you feel like checking.

was far too depressing for readers, who would want to be assured that Pip and Estella would finally be united;* the last sentence is the last sentence of *Middlemarch*, which brings the grave-digger's shovel down good and hard by ending on the word 'tombs'. Which reminds me to point out that the very last word of a literary work will quite often be some metaphor about death, or completion, or valediction; many a composition ends with some synonym for the word 'end'. I'm not sure about the Danish original, but the English translation of Peter Høeg's thriller *Miss Smilla's Feeling for Snow* does just this:

> There will be no conclusion.
> THE END†

Alastair Gray ends at least two of his books with the word GOODBYE, printed in giant block capitals which I will spare my poor, long-suffering publisher the labour of reproducing; and Flann O'Brien ends *At Swim-Two-Birds* with a suicide cutting his throat and writing the words '. . . goodbye, goodbye, goodbye'.

Earlier in these lucubrations I made bold to award the prize for Best First Lines to one J. A. Joyce, Esq., so it would be a howling omission not to return to the fellow as this book draws steadily nearer to its own close and see (i)

---

* Dickens responded to this by revising that last line to 'I saw no shadow of another parting from her', which, as many readers have pointed out, is hardly less ambiguous than the early version.

† Op. cit., p. 410 of the Harvill edition (London: 1993). I'll just use this footnote to lament the decline of 'The End', 'Finis', 'Fin' etc. in both books and films.

whether he manages to finish novels in the same high form in which he began them, and (ii) how far the old rule-breaker manages to make nonsense of everything I've been driving at so far about death and such. Can you quote his last lines from memory? They're easy enough. The last line of *A Portrait of the Artist as a Young Man* is:

> Dublin, 1904
> Trieste 1914

The last line of *Ulysses*:

> *Trieste-Zurich-Paris, 1914–1921*

And the last line of *Finnegans Wake*:

> Paris,
> 1922–1939.

Well, the dateline is an IF that might bear a little investigation in its own right, but instead let us straighten up, fly right and go back to the last of the stories in *Dubliners*, which might have been composed to vindicate my deathly crotchets: it's called, of course, 'The Dead':

> His soul swooned slowly as he heard the snow falling faintly through the universe and faintly falling, like the descent of their last end, on all the living and the dead.

Lovely prose, Jimmy, simply lovely; not a dry eye in the parlour the last time I read it out to the servants. But all that falling faintly and faintly falling and failing faulty and feeling failing felling, not to mention the soul swooning slowly in the slippery sloppery snow . . . strictly *entre nous*, would you not admit it's all, how can I put it, a bit much?

It's a fair bet he did, for he never went that twilit way again. The three works to which Joyce devoted the rest of his life not only cut the schmaltz but deny death as decidedly as did dear doomed Dante; only alliteration lingered lovingly to give a lulling lilt to his last last line. The real finale of the *Portrait*, for all its prayerfulness, is almost abrupt in context:

> Old father, old artificer, stand me now and ever in good
> stead.

The final sentence of *Ulysses* . . . well, I despair of hunting right the way through Molly Bloom's novel-length soliloquy in search of a rogue full stop or two* that may or may not be tucked away somewhere in her frilly drawers, so I'll assume that the book really does possess the longest of all last lines, and will just fade in round about the part critics all used to call 'life-affirming' before such displays of sticky humanism could cost an assistant prof. his or her stab at tenure:

> . . . . and how he kissed me under the Moorish wall and I
> thought well as well him as another and then I asked him
> with my eyes to ask again yes and then he asked me would
> I yes to say yes my mountain flower and first I put my
> arms around him yes and drew him down to me so he
> could feel my breasts all perfume yes and his heart was
> going like mad and yes I said yes I will Yes.

No: I said No: even I can't find anything much in the way of a skull beneath that warm and perfumed skin. Finally,

---

* I seem to recall that this last chapter is divided into eight – or was it nine? – sentences. *Ars longa, vita brevis* . . .

there's the *Wake*, which defies mortality just as it defies finality:

> A way a lone a last a loved a long the

No full stop. (Beckett aided Joyce in the years when the *Wake* was known as *Work in Progress*.) Before settling on this, Joyce had come up with an earlier version, less alliterative:

> A bit beside the bush and then a walk along the

No full stop. Another of Joyce's novels ends in mid-sentence, though by accident rather than design, the abandoned draft of *Stephen Hero*:

> He remained behind gazing into the canal near the feet of the body, looking at a fragment of paper on which was

Now we'll never know. What we do know is that Joyce devoted a great deal of thought to constructing his last lines. He wrote to a friend that:

> In *Ulysses*, to depict the babbling of a woman going to sleep, I had sought to end with the least forceful word I could possibly find. I had found the word 'yes', which is barely pronounced, which denotes acquiescence, self-abandon, relaxation, the end of all resistance. In *Work in Progress*, I've tried to do better if I could. This time, I have found the word which is the most slippery, the least accented, the weakest word in English, a word which is not even a word, which is scarcely sounded between the teeth, a breath, a nothing, the article *the*.*

---

* In Ellmann, *James Joyce* (Oxford: Oxford University Press), p. 712n.

The 'the' might be effortless, but the struggle to reach it was not: *Finnegans Wake* cost Joyce seventeen years of labour, the incomprehension and hostility of some of his former supporters and periods when he doubted not just the point of the exercise but its sanity. On the day when he finally reached that long-awaited 'the', he told Eugene Jolas:

> I felt so completely exhausted, as if all the blood had run out of my brain. I sat for a long while on a street bench, unable to move.*

It's not hard to sympathize with Joyce's state of numbed fatigue. Unless you're a Jack Kerouac, slamming out the lines on a continuous roll of paper in the space of a couple of weeks of benny-fuelled frenzy, every book takes a fair amount of one's allotted span to write; and if I'm not wholly a crackpot in insisting that the last line of any book is a *memento mori*, how much so must that be the case when the book in question has taken many, many years? The composition of *Finnegans Wake* cost Joyce seventeen years. It took Edward Gibbon twenty years to attain the final sentence of *The Decline and Fall of the Roman Empire*, a sentence which (ah, but look at that word 'ruins') appears to look backwards at conception and birth ('deliver') rather than forwards to the grave.

> It was among the ruins of the Capitol that I first conceived the idea of a work which has amused and exercised near twenty years of my life, and which, however inadequate to

* Ibid., p. 713.

my own wishes, I finally deliver to the curiosity and candour of the public.

(Joycean date-line: 'Lausanne. June 27, 1787'.)

Cheerful enough on the face of it, I'd admit. But my main contention in this pseudo-final piece has not been that every last sentence is directly *about* death, but that the composition of such sentences is always touched with intimations of mortality – mildly for the reader, more forcibly for the author.* And there is no more eloquent account of this *memento mori* effect than Gibbon's reminiscence of completing *Decline and Fall* in his *Memoirs* – a book, not so incidentally, only edited and published after Gibbon's death:

It was on the day or rather the night of the 12th June 1787, between the hours of eleven and twelve, that I wrote the last lines of the last page in a summer-house in my garden. After laying down my pen, I took several turns in a *berceau* or covered walk of acacias which commands a prospect of the country, the lake and the mountains. The air was temperate, the sky was serene; the silver orb of the moon was reflected from the waters, and all nature was silent. I will not dissemble the first emotions of joy on the recovery of my freedom, and perhaps the establishment of my fame. But my pride was soon humbled by the idea that I had taken my everlasting leave of an old and agreeable com-

---

* Which is surely one of the reasons why so many otherwise industrious writers find it hard to complete books they've been living with for years.

panion, and that, whatsoever might be the future date of my History, the life of the historian must be short and precarious.

That's all, folks.

Appendix

Nothing gives such weight and dignity to a book as an appendix

Herodotus*

According to the *OED*, the literary sense of the word appendix (from the Latin *appendere*, 'to hang', so, literally 'that which is attached as if by being hung on') is 'An addition subjoined to a document or book, having some contributory value in connexion with the subject-matter of the work, but not essential to its completeness'. The earliest citation is from the mid-sixteenth century – a collection of sermons by Latimer: 'The commentaries, contaynyng the solemnities of their religion wyth manye other appendixes.' (The anatomical/biological sense appears in the early seventeenth century, which means that people have been able to make the little pun enshrined in the title of Brian Eno's published diaries, *A Year With Swollen Appendixes*, for nearly four centuries now. Though, as far as I know, no one has bothered.)

Since the main body of my digressions is now very close to being as complete as my format permits, I have decided, rather than discourse on the Appendix as IF, to

---

* A double-exposed epigraph, this: Mark Twain used it in *The Gilded Age*.

indicate something of its functions by providing an appendix to the chapter on Imaginary Authors and Imaginary Books – which mentions its subject in passing. Those who have never read Max Beerbohm's story 'Enoch Soames' should at once put down this book, and give themselves the treat of finding and reading a copy of *Seven Men* (better libraries have it, and it crops up in second-hand bookshops quite frequently).

(Pause for the space of a day or so.)

Good, isn't it? Well, as most of us are now aware, 'Enoch Soames' is the tale of a conspicuously giftless minor poet of the 1890s, who in 1897 is finally driven by his lack of success to strike a bargain with the Devil. In return for Soames's immortal soul, His Satanic Majesty agrees to transport the poet a century into the future, so that he can visit the reading room of the British Library, consult the index and bask in the approbation of posterity. Alas, his short burst of time travel proves bitterly disillusioning, and the agonies of his endless perdition are sharpened by the knowledge that future ages will remember him, if at all, as no more than the hero of a light fiction by Max Beerbohm.

But the story does not end in 1897, nor even in 1919, the year in which *Seven Men* was first published. In the early months of 1997, the art historian Stephen Calloway recruited a number of writers and artists for a (literally) singular project. According to Beerbohm's report, the date on which Soames would manifest himself in the British Library was to be 3 June 1997, some time in the afternoon. So as to give the poet a small crumb of solace for the rest of eternity, Mr Calloway had come to the compassionate decision that both the past and the future should be rewritten in Soames's favour. Accordingly, a volume of essays, drawings and portraits entitled *Enoch Soames: The Critical Heritage* was printed, handsomely bound and deposited in the Library just in time for Soames's visit. Came the day, came the man: Soames became dimly but indisputably apparent in the Reading Room, consulted the catalogue, perused the essays and departed – we must hope, content. (The whole affair was captured on videotape.)

This seems to me an incident more than worthy to stand beside, say, Ern Malley's fleshly appearance in March 1988; and the hundred or so admirers of Soames's slight but distinctive *œuvre* who remained in the Reading Room for drinks and other festivities that fine June evening would, I am sure, agree. In commemoration of a strangely moving day, I reproduce here a short essay from *Enoch Soames: The Critical Heritage* which investigates some hitherto unsuspected aspects of the poet's life and work. I should explain that its author, though my namesake, is not to be confused with me, but is (or was, until his recent hasty departure from the institution under circumstances that remain unclear) a lecturer in the Department of Cultural Studies at the University of Preston. That town was, of course, Soames's birthplace.

*   *   *

ENOCH'S CASTLE: SOAMES, SATANISM AND
SYMBOLISME, 1887–1892
by Kevin Jackson, B.A. (*aegrot.*)

For several years before his transformation into a veritable shade, Enoch Soames had flitted through the poetic, painterly and occultist circles of *fin de siècle* Paris, an English spectre – albeit a rather *dim* spectre – stalking the margins of the Banquet Years. Certain facts about this period have long been acknowledged by Soames scholars: his meetings with Rothenstein and Harland at the Café Groche and elsewhere; his touching friendship with the dying Villiers de l'Isle Adam (one of the few contemporaries to whom he would concede any artistic merit); his bitter quarrel with that '*épicier malgre lui*' Verlaine; and so on. Until the late months of 1996, however, long stretches of Soames's crucial Parisian years were a matter for speculation, educated guess and heated debate.

But blazing light has now been cast into this tantalizingly crepuscular zone by a chance discovery which may, in the next few years, bring about nothing less than a revolution in Soames studies. Last August, a M. Charles Montel, one of the under-librarians involved in the epic task of relocating stock from the former Bibliothèque Nationale to its imposing new home on the banks of the Seine, happened upon a set of autograph manuscripts bearing dates between 1864 and 1916. Though the hand was hard to decipher, and the contents appeared at first sight to consist of little more than the disjointed, indeed paranoid ravings of some justly failed writer, M. Montel soon recognized that these texts must be

the intimate journal of Hugo Vernier (1836–1916/17?), author
of a single, uniquely influential masterpiece: *Le Voyage d'hiver*,
published by Hervé Frères of Valenciennes in 1864 – the
date, that is, at which the MS begins.[1]

M. Montel is still hard at work deciphering Vernier's
crabbed scribblings, and many of his readings must remain
conjectural for some time to come. For all this, his prelimi-
nary explorations of the manuscript have already helped
settle a number of fiercely contested disputes concerning
some five decades of French cultural life; and though M.
Montel frankly concedes that he has little personal interest
in *'ce petit poète Prestonien'*,[2] his generosity in sharing the
fruits of his continuing research with British colleagues has
been heartening. A new century will have dawned before his
labours come to an end; for now, we can be more than
content – indeed, we must be astonished – with the handful
of revelations M. Montel has granted us so liberally.

Put simply, our interim conclusions are twofold. Despite
Soames's proud boast that 'I owe nothing to France', it is
now more plain than ever (a) that he was not only influenced
by his Parisian contemporaries, but left his own mark on
French letters; and (b) that, despite widespread claims that
Soames's early leanings towards diabolism amounted to little
more than fashionable affectation,[3] it is now undeniable that
he grew ever more deeply involved in many forms of occult
science, from Rosicrucianism to Black Magic, throughout his
stay on the other side of the channel.

To consider the latter point first: it now appears beyond
reasonable dispute that the 'smooth-shaven, melancholy
man' seen at the Black Mass attended by the hero of
Huysmans's *roman à clef* about contemporary Satanism,

Là-bas (Chapter XIX), can have been none other than our poet. This possible attribution has long been rejected on the grounds that Soames, far from being smooth shaven, habitually cultivated a beard, albeit a scanty one. The Vernier documents, however, show that Huysmans – who appears to have encountered Soames several times at one of the celebrated *Mardis* at 87 rue de Rome – was fond of mocking Soames's inability to achieve a fine facial growth comparable to Mallarmé's, and would pretend to admire Soames's skill with cut-throat razor and shaving soap in terms as loud as they were humiliating.

Soames bore the verbal mockery with relative good grace, but when the joke was immortalized in print in 1891, with the publication in serial form of *Là-bas* in the *Echo de Paris*, he took violent exception, ceased to attend the *Mardis* and would cut Huysmans whenever they encountered each other in the street. Before this time, their relations had been warm. A precocious reading of Huysmans's breviary of Decadence, *À rebours*, had indeed been one of the lures which first brought Soames to Paris. In 1889, for example, Huysmans and Soames had joined Mallarmé and Diercx as witnesses to the marriage *in extremis* of Villiers de l'Isle-Adam; Soames was a last-minute replacement[4] for Coppée, who declined to attend. Soames also joined Huysmans and Mallarmé in editing *Axël*, the work which, thanks to Edmund Wilson's *Axel's Castle*, is now Villiers's best-known production. It was published some five months after the writer's death, in January 1890. How sublimely fitting that Soames – so neglected a figure in his own day, so haunting for us today – should have been an unacknowledged presence in the work which is now seen as the paradigm of *Symbolisme*!

Huysmans's own reaction to the 'smooth-shaven' episode remains cloudy. What is definite, however, is his dismay at the extent to which Soames had become involved in diabolism. Piecing together hints in the Vernier MSS, we can establish that Soames must have been recruited to the Black Mass by Charles Buet, the Catholic historian who provided Huysmans with the original of his villain M. Chantelouve.[5] Vernier, who among other epithets refers to Soames as a 'lanky, dishevelled demonologist',[6] also shows that the English poet first drifted towards the Dark Arts by way of a more benign occultist, the Sâr Peladan. One of the final clear glimpses of the Parisian Soames comes in Vernier's account of Peladan's inaugural *Salon des Rose + Croix* at the Durand-Ruel gallery in 1892. No longer do historians have to speculate as to the identity of the 'abusive Englishman' whose insults and howls of rage could be heard above the sound of Eric Satie's trumpet fanfare, and who had to be forcibly ejected into the night.[7]

A great deal of work remains to be done on Soames's career as diabolist, and we must assume that not all of the findings will be agreeable. In the meantime, therefore, let us conclude with a note more appropriate to a volume of celebration, and recall some of the happier episodes in our poet's brief and tragic life. For thanks to Vernier – yet another writer who did not, alas, seem to like Soames greatly – we can warm ourselves with the knowledge that Paris proved to be the home for the closest, perhaps the only profound friendships Soames was ever to know.

It was at the café Chat Noir, now best remembered as the favoured watering hole of the Neuropath poet Maurice Rollinat,[8] that Soames first came face to face with Adoré

Floupette, scandalous author of *Les Déliquescences: Poèmes decadents* (1885) and the controversial critic Jacques Plowert, whose *Petit Glossaire pour servir à l'intelligence des poètes decadents et symbolistes* created such a stir in *Symboliste* circles on its publication in 1888. It was Floupette who introduced Soames to the allures of the *sorcière glauque* in long drinking sessions with the Hydropath circle, and, more important to our writer's sometimes faltering sense of his literary mission, welcomed him as a brother poet. It was Plowert who wrote the earliest Francophone appreciation of Soames's verse, in his column for *Le Symboliste*.[9]

We can confidently expect that further decipherings of the Vernier MSS will yield further and perhaps still more remarkable discoveries for students of *fin de siècle* art, literature and hermeticism. Few, though, will be quite as extraordinary as one of the latest of M. Montel's gleanings. Three years before their earliest absinthe-soaked encounter in the flesh, Soames and Floupette had begun a long and impassioned correspondence; each man somehow saw in the other a *semblable*, a *frère*. Unknown to the fashionable world, this correspondence grew into a collaboration, for we now know that the 'Marius Tapora' who wrote the introduction to Floupette's *Déliquescences*, purporting to be a pharmacist friend of the poet's, was in fact none other than ... Enoch Soames! Unkind as the sentiment may be, it is hard not to relish the prospect of the dismay with which Soames's detractors – who have sought so strenuously to deny our writer's manifest qualities of wit, vivacity and ingenuity – will greet the revelation that Enoch Soames was in fact the author of the late nineteenth century's most gleeful literary hoax.

Notes

1. For more on Vernier, see the article by G. Perec in *Hachette Informations*, no. 18, March–April 1980; reprinted in *Magazine littéraire*, no. 193, March 1983.

2. Charles Montel, private communication to the author, 3 January 1997.

3. For a survey of sceptics, see my article 'Better the Devil He Didn't Know: Was Soames a True Diabolist?', *The Journal of Victorian Satanism*, Vol. 6., No. 4, November 1992. Some of my conclusions will, of course, have to be modified in the light of the Vernier MSS.

4. For a fuller account of these mournful nuptials, published too early for the identity of the 'person replacing Coppée' to have been established, see Gordon Millan, *Mallarmé: A Throw of the Dice* (London: Secker & Warburg, 1994), p. 270.

5. See Robert Irwin's 'Introduction' to the Dedalus European Classics edition of *Là-bas* (London: Dedalus, 1986).

6. M. Montel's translation; oddly, the phrase anticipates Aleister Crowley's scornful description of W. B. Yeats.

7. On Sâr Peladan and related figures, see Phillipe Jullian, *Dreamers of Decadence* (2nd edition, London: Phaidon, 1974), pp. 75–85.

8. For a fascinating, and, to my mind, entirely convincing account of the origins of Soames's poem 'Nocturne' ('Round and round the shutter'd Square . . .') in one of Rollinat's Satanic verses, see Patrick McGuinness, *Journal of Victorian Satanism*, Vol. 8, No. 1, Feb–Mar 1994. See also the *Cahiers des amis de Maurice Rollinat, passim*.

9. See Patrick McGuinness, 'New Bearings in Deliquescent Poetry: Floupette, Soames and their Exegetes' in *Floupettiana* (PUP, forthcoming). I am grateful to Dr McGuinness for the many enlightening discussions we have enjoyed on these and related subjects, and particularly those at the conference on Deliquescence he organized at Jesus College, Oxford in January 1997.

Bibliographies & Selected Bibliography

> The compiling of bibliographies implies an active opposition to censorship, related to our faith in the importance of human diversity.
>
> D.W. Krummel

It is required by law that everyone who undertakes to write about bibliography, no matter how perfunctory or ephemeral the survey, should begin by pointing out that our free and easy everyday use of the word (to mean 'book list', or 'a particular type of book-list', or 'the making of book-lists, catalogues etc.' or, the *ex cathedra* definition of an eminent bibliographer, Sir Walter Greg, 'the study of books as material objects') flies in the face of etymology, history and horse sense. Break the word up into its basic Greek bits and you will find that 'bibliography' ought to mean 'the writing of books'. Cross-check with the *OED* and you will discover that it once used to mean precisely that; the editors will refer you to the example of one Edward Phillips in 1678. But *OED* also warns that this first sense is 'obs.': i.e., dead as a dead fish.

'Bibliography' settled down into its three or four principal modern senses early in the nineteenth century, largely thanks to the influence of Thomas Frognall Dibdin, author of *The Bibliographical Decameron* (1817). Not everyone was quite happy with this. Robert Southey fought hard for the more

logical (and more -logical) 'bibliology', while our old friend
Isaac D'Israeli, though allowing that the correct term for 'a
describer of books and other literary arrangements' was
indeed a *bibliographe,* coined* the lovely word *bibliognoste* to
designate 'one knowing in title-pages and colophons, and in
editions; the place and year when printed; the presses
whence issued; and all the *minutiae* of a book'†. By the end
of the nineteenth century, all the rival terms had become
obs. in their turn, and everyone knew what bibliography was
and bibliographies were; which is, of course, why there is
now a vast and steadily proliferating literature bursting with
impassioned explanations of what bibliography and bibliographies is and are and should be, world without end, amen.

Well, fools rush in and all that, but I have no intention
of stepping into professional crossfire again this late in the
book, and plan to use this, my all too rapidly diminishing
space, for a few humble chores. Four of them, to be exact.

1. Bibliography: An Extremely Short History

a. BC (third century onwards): According to an influential
   essay, 'The Aims of Bibliography', published by Stephen
   Gaselee in 1933, the lists drawn up by scribes and such to
   keep tabs on the Alexandrian Library's holdings may be
   counted as 'the first real example in the field'. Did they

---

* So the reference books say, but if you look it up you find that he
attributes the coinage to the Abbé Rive.

† *Curiosities of Literature,* Vol. III (1881), p. 343.

survive the burning, though? I consulted Luciano Canfora's much-lauded *The Vanished Library* and was left not much the wiser. My guess: no.

b. AD: second century: Galen, the influential writer on medical matters, compiles a list of all his own works, and as far as most people know is the first author to undertake such a task. This autobibliography is considered by posterity to be a significant enough production in its own right that it is included in the first collected edition of Galen's works in 1525. (*OED* informs us that its fourth principal definition of 'bibliography', 'A list of the works of a particular author, printer, or country . . .', etc. etc., becomes current in English from 1869.)

c. Fifth century: St Jerome (*c.* 341–420), the most sarcastic of the Church doctors, gives his lion a saucer of milk, adjusts his cardinal's hat and writes *De illustribus viris* (a.k.a. *De scriptoribus ecclesiasticus*, the saint's preferred title), which sounds as if it should be a biographical collection of Church worthies with special emphasis on feats of piety, but is mainly a list of said worthies' writings.

d. Eighth century: The Venerable Bede concludes his *Historia ecclesiastica gentis Anglorum* with a list of forty works under the heading '*Notitia de se ipso e de libris suis*', including:

> *A Book of Hymns* in various metres or rhythms.
> *A Book of Epigrams* in heroic, or elegiac, verse.
> *On the Nature of Things*, and *On Times*; a book on each.*

---

* Bede, *A History of the English Church and People*, trans. Leo Sherley-Price (Harmondsworth: Penguin, 1955), p. 331.

Is this the beginning of the convention that bibliographies should be placed at the back of a book? I will conclude so until someone tells me otherwise.

e. Fifteenth century. John Boston of Bury compiles what may well be the first fully realized union catalogue, the *Catalogus scriptorum ecclesiae*. The distinguished bibliographer Roy Stokes refers to Boston's work as 'a location list of considerable sophistication'.

f. Sixteenth century. First rumblings of the coming information explosion, and beginnings of the specialized bibliography: Champier (1506) on medicine; Nevizzano (1522) on law; Erasmus (1523) on himself; and Gesner on everything. Conrad Gesner (1516–65) is sometimes referred to as the 'father of bibliography'.

His *Bibliotheca universalis* is published in 1545; Gesner attempted to list every book so far published, but ignored everything in vernacular literatures, confining himself to works in Greek, Latin and Hebrew. Given this restriction, he didn't do too badly. Stokes: 'The desire to be able to produce a complete listing of the world's literature has been a day-dream of bibliographers ever since.'

g. Eighteenth century: Samuel Johnson gives no entry for 'bibliography' in his *Dictionary of the English Language*, but, following the examples of Messrs. Blount (1656) and Fenning (1761), defines a 'bibliographer' as 'a writer of books; a transcriber'. On his death, the dealers at Christie's compile a *Sales Catalogue of the Valuable Library of Books of the Late Learned Samuel Johnson Esq., LL.D.*,

Deceased for their auction on 16 February 1785. Though the intentions of this publication are commercial rather than scholarly, it is one of the most celebrated examples of a bibliography describing the books an author has owned rather than those he has written. Jonathan Swift, Adam Smith, John Locke, Horace Walpole have all been given the library-list treatment, as, more recently, has James Joyce, in Richard Ellmann's *The Consciousness of Joyce*.

h. Nineteenth century: see remarks about Thomas Frognall Dibdin, above. Bibliography flourishes, but even as the Victorian age grows old and grey and full of years, scholars prove reluctant to apply this science to anything published before 1800.

i. Twentieth century: in 1922, the *annus mirabilis* of literary modernism (*Ulysses* and *The Waste Land* both published), the bibliographer Michael Sadleir brings his own literary discipline howling into the new age by being the first to apply its techniques to certain Victorian writers. The floodgates are opened. You can take it from there.

2. The Joy of Bibliography

Most lists have at least a sliver of aesthetic interest; book lists often have more than a sliver; great book lists are better still. I have in mind such diverse flowerings of the short bibliographical form as Edgar Allan Poe telling the rosary of Roderick Usher's personal collection, a passage already cited in this book;* Marianne Moore's list of her hundred best-loved volumes, put together at the request of Raymond Queneau for his book about an ideal *bibliothèque*, or what might be called (following André Malraux's Museum Without Walls) a Library Without Walls; Paul Masson's erudite catalogue, prepared for the Bibliothèque Nationale, of Latin and Italian books of the fifteenth century, none of which, alas, existed – he had invented them to 'save the prestige of the catalogue';† the more frankly fantastical catalogues of imaginary works by Donne, Sir Thomas Browne and others; the contents of Charles Olson's *A Bibliography on America for Ed Dorn*; Cyril Connolly's brief roll-calls of masterpieces in *The Unquiet Grave*; or, to conclude with a recent example, the exquisitely slight catalogue of just eleven texts, each one bound in grey paper, treasured by the murderous protagonist (inspired by Ernst Jünger?) of Bruce Chatwin's short story 'The Estate of Maximilian Tod', including Hsien Yin Lung's *Essay on Living in the Mountains*, John Tyndall's *Notes on the Colour of Water and Ice*, Cassian's treatise on Accidie and – to bring us full circle – 'Landor's Cottage', by Edgar Allan Poe.

3. A Selected Bibliography on Bibliography

Not so much selected as pared down to the bone, or even marrow; but these are the four main texts from which I

---

* See 'Epigraphs', above, p. 86n.

† See Manguel, op. cit., p. 198.

pillaged a good part of the material found in the 'Extremely Short History':

Krummel, D. W., *Bibliographies: Their Aims and Methods* (London: Mansell, 1984)

Newton, A. Edward, *Bibliography and Pseudo-Bibliography* (London: Humphrey Milford/Oxford University Press, 1936)

Stokes, Roy, *Michael Sadleir, 1888–1957* (Metuchen, N.J. and London: The Scarecrow Press, Inc., 1980)

Stokes, Roy, *The Function of Bibliography* (second edition, Hants: Gower, 1982).

4. A Selected Bibliography for *Invisible Forms*

Paul Fussell, who, as I explained in the Introduction, was the critic who unwittingly started me off on all this paratextual business years ago with a couple of paragraphs in his study of Johnson, has complained in a more recent book – *The Anti-Egotist: Kingsley Amis, Man of Letters* (Oxford: Oxford Universty Press, 1994) – about the casual, not to say downright slovenly appearance of bibliographies in British books these days. OK, Prof. Fussell, you've given me hours of pleasure over the years, so I'll do my best not to make too much of a hash of it.

I'd initially planned to draw up a bibliography of quite preposterous dimensions, citing not only every single work mentioned in passing and every unnamed text which might be in some way pertinent, but also a vast array of additional volumes, existent and non-existent, in languages from

Albanian to Zulu (of which last tongue I have, admittedly, no more than a modest working knowledge). Instead, I've opted for mercy and utility, and given details of no more than a few of the books that readers may be interested to consult if they have been diverted by some of the preceding chapters. In homage to the Venerable Bede, there are forty of them; forty-one if you count the Genette translation as a separate book. Genette, again, apart, I haven't cited any works not available in English; I've only smuggled in plugs for one or two books by chums, and I've abstained entirely from parading my own back catalogue . . . which makes this the final time in this volume that I'll have failed to meet the full generic requirements of an IF.

Adair, Gilbert, *Surfing the Zeitgeist* (London: Faber and Faber, 1997)

Baker, Nicholson, *The Mezzanine* (Cambridge: Granta, 1989)

——, *The Size of Thoughts* (London: Chatto & Windus, 1996)

Barth, John, *The Friday Book* (Baltimore and London: Johns Hopkins University Press, 1997)

Beerbohm, Max, *Seven Men* (London: Heinemann, 1919)

Bellos, David: *Georges Perec: A Life in Words* (London: Harvill, 1993)

Benabou, Marcel, *Why I Have Not Written Any of My Books*, trans. David Kornacker (Lincoln & London: Bison Books, University of Nebraska Press, 1997 (hardback), 1998 (paperback): from *Pourquoi je n'ai ecrit aucun de mes livres* (Paris: Hachette, 1986).

Bernard, André, *Now All We Need is a Title* (New York and London: W. W. Norton, 1995)

Bombaugh, C. C., *Oddities and Curiosities of Words and Literature*, edited and annotated by Martin Gardner (New York: Dover, 1961)

Breakwell, Ian and Hammond, Paul: *Brought to Book: The Balance of Books and Life* (Harmondsworth: Penguin, 1994)

Brotchie, Alastair (ed.), *Oulipo Laboratory* (London: Atlas, 1995)

Burton, Robert, *The Anatomy of Melancholy*, ed. Floyd Dell and Paul Jordan-Smith (New York: Tudor, 1927)

Coleridge, S. T., *Marginalia I, Abbt to Byfield*, edited by George Whalley, as Volume 12 of *The Collected Works of Samuel Taylor Coleridge* (Bollingen Series LXXV), (Princeton and London: Princeton University Press, Routledge and Kegan Paul and the Bollingen Foundation, 1980)

Cortázar, Julio, *Around the Day in Eighty Worlds*, translated from *Le Tour du jour en quatre-vingts mondes* (Paris: Éditions Gallimard, 1980) by Thomas Christensen (San Francisco: North Point Press, 1986)

Cuddon, J. A., *A Dictionary of Literary Terms and Literary Theory* (Fourth edition, revised by C. E. Preston, Oxford: Blackwell, 1998)

Davenport, Guy, *The Geography of the Imagination* (North Point, 1981, repr. London: Picador, 1984)

D'Israeli, Isaac, *Curiosities of Literature*, Vols 1–3 (London: Frederick Warne and Co., 1881)

Forbes, Peter (ed.), *Poetry Review: The Hoax Issue*, Vol. 87, No. 2, Summer 1997

Fussell, Paul, *Samuel Johnson and the Life of Writing* (New York: Harcourt Brace Jovanovich, 1971)

Genette, Gérard, *Seuils* (Paris: Éditions du Seuil, 1987)

——, *Paratexts: Thresholds of Interpretation*, translated by Jane E. Lewin (Cambridge: CUP, 1997)

Gere, J. A., and Sparrow, John (eds), *Geoffrey Madan's Notebooks* (Oxford: Oxford Universty Press, 1981)

Grafton, Anthony: *The Footnote: A Curious History* (London: Faber and Faber, 1997)

Heyward, Michael, *The Ern Malley Affair* (London: Faber and Faber, 1993)

Irwin, Robert, *The Arabian Nights: A Companion* (Harmondsworth: Penguin, 1994)

Kell, Thomas, *Every Verb a Glerb* (London: Alces Press, 1999)

Kenner, Hugh, *The Counterfeiters* (Baltimore and London: Johns Hopkins University Press, 1968)

—— *The Stoic Comedians: Flaubert, Joyce and Beckett* (Berkeley, Los Angeles, London: University of California Press, 1962; paperback edition, 1974)

Korn, Eric, *Remainders* (Manchester: Carcanet, 1989)

Mahony, Patrick J., *Freud as a Writer* (New Haven and London: Yale, 1987)

Manguel, Alberto, *A History of Reading* (London: Harper-Collins, 1996)

Norwich, John Julius, *Christmas Crackers* (Harmondsworth: Penguin, 1982)

—— *More Christmas Crackers* (Harmondsworth: Penguin, 1990)

Ogden, James, *Isaac D'Israeli* (Oxford: Clarendon Press, 1969)

Pessoa, Fernando, *A Centenary Pessoa*, ed. Eugénio Lisboa with L. C. Taylor (Manchester: Carcanet Press, 1995)

Room, Adrian, *Naming Names: Stories of Pseudonyms and Name Changes, with a Who's Who* (London and Henley: Routledge and Kegan Paul, 1981)

—, ed., *Bloomsbury Dictionary of Dedications* (London: Bloomsbury, 1990)

Said, Edward, *Beginnings: Intention and Method* (London: Granta, 1997)

Tournier, Michel, *The Wind Spirit*, trans. Arthur Goldhammer (London: Methuen, 1991)

Wallen, Martin (ed.), *Coleridge's Ancient Mariner: An Experimental Edition of Texts and Revisions 1798–1828* (Barrytown, N.Y.: Station Hill, 1993)

Wellisch, Hans H., *Indexing from A to Z* (New York: H. W. Wilson, 1995)

Afterword *

Every finished work is the death mask of its intuition.

Walter Benjamin

---

* This chapter originally contained a medium-long discussion of the afterword as an IF, written in the form of a dialogue between the author and himself – a pastiche, that is, of Rousseau's extraordinary afterword to *Julie, or the New Heloise.* You've had a narrow escape.

Indexes

And in such indexes, although small pricks
To their subsequent volumes, there is seen
The baby figure of the giant mass
Of things to come at large . . .

Troilus and Cressida, I, iii, 343–6*

It's curious that Gerard Genette, master theoretician of the paratext, has next to nothing to say about indexes† – a bare six lines of italics, to be exact, as though they were all but insignificant ('unsignifying'?) works of technology rather than of art. His reticence is baffling, and not only because our copyright laws now acknowledge that an index may qualify as an item of intellectual property in which the indexer has

---

* This is a tricky passage to gloss, even for late Shakespeare, though Kenneth Palmer has a brave stab in his notes for the Arden edition (p. 147). I place it here by way of obeisance to all the other writers on indexes who are fond of quoting it; and also because it showed the English that the proper plural is *indexes*; 'indices' are for the mathematicians and boffins.

† What he does say is this: '*Tel qu'il est, comme la plupart, sa véritable fonction est d'éviter à l'auteur la marque infamante:* no index.' (*Seuils*, p. 381. Why the lapse into English?)

full rights of ownership.* Indexes aren't simply literary
conveniences or amenities . . . although most habitual readers know how irritating it can be to turn to the back of a
book in search of directions and discover that the publisher
has been too cheap or perverse or calculating† to include
one. (In recent years, I've taken to scribbling my own
customized indexes in the endpapers of offending volumes,
such as Guy Davenport's *The Geography of the Imagination*, a
work which screams out for proper indexing and goes
unheeded.) A good index has the satisfying qualities of all
skilled workmanship; an inspired index may be a thing of joy
– sometimes wittier, more eloquent and more enlightening
than the book in whose train it follows with such deceptive
humility. Should you doubt the sanity of this proposition,
take a look at a couple of recent publications by Joe
Queenan, the acerbic commentator on the American movie
industry (*If You're Talking to Me, Your Career Must be in
Trouble*) and other garish symptoms of the ever-accelerating
Decline of the West (*Red Lobster, White Trash and the Blue
Lagoon*). Mr Queenan's essays consist of little more than a
string of cheap, nasty, bitter, snotty, *ad hominem* snipings and
sneerings at popular entertainers and their gullible fans; and
his indexes are even better. I cite more or less at random,
from names listed under 'T':

---

* See Leonard Montague-Harrod, ed., *Indexers on Indexing* (New York and
London: R. R. Bowker, 1978), pp. 106–11.

† Why 'calculating'? Because some readers only want to gut the book for
a reference or two, and will be able to do so in the bookshop if there's a
decent index. Thwart this character's meanness and he'll have to buy the
thing.

Having subjected Queenan's indexes to rigorous scientific testing (viz., by reading them out loud to innocent bystanders), I am in a position to confirm that they are capable of inducing unseemly fits of laughter in adult bipeds. In this regard, they stand in a noble tradition. Whether or not Mr Queenan is aware of the fact, his mordant listings are no more, if no less, than the latest avatars of a satirical spirit that has breathed through creative index makers for the better part of five centuries. The scope that an index format offers for mischief ought to be apparent to anyone who has heard the old chestnut about the Jesuit encyclopaedia which includes the entry 'Woman: *see under* Sin'; and while Queenan's best indicial jokes are achieved by a kind of cod-scholasticism, in which he mingles the expected note of coolly detached pedantry with incongruously demotic bursts of abuse ('Cassidy, David: hootiness of, 163–165'), wicked indexers have more typically gone about their destructive

---

* *Red Lobster*, etc., p. 194. The index entry on that popular seafood restaurant ('children's tragic inability to detect lack of point of, 104 . . .') is among Queenan's most satisfying touches.

tasks a little more slyly, as in the index for D. B. Wyndham Lewis & Charles Lee's *The Stuffed Owl: An Anthology of Bad Verse*:

> Angels: not immune from curiosity, 31, 162;
> give Mr. Purcell a flying lesson, 37; patrol
> the British sky, 47; invited to take up
> permanent quarters at Whitehall, 50; and
> Britons, mixed choir of, ibid.

Compare, to take a still quieter example, the index to Sidney Wolfe Cohen's gathering of dud prophecies, mostly technological, *The Experts Speak*:

> computers, home, no reason seen for —
> germs, as fictitious —; heat generated by
> kisses as destructive of —
> Pickering, William Henry: on fallacy of
> expecting airplanes to reach speed of
> trains and cars —; on uselessness of
> airplanes in war —; on visionary notion
> of transatlantic passenger flights —*

This list of sardonic indexes might be extended until it achieved the dimensions of an index in its own right. What's more, there also seem to be some more subtle and pervasive affinities between indexes and satirists than can be accounted for simply by the handiness of the device. At any rate, most of the references I came up with when I first set about pondering this section were to satirical writers of one kind or another. To Swift, for example, whose *A further account of the most deplorable conditions of Mr Edmund Curll, since his*

---

* I owe both these examples to Hans H. Wellisch's *Indexing from A to Z* (New York: H. W. Wilson, 1995), p. 321.

being poisoned on the 28th March (1716) reveals that, in the eighteenth century as in our own day, there was a thriving class of literary journeymen who provided the indexes to other writers' works. On second thoughts, perhaps 'thriving' isn't the *mot juste*:

> At the laundress's at the Hole in the Wall in Cursitor's Alley up three pairs of stairs ... you may speak to the gentleman, if his flux be over, who lies in the flock bed, my index maker.

And then there is Pope, deriding in *The Dunciad* the kind of bone-idle scholar who gathers all his learning, such as it is, from the rear end of books:

> How index-learning turns no student pale,
> Yet holds the eel of science by the tail.

And, more topically, there is Gore Vidal, who beguilingly* admits to a penchant for starting books from the back if there is any likelihood that his name might be listed there, as when the work is by an old friend, or enemy, or both. He recalls, for example, looking his name up in the index to Tennessee Williams' memoirs to find out how grossly he has been defamed by the Great Bird (hardly at all, at it happens).† Here I should own up to a small disappointment. I was informed by a usually reliable source that Vidal had once published a book of essays which had an index that

---

* Mr Vidal, like Logan Pearsall Smith, is fond of adverbs; I offer this one by way of *hommage*.

† 'Some Memories of the Glorious Bird and an Earlier Self', in *United States: Essays 1952–1992* (New York: Random House, 1993), p. 1134.

was perfectly conventional save in one particular: next to 'Mailer, Norman' was printed not the appropriate page number(s) but the cheerily knowing salutation 'Hi, Norm!' Thus far, I have been unable to confirm this pleasing tale.

Why, a shrink might fairly ask, did my associations hop so neatly from Swift to Pope to Vidal? Best guess: because all three have harsh words for sluggish-witted pedants (Pope called them dunces, Vidal calls them the hacks of academe), all three morosely relish the badness of egregiously or gregariously bad books, from title page to index, and all three are therefore likely to turn to the terminal lists in search of malice and/or with malice in mind. Before flogging this particular hobby horse to splinters, it's worth recalling that not all satire is intentionally humorous in effect, and that one of Joe Queenan's spiritual ancestors – far more appalled by the popular entertainers of his day than Queenan is by Billy Joel or even by Andrew Lloyd-Webber – was the seventeenth-century barrister and killjoy William Prynne,* whose attack on all things theatrical, *Histrio-Mastix: the players scourge* ('unreadable': Thomas Carlyle), boasts one of the most insanely splenetic indexes of all time, forty pages long and bursting at the seams with bile, as may be gathered from this considerably abbreviated extract from his entry on actresses:

> Women-Actors notorious whores ... and dare then any
> Christian women be so more than whorishly impudent as
> to act, to speak publikely on a stage perchance in man's

---

* 1600–1669; a tireless and stubborn curmudgeon who is, I suspect, the only English writer ever to have had his ear cut off twice. (*Histrio-Mastix* offended Charles I, who put him in the Tower.)

apparell and cut haire here proved abominable in the presence of sundry men and women? ... O let such presidents of imprudency, of impiety be never heard of or suffered among Christians, 385.*

A suitably cranky note on which to end this brief and modest proposal on the satirical ways of the indexer. For, let it be stressed, the pleasures of the index are greatly more various than this highly prejudicial sampling has thus far suggested. John Julius Norwich has included a couple of quite different indexes in his two *Christmas Cracker* anthologies of literary goodies, delighting in the morbid surrealism of the index to John Carey's study of Dickens' imagination *The Violent Effigy*,† and reminding us of the ways in which a good index to a diary such as Boswell's or Pepys's will contain any number of miniaturized yarns, usually of an amatory nature;‡ Paul

---

* Cited by G. Norman Knight, 'Book Indexing in Britain: A Brief History', *Indexers on Indexing*, p. 10.

† Try these for size: 'babies, bottled, 82; beheading, 21; boiling spirit, 25–6; boots, 61; caged birds, 44, 46, 116–19; cannibalism, 22–4, 175; capital punishment, 38; caravans, 42–3, 48; cleanliness, excessive, 36–7; climbing boys, 72; clocks and watches, 133–4; coffins, walking, 80–1; combustible persons, 14, 165; conservatories, 112–3; corpses, 30, 80–3 . . .' The last entry in this flesh-creeping list is 'zoo, feeding time at, 68–9'.

‡ Here's one not used as a cracker, from R. C. Latham's index to Pepys: 'BAGWELL—; wife of William: her good looks—; P plans to seduce—; visits—; finds her virtuous—; and modest—; asks P for place for husband—; P kisses—; she grows affectionate—; he caresses—; she visits him—; her resistance collapses in alehouse—; amorous encounters with: at her house— . . .' Unsurprisingly, Mr Latham won the Society of Indexers' Wheatley Medal for 1983 with this fine work.

Fussell has shown how the great Hill–Powell index to the *Life of Johnson* dramatizes the rich inconsistencies of the Great Cham's mind ('Roman Catholicism. . . . Johnson . . . respects it, ii, 105; attacks it, iii, 407').* Incidentally, Johnson himself was keen on indexes, so much so that he encouraged Richardson to add an index to his novel *Clarissa*, to be 'occasionally consulted by the busy, the aged, and the studious'. Richardson obliged: he added an *Index rerum* to the third edition of *Clarissa*, and three years later published a general index for a combined edition of *Clarissa*, *Pamela* and *Sir Charles Grandison*, titled *A collection of the moral and instructive sentiments, maxims, cautions, and reflexions, contained in the histories of Pamela, Clarissa, and Sir Charles Grandison.: Digested under proper heads, with references to the volume and page, both in octavo and twelves, in the respective histories. To which are subjoined, two letters from the editor of those works: the one, in answer to a lady who was solicitous for an additional volume to the history of Sir Charles Grandison. The other, in reply to a gentleman who had objected to Sir Charles's offer'd compromise in the article of religion had he married a Roman Catholic lady.* Sample:

> *Aged* persons should study to promote in young people those innocent pleasures which they themselves were fond of in youth, VI, 859. *See* Mrs. Shirley.

Very few novelists have followed Richardson's example;† fortunately, no doubt. Anyway, to resume our litany: Paul Fussell is also alive to the lugubrious splendours, and valu-

---

* *Samuel Johnson and the Life of Writing*, p. 179.

† Though others have done the job for them: Terence Kilmartin's concordance to Proust is an excellent instance.

able moral for would-be writers, contained in the index to
Isaac D'Israeli's* *Calamities of Authors.* Here is my own brief
selection:

> BAYNE, Alexander, died of intense
> application 72
> CASTELL, Dr, ruined in health and
> fortune by the publication of his
> Polyglott 189
> CHURCHYARD, Thomas, his pathetic
> description of his wretched old age .. 26
> COTGRAVE, Randle, falls blind in the
> labour of his 'Dictionary' 73
> DRAKE, Dr John, a political writer, his
> miserable life 11
> DRYDEN, in his old age, complains of
> dying of over-study 204
> GREENE, Robert, a town wit, his
> poverty and death 23
> HENRY, Dr., the Historian, the sale of
> his work, on which he had expended
> most of his fortune and his life,
> stopped, and himself ridiculed, by a
> conspiracy raised against him 136
> HERON, Robert, draws up the distresses
> of a man of letters living by literary
> industry, in the confinement of a
> sponging-house, from his original
> letter 81

An enlightened Arts Council would have this index reprinted
in pamphlet form and issued gratis to any young person
contemplating a career as an *homme* or *femme de lettres*.

Tragic, comic, surrealist or erotic, almost all the indexes
I have so far cited have one thing in common: they would
be classified by the professionals as Narrative Indexes, rather

---

* Fussell, op. cit., p. 270. And see my chapter on Isaac D'Israeli, below.

than straightforward indexes of proper names. According to Hans H. Wellisch's chapter on the subject in his magisterial *Indexing from A to Z* – incidentally, far and away the best introduction I managed to find not only to the practical techniques of indexing but to its history, philosophy and folklore – such narrative indexes have their murky origins some time in the thirteenth century, when itinerant Dominican and Franciscan monks from Oxford put together their own pocket guides to citations from scripture or the Church Fathers. (If you've ever wondered idly about the origin of the term *vade mecum* for a pocket guide, your quest is done.) This business of do-it-yourself indexing continued until the advent of printing in the mid-fifteenth century, when the practice was adapted for the page and so gave birth to what appears to be the very first printed index, provided at the end of an edition of St Augustine's *De arte praedicandi*, 'On the art of preaching', published in 1467. Thanks probably to its centuries of refinement in the hands of wandering divines, the modern index was born fully grown, or very nearly; this proto-index could readily pass for a modern one:

> Goodwill of listeners, gaining of
> Listeners, how to teach them
> Study of the art of preaching, not to be
>   neglected . . .*

Unassuming as it appears, such a minor addendum to Augustine's text affected habits of reading radically. As Mr Wellisch emphasizes, though the word 'index' is old, the

---

* Wellisch, pp. 317–18.

thing as we know it was unknown in antiquity, extremely rare even in the years after the advent of printing and not at all common until the middle of the sixteenth century, at which point it settled down comfortably at the end of the book instead of near the front, after a table of contents. When Cicero writes to Atticus of an *index*, he means a little slip on which the title of a papyrus roll was written, so that it could be identified without having to be dragged down from the shelf; hence the development of the Latin word into a general term for 'title'. Later on, during the first century AD, *index* also came to mean 'a table of contents' or 'a list of chapters', 'a bibliography' or simply 'a list'. Largely because of the physical make-up of books in the classical period, however, these lists did not provide accurate locations for names or concepts: not only was it practically difficult to plot a path through a text that wasn't chopped up into pages, but there wasn't a lot of point in trying, at great expense, to give fixed points of reference for scrolls that would vary considerably from copy to copy.

Flash forward to 1467. It would be hard, some scholars are now saying, to overestimate the effect this invention had on the advancement of learning: as the map to geographical voyages of discovery, so the index to their intellectual counterparts. In the early summer of 1998 I spent a couple of days eavesdropping on a conference at St Andrews University entitled 'The Renaissance Computer', at which literary critics and historians discoursed learnedly on the printed index as a form of what we would now call a search engine; on the relationship of alphabetical modes of ordering knowledge to other forms of taxonomy; on the ways in which indexes opened up non-linear modes of reading and thus of conceptual organization. Expect a deal of publication on these matters in specialist journals in the next few years.

In the meantime, anyone interested in the contemporary art of indexing – and its practitioners insist that it *is* an art rather than a science, which is why no computer will ever put an indexer out of work – should consult Mr Wellisch's work, or the diverting series of case histories and other articles collected in *Indexers on Indexing*,* or any good introductory handbook, such as G. Norman Knight's *Indexing: the art of*.† In their pages, you will meet with such exotica as Locators, KWIC, KWAC and KWOC (referred to by Mr Wellisch as 'the three stooges'; KWIC stands for Key Word in Context, take it from there), Bad Breaks, Lead Terms, Homographs, PRECIS (Preserved Context Index System), Grouped Order and And. Yes, And. All the hazards, in fine, that a skilled indexer must negotiate if she or he is ever to attain the highest accolade awarded by the Society of Indexers, the annual Wheatley Medal, named in commemoration of H. B. Wheatley (1838–1917), author of *How to Make an Index*, widely acknowledged as the father of modern indexing. But these are mysteries too profound for cursory attention, so let's conclude with the best known of all poems – the *only* existing poem? – on indexing:

> *Absente auxilio perquirimus undique frustra*
> *Sed nobis ingens indicis auxilum est.*

---

* I particularly enjoyed G. V. Carey's story about Noel Coward and the Hot Tadpole on p. 44.

† London: Allen & Unwin, 1979.

(Without a key we search and search in vain
But a good index is a monstrous gain.)*

And with at once the most judicious and the most fervent defence of indexes, by Thomas Fuller (1608–61):

An INDEX is a necessary implement, and no impediment of a book, except in the same sense wherein the carriages of an army are termed *Impedimenta*. Without this, a large author is but a labyrinth without a clue to direct the reader therein. I confess there is a lazy kind of learning which is *onely Indical*; when scholars (like adders which only bite the horse's heels) nibble but at the tables, which are *calces librorum*, neglecting the body of the book. But though the idle deserve no crutches (let not a staff be used by them, but on them), pity it is the weary should be denied the benefit thereof, and industrious scholars prohibited the accomodation of an index, most used by those who most pretend to contemn it.

Couldn't agree more. Kind reader, now proceed to the index – prepared, as is often the case, not by the bumbling author but by another writer – and regard it with renewed affection and respect.

---

* G. Norman Knight tried to track down the authorship of this distich via the *TLS*, but without luck. He used it on the title page of his *Indexing: the art of.*

Index Nominum